Teachers in Anglophone Africa

Teachers in Anglophone Africa

ISSUES IN TEACHER SUPPLY, TRAINING, AND MANAGEMENT

Aidan Mulkeen

THE WORLD BANK
Washington, DC

Contents

BOXES

TABLES

FIGURES

Foreword

T he last two decades have seen a profound change in participation in education in Sub-Saharan Africa. Enrollment in primary education has grown rapidly, there are now more children in school in Africa than at any other time in history, and most African children now enroll in school at some point. This remarkable achievement has involved increases in the number of teachers and has placed national systems for teacher provision and management under increased stress. Countries have struggled to recruit sufficient qualified teachers, to deploy them to where they are needed, and to provide the management and support structures to ensure that quality education is delivered.

For many countries in Sub-Saharan Africa, the challenges of education expansion are changing. Following the rapid expansion of access to primary education, countries are now striving to complete the drive to universal primary education, consolidate gains by improving the quality of learning, and build on the successes in primary education by expanding access to secondary education.

As these new priorities emerge, it is an opportune time to review the policies that guide the provision of teachers. Teacher policy is a complex and multi-faceted area, and often evolves through historical events rather than systematic planning. This book examines teacher policies and issues in eight anglophone countries in Sub-Saharan Africa. These case studies provide a synthesis of the major issues in teacher supply, deployment, training, management, and finance.

This book is intended to underline the need for careful planning for the provision of teachers. Many of the difficulties in teacher provision can be anticipated and ameliorated through appropriate policies. Nevertheless, teacher policies form a complex interconnected system, and policy development should be based on an overview of the issues, as policies to address one difficulty can easily have an adverse impact on another.

Readers may find this synthesis useful in four different ways. First, it provides a body of comparative information on teacher issues in the eight case-study countries. Second, it describes the policies currently in use and the indications of their impact. Third, it provides a model of the interlinked nature of teacher policies. Fourth, it draws together a series of promising actions that can serve as positive suggestions for countries seeking to improve their teacher policies.

We hope that the developments in these countries, and the lessons drawn from them, will be of assistance to policy makers throughout the region as they address the challenges of the next phases of expansion in education.

Yaw Ansu
Sector Director, Human Development
Africa Region
The World Bank

Acknowledgments

This synthesis was prepared by Aidan Mulkeen, based on case studies in eight countries. Megan Haggerty provided invaluable assistance in the writing and editing of the text, and Michelle Duvall-Kalinski assisted in the analysis of the data. The eight cases studies were prepared by Aidan Mulkeen with the assistance of Andy Burke (The Gambia), Suzanne Miric and Puleng Mapuru (Lesotho), Padraig Carmody and Demis Kunje (Malawi), Colin Bangay (Uganda), and Fiona Edwards (Zambia).

Special thanks are due to the numerous staff in the ministries of education in each of the countries, who gave their time in providing both data and their perspectives, which contributed greatly to the case studies. Thanks are also due to the World Bank task team leaders and education specialists who facilitated the case studies in each country: Dandan Chen (Eritrea and Zambia), Lily Mulatu (The Gambia), Xiaoyan Liang (Lesotho), Peter Darvas and Nathalie Lahire (Liberia), Michael Mambo (Malawi), Harriet Nannyonjo (Uganda), and Ivar Strand (Zanzibar).

The synthesis benefited from reviews by Jee-Peng Tan, Luis Benveniste, Emiliana Vegas, Helen Craig, Lily Mulatu, Michel Welmond, and Bob Prouty.

The case studies, the analysis, and this publication were supported by the World Bank's Africa Region and the Irish Education Trust Fund.

Abbreviations

ATEI	Asmara Teacher Education Institute
BETUZ	Basic Education Teachers Union of Zambia
CCT	coordinating center tutor (Uganda)
CDSS	Community Day Secondary Schools (Malawi)
CEF	Campaign for Education Forum (Lesotho)
COSC	Cambridge Overseas School Certificate (Lesotho)
CPD	continuing professional development
CPS	cost per student
CSCQBE	Civil Society Coalition for Basic Education (Malawi)
DAPP	Development Aid from People to People
DEBS	district education board secretaries (Zambia)
DEM	district education manager (Malawi)
DIC	District INSET Coordinator (Zambia)
DoSE	Department of State for Education (The Gambia)
DRC	District Resource Center (Zambia)
DRT	district resource teacher (Lesotho)
DTEP	Distance Teacher Education Programme (Lesotho)
EFA	Education for All
EIT	Eritrea Institute of Technology
EMAS	Education Methods Advisory Service
EMIS	Education Management Information System
ESA	Education Standards Agency (Uganda)
FENU	Forum for Education NGOs in Uganda
FTI	Fast Track Initiative
GER	gross enrollment rate
GMD	dalasi (currency, The Gambia)
GPA	grade point average
GTU	Gambia Teachers' Union
HTC	Higher Teacher's Certificate (The Gambia)

INSET	in-service education and training
LAT	Lesotho Association of Teachers
LCE	Lesotho College of Education
LETCOM	Liberia Education for All Technical Committee
LRD	Liberian dollar (currency)
LTTU	Lesotho Teachers Trade Union
LSL	loti (currency; plural maloti, Lesotho)
MIITEP	Malawi Integrated In-service Teacher Education Programme
MoE	Ministry of Education
MoES	Ministry of Education and Sports (Uganda)
MoET	Ministry of Education and Training (Lesotho)
MoEVT	Ministry of Education and Vocational Training (Zanzibar)
MSSSP	Malawi School Systems Support Programme
MWK	Malawi kwacha (currency)
NGO	nongovernmental organization
NISTCOL	National Distance Education College for Teachers
NTAL	National Teacher's Association of Liberia
NTC	National Teachers College (Uganda)
OECD	Organisation for Economic Co-operation and Development
OSC	Orientation Secondary Class (Zanzibar)
PEA	primary education adviser
PEO	primary education officer (Zambia)
PER	public expenditure review
PPP	purchasing power parity
PSEUM	Private Schools Employees Union of Malawi
PTA	parent teacher association
PTC	Primary Teacher's Certificate (The Gambia)
PTC	Primary Teacher College (Uganda)
PTC-E	Primary Teacher's Certificate, Extension (The Gambia)
PTDDL	Primary Teacher Diploma by Distance Learning (Zambia)
PTR	pupil-teacher ratio
RIFT	Remedial Initiative for Female Teachers (The Gambia)
SES	Social and Environmental Studies (The Gambia)
SESTUZ	Secondary School Teachers Union of Zambia
SIC	School INSET Coordinator (Zambia)
SMC	school management committee
SUZA	State University of Zanzibar
TAE	Teachers' Association of Eritrea
TDC	Teacher Development Center (Malawi)
TSC	Teaching Service Commission (Lesotho and Malawi)

TUM	Teachers' Union of Malawi
TZS	shilling (currency, Zambia)
UACE	Uganda Advanced Certificate of Education
UNATU	Uganda National Teachers' Union
UPE	universal primary education
WASSCE	West African Senior School Certificate Examination
ZAOU	Zambia Open University
ZATEC	Zambia Teacher Education Course
ZATU	Zanzibar Teachers' Union
ZIC	Zonal INSET Coordinator (Zambia)
ZMK	Zambian kwacha (currency)
ZNUT	Zambia National Union of Teachers

Overview

Teacher policy is central to the challenges of both expansion and quality of education in Africa. Provision of an effective teacher in every classroom requires a set of policies that ensure: (i) an adequate supply of teachers; (ii) the ability to locate teachers where they are required; (iii) training systems that equip teachers with the required skills; and (iv) management and career structures that result in consistent, high-quality performance by teachers. Low-income countries in Africa must address these policy challenges in the context of severely constrained education budgets. While it is tempting to view these challenges in isolation, in reality they are interlinked. Interventions intended to solve problems in one of these areas frequently have unanticipated impacts in another area of teacher provision. Developing an appropriate balanced set of policies requires a holistic view of the issues.

With the international drive toward Education For All, low-income countries in Africa have seen rapid expansion of access to education, and an increased social and geographic diversity of school enrollment. These historically unprecedented expansions in access require greater numbers of teachers, pose challenges for teacher deployment and management, and strain the financial resources available. In the context of these challenges, this book aims to support the development of teacher policies, particularly in the Anglophone countries in Sub-Saharan Africa, by providing a holistic view of contemporary trends, issues, and policies. The work is a synthesis of eight case studies conducted in Eritrea, The Gambia, Lesotho, Liberia, Malawi, Uganda, Zambia, and Zanzibar between 2006 and 2008. The synthesis examines the issues of teacher supply, deployment, training, and management in each of the eight cases. Based on this analysis, it identifies common challenges and promising practices.

SUPPLY

These case studies highlight the need for better planning and management of teacher supply. In all of the case-study countries there was a mismatch between the national requirement for new teachers and the output of newly qualified teachers. In six of the eight cases, the annual output of trained primary teachers was less than 6 percent of the teacher workforce (which might be considered a normal attrition rate). Shortages of primary teachers resulted in widespread use of unqualified teachers. Shortages of qualified secondary teachers led to use of underqualified teachers, use of primary teachers in secondary schools, and in two countries, led to reliance on expatriate teachers. The proportion of secondary teachers specialized in each subject was poorly matched with needs, resulting in oversupply in some subjects and shortages in others. Systems for management of supply were often weak and, as a result, intake to teacher colleges was often not adjusted in response to the national needs. In some cases the ability to control teacher supply was being reduced with increasing autonomy of the teacher-training institutions.

Management of teacher supply will require the monitoring of teacher attrition. Attrition rates seem likely to fluctuate with labor market opportunities, as in most of the countries where data were available, the most frequent cause of teacher attrition was voluntary resignation, presumably to take another job. In general, the attrition rate of secondary teachers was higher than that of primary teachers. There were also reports that attrition was higher for better-educated teachers, and teachers of mathematics and science.

In several of the countries, particularly Lesotho, The Gambia, and Eritrea, the supply of teachers was constrained by the limited output of suitably qualified school leavers. As a result, the available places in teacher colleges could not be filled without a reduction of entry standards. This pattern reflects a structural imbalance in education systems, with a limited output from secondary education, insufficient to fill the available places in higher education and teacher training. This problem had been exacerbated by both the expansion of the capacity of higher education systems and the increasing demand for primary teachers.

There were particular difficulties with the supply of teachers of mathematics and the sciences. This was reflected in shortages of mathematics and science teachers at the secondary school level and in primary teachers with poor understanding of mathematical and scientific content. There is a vicious cycle where poor teaching of mathematics and sciences results in poor performance in these subjects, limited availability of student teachers with understanding of mathematics and science, and a shortage of teachers in these subjects.

DEPLOYMENT

Teacher deployment presented challenges in all of the case-study countries, with teacher shortages in certain locations, usually remote rural areas. There were often greater differences between schools within a district than between districts, and these intradistrict inequities were often masked by the use of district averages in reporting. The distribution of the better-qualified teachers, and teachers of mathematics and sciences, was highly inequitable, as these teachers were more concentrated in the urban areas. There was a strong gender pattern in deployment, with female teachers underrepresented in the rural schools. In countries with multiple linguistic and ethnic groups, deployment of teachers to areas of linguistic minorities seemed particularly difficult.

Attempts to deploy teachers rationally through central planning did not appear to be effective in most cases. Teachers assigned to unpopular posts often failed to take up the post, or quickly arranged to transfer. For remote schools, this resulted in more unfilled posts, higher turnover, and less experienced staff. Financial incentives to encourage teachers to accept hardship posts were provided in most countries, but their impact was limited. One exception suggested that incentives can attract teachers, if both substantial and well targeted. In The Gambia, a carefully targeted hardship bonus of up to 40 percent of salary had resulted in large numbers of teachers already in rural schools, requesting transfer to a hardship school.

Giving teachers some choice of location also appeared to improve the equity of teacher deployment. In Lesotho, a system of local recruitment, where schools advertise for and recruit their own teachers, has resulted in relatively even teacher distribution. Zambia and Uganda were both using more location-specific recruitment in an attempt to fill places in remote schools. In some countries, the practice of recruiting unqualified teachers and then providing in-service training was an important mechanism for provision of teachers, as schools in remote areas were often able to recruit unqualified teachers locally. Providing training and a career path for local people willing to work in remote schools may be part of an effective response to the deployment problem.

UTILIZATION

Primary teacher utilization varied widely, with teachers expected to teach between 12.5 and 27 hours per week. In practice, real workloads were often lower than the official expectation, reduced by an oversupply of teachers in some places, unofficial shortening of the school week, and unauthorized absences. Primary teachers were generally expected to teach all subjects to one class, but there was some informal teacher specialization, especially in the upper grades of primary education. Multigrade teaching was widely used, particularly in rural areas. In some cases, this was a result of a deliberate teacher deployment policy; in other cases, it was a necessity resulting from failure to deploy teachers to remote schools. Despite its widespread use, multigrade teaching was not well integrated into policy or teacher training.

In general, the efficiency of utilization was lower at the secondary level, both because secondary teachers generally had shorter working hours than primary teachers, and because of smaller classes resulting from the provision of multiple optional subjects. The pattern of teacher utilization at the secondary level had a very significant impact on the cost per student of teacher provision, which in some countries was more than ten times the cost per student at the primary level. These cost structures are a barrier to the expansion of secondary education.

IMPACT OF HIV

HIV infection rates varied widely across the eight case-study countries, ranging from 1.2 percent to 27 percent. Teacher death and illness (from all causes) accounted for attrition of between 0.66 percent and 3 percent of the teacher workforce annually. HIV/AIDS was often a factor in teacher deployment, as ill teachers were transferred to schools near medical facilities, predominantly in urban areas. As a result, the percentage of sick teachers in urban areas was higher, contributing to higher absenteeism in these areas.

The burden of the HIV pandemic also fell on the education system in a variety of other ways. In Malawi, high attrition of district education officials due to illness was reported, reducing the management capacity. Further, teachers needed to leave their posts to assist ill friends and relatives, and attend funerals. In Malawi, when teachers or their relatives die, the Ministry of Education pays for the transportation of the body to the home area. Given the large number of deaths, this imposes a considerable cost, absorbing much of the discretionary budget of some districts and reducing the availability of ministry vehicles for other purposes.

TEACHER TRAINING

Pre-service training of primary teachers ranged from 12 weeks to three years, following either upper or lower secondary education. For secondary teachers, most countries had dual systems, with diploma courses of two or three years, and degree courses of three or four years. Entry to teacher training was mostly based on academic performance alone. The academic performance required to enter teacher training was quite low, and in some cases declining. As a result of the poor perceptions of the teaching career, teacher training tended to absorb the school leavers who had failed to get places in other higher education courses. The teaching courses had particular difficulty in attracting sufficient students with qualifications in mathematics and science. The poor educational standard of entrants presented quality problems, reflected in high failure rates in some cases.

The teacher-training curriculum was not always well matched to the needs of student teachers. First, training in pedagogical methods was often theoretical, making it less likely to have an impact on classroom practices. Second, the teaching of the content knowledge was often not closely aligned to the school curriculum. Third, the difficulties were often compounded by the students' poor proficiency in the language of instruction (English). In addition, teacher trainers were not always well equipped to deliver training in a practical and relevant manner. Some, particularly in primary teacher training, had little experience teaching at the appropriate level. Several countries were attempting to reform initial teacher education to improve its quality and relevance.

In-service training: In almost every case there was an in-service training system for unqualified teachers. These varied in duration and structure, but typically involved a mix of text materials, residential training sessions in a teacher training college, and some tutorials provided locally. Where in-service systems were implemented well, they provided a second pathway into teaching, and had particular advantages for teacher deployment, as they provided opportunities for people from rural areas to gain a professional qualification while remaining in their home areas. Although there was little objective comparative data, in-service training systems seemed to result in quality comparable to that of pre-service training. The scale of the in-service teacher training courses makes it unlikely that all of the unqualified teachers can be trained quickly. In Lesotho, for example, each cohort of teachers taken into the in-service course was approximately 10 percent of the total of unqualified teachers.

Continuing professional development: Systems for continuing professional development of qualified teachers were relatively undeveloped. The most common modality was centrally planned delivery of short courses on specific topics, such as the introduction of a new curriculum. A few countries had developed alternative systems. In Zambia, for example, there were zonal resource centers, serving small numbers of schools, and staffed by a teacher on a volunteer basis. Teachers within the zone were expected to identify their own training needs, usually drawing on locally available expertise.

MANAGEMENT

Systems for managing teachers were weak. Head teachers were recognized to play important roles in managing, supervising, and mentoring teachers, but in practice head teachers devoted much of their time to relations with administrative authorities outside the school. Training for head teachers was sporadic and did not reach the majority of head teachers.

All of the countries had systems for external monitoring or inspection of schools, but in most cases the frequency of visits was too low to effectively monitor quality. Teacher-inspector ratios were as high as 700:1, and in six of the eight countries schools were visited once a year or less. Some countries had achieved much more frequent supervision by locating supervisors at small clusters of schools. In The Gambia, schools were visited every week or two by cluster monitors who were responsible for approximately ten schools each, and traveled by motorbike. In Eritrea, cluster supervisors were responsible for 80 teachers each, and traveled by bicycle or on foot, managing to visit each *teacher* twice per year.

Absenteeism was not well recorded, but reported to be as high as 25 percent in some countries. Few practical measures were in place to reduce absenteeism. In most countries teacher attendance was recorded at the school level, but not analyzed or reported. There was some indication that teacher absence was responsive to monitoring. In The Gambia, with the introduction of cluster monitors and regular external visits to schools, it was reported that teacher absence had fallen. Some of the teacher absence was work related, including absence to address administrative issues, and absence to attend training. Improvements in administrative systems and policies on provision of training could contribute to reducing teacher absence.

Disciplinary systems were generally perceived to be too slow, unpredictable, and "high stakes" to be used to address absenteeism. There were some suggestions that simple "low-stakes" sanctions could also be effective. In Liberia, schools were able to withhold the salary of a teacher who had been absent until a small fine was paid at the local revenue office. In The Gambia, unqualified teachers were paid in cash, and head teachers had the discretion to withhold payment in cases of absence.

Ensuring efficient delivery of pay may also reduce absenteeism. In Liberia and Zambia, some remote schools routinely closed for up to a week each month as teachers traveled to collect their pay. Increasingly countries (including The Gambia, Lesotho, Uganda, and Zambia) are migrating to the use of electronic transfers into teachers' bank accounts. This improves the efficiency of delivery, but without adequate controls, it may reduce the ability of the system to respond quickly to teacher absenteeism or movement to other schools.

Parent teacher associations or school management committees had little involvement in monitoring the schools, and were mainly involved in fundraising activities. There were some isolated reports of parents monitoring teacher attendance or taking action in cases where absenteeism was unacceptably high. In Uganda, one district officer reported pressure from parents to address teacher absence. In Malawi, some school management committees were very active, in part because of training through nongovernmental organizations (NGOs).

Teacher unions were also present in all countries, with the majority of public teachers represented. All had some role in advocacy for better pay and conditions for teachers, but many were also involved in professional development activities, providing training opportunities for teachers or helping to define codes of professional conduct.

THE TEACHER CAREER STRUCTURE

In all of the case-study countries, most teachers were employed as permanent public servants, with incremental salaries based on a fixed salary scale. There was no significant use of contract teachers. Teachers were employed on short-term contracts only when unqualified, or in some cases where retired teachers were offered opportunities to work after retirement age.

The career structures tended to reward improved academic credentials more than performance or even attendance in the classroom. In some cases this provided perverse incentives, encouraging teachers to neglect their duties in pursuit of additional qualifications. Opportunities were limited for promotion within the classroom. Some countries had a grade of senior teacher, but few had robust merit-based systems for selection to this grade. In some cases the provision of paid study leave allowed some of the most able teachers to upgrade their qualifications and leave the profession, sometimes spending almost as much time on paid leave as they did teaching. The scale of paid study leave was in some cases very significant. In The Gambia in 2007, the number of teachers leaving to start full-time study leave was almost half of the number of newly qualified teachers recruited.

TEACHER FINANCE

While teacher remuneration varied, it was generally much higher than the national average and a multiple of per capita GDP, but lower than the alternative opportunities open to graduates or similarly educated people. Starting pay for a qualified primary teacher ranged from $490 per year in Zanzibar to $3,292 in Zambia. These salaries allowed a very modest standard of living. In Zanzibar and Liberia, a teacher with one dependent would have a per-person income of less than $2 per day (purchasing power parity). Even in Zambia, the starting salary of a primary teacher was only two-thirds of the cost of the basic basket of needs for a family of six. On the other hand, these salaries represented multiples of GDP per capita, ranging from 1.5 times GDP per capita in Zanzibar to five times GDP per capita in Uganda.

In general, teaching was perceived as less attractive than other government jobs with the same entry qualifications. Teaching was seen as having a slower pay progression, fewer opportunities for promotion, and sometimes fewer opportunities for additional benefits. As a result, teaching tended to be the "profession of last resort," absorbing those who had attained the minimum qualifications but failed to get any of the jobs seen as more desirable. This pattern of recruiting contributed to the difficulty of attracting teachers for subjects where there was a labor market shortage, such as mathematics and science.

In some cases the *per-student* cost of teacher provision was much higher at the secondary level than at the primary. Shorter working hours, multiple optional subjects, and inefficiencies resulting from specialization resulted in lower student-teacher ratios, while the higher qualifications for secondary teachers resulted in higher costs. In extreme cases, the cost per student was more than ten times the cost at the primary level. Cost differentials of this magnitude will severely constrain the expansion of secondary education, unless addressed by improved teacher utilization.

TEACHER ISSUES—AN INTERCONNECTED SYSTEM

The case-study countries face multiple challenges in teacher policy. These can be grouped into four major areas:

1. **Supply:** More teachers need to be trained, particularly in specific subjects.
2. **Distribution:** More and better-qualified teachers, and possibly more female teachers, are required in remote schools.
3. **Quality:** To improve the quality of learning outcomes, the quality of teaching must be improved. This may involve recruiting better-educated teachers, provision of better training and continuous professional development, and improved support, management, and supervision systems.
4. **Cost:** These challenges must be met within constrained budgets.

These four dimensions of teacher policy are closely interrelated. Measures to improve teacher supply or improve deployment may require recruitment of teachers with lower entry standards, with implications for quality. Conversely, measures to improve quality by raising the certification requirements, such as requiring a degree for secondary teaching, may reduce supply and exacerbate deployment problems by drawing in more teachers from urban backgrounds. Any measure involving financial incentives, accelerated promotion, or increased training or supervision has cost implications. Figure 1 illustrates the interrelationships of these four dimensions.

Figure 1 Teacher Policy: Four Interrelated Dimensions

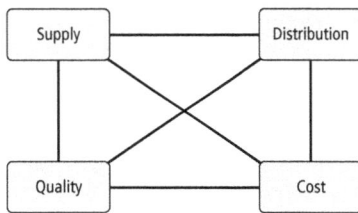

Developing the right teacher policies is likely to require careful examination of the range of challenges, and making difficult trade-offs between these four dimensions. While no single response will be appropriate in every case, the case studies suggest a series of promising practices.

PROMISING PRACTICES

Planning for teacher supply: Significant improvements in teacher supply could be attained by better planning and regulation of teacher training. Three components are required to achieve this. First, education sector plans should include forecasts of the number of newly trained teachers required. Second, teacher attrition should be monitored on an annual basis, for each level and subject specialization. Third, on an annual basis, the entry to teacher training should be adjusted in response to analysis of requirements and attrition.

In some countries, planning alone will not end the shortages, as there are insufficient qualified applicants for teacher training. In such cases there is little choice but to adjust entry requirements until sufficient student teachers can be recruited.

Where this has to be done, it should be done in conjunction with an adjustment of the teacher-training curriculum, to take account of the lower standard of entry of the intake.

In planning for teacher supply, targets and expectations must be realistic. In a number of cases where unrealistic aspirations appeared to be damaging the quality of education. In many countries, for example, it was expected that all upper secondary classes would be taught by university graduates, while in practice the majority of upper secondary classes were taught by diploma holders. In line with the policy, diploma courses for secondary teachers were precluded from preparing teachers to teach at the upper secondary level.

The second path into teaching: Recruiting unqualified teachers locally, and providing them with training while they remain in-service is a promising interim solution for addressing both supply and deployment problems. Where the current output of primary teachers is inadequate, some recruitment of unqualified teachers is inevitable. Recruiting unqualified teachers locally, and then providing opportunities for them to upgrade to qualified status through in-service training, has become a second path into the profession. If good-quality in-service training can be provided, this second path can help address the problem of teacher distribution by recruiting teachers already resident in the areas where there are teacher shortages. Building the capacity of people who are from the remote areas seems a better long-term solution than providing subsidies to encourage teachers from other areas to move to places they consider undesirable. This can also contribute to addressing the teacher gender gap in rural areas by providing access to teaching jobs for female teachers already living in the area, and thus avoiding the specific difficulties of deploying female teachers to remote areas. However, this approach does present some quality risks, and is dependent on the availability of people with sufficient levels of educational achievement to adequately understand the subject matter they will have to teach.

Location-specific teacher recruitment: Recruiting teachers for specific locations seems to improve the probability of filling unpopular posts, and may also improve retention and gender balance. Central recruitment of teachers, followed by planned deployment, has consistently caused difficulties, as teachers resist moving to the least-desired locations. Location-specific recruitment provides teachers seeking employment with a strong incentive to accept a remote location, and allows them some choice of location. This enables some teachers to work in their home areas or areas where they have some relatives, thus increasing the probability of retention. Similarly, the element of choice enables female teachers to apply for jobs in areas close to their families, and may increase the proportion of female teachers in rural schools. Where schools have a say in the selection of teachers, they are likely to favor local candidates, further improving take-up and retention. Lesotho, Zambia, and Uganda have all had positive experiences with local recruitment.

Specific interventions for mathematics and sciences: Breaking the cycle of poor performance in mathematics and sciences is likely to require some specific interventions. One promising option is the provision of booster courses in teacher colleges, to improve the mathematical and scientific understanding of student teachers. Such booster courses are planned in Lesotho and are being implemented in The Gambia.

Broader criteria for selection into teacher training: Selecting into teacher training on the basis of willingness to work in rural areas, as well as academic performance, can help alleviate deployment difficulties. Selection into teacher training has traditionally been based mainly on academic performance. In some cases this biases the selection toward students from more urban and better-off backgrounds, who are more likely to have better academic results. These students are less likely to see primary teaching as their long-term career goal, or to be willing to accept a post in a remote rural school. Yet the success of the teacher training college in Malawi (and similar colleges in Mozambique and Angola) operated by the NGO Development Aid From People to People (DAPP) in attracting students who want to work in rural areas demonstrates that there are people who both are willing to teach in rural schools and have the ability to succeed in pre-service teacher training. Broader selection criteria, including both academic performance and interview, offer an opportunity to draw into teaching more of those who want teaching as their career, more of those who are willing to work in rural areas, and more students from linguistic and ethnic minorities who are underrepresented in teaching.

Targeted incentives for teachers in remote areas: Use of incentives to encourage teachers to take up posts in rural schools can be effective if carefully targeted. The case of The Gambia illustrates the effectiveness of incentives. In The Gambia, following the introduction of a carefully targeted hardship bonus of up to 40 percent of salary, experienced teachers began requesting transfers to hardship schools. In 2008, more than one-third of the teachers in regions 3, 4, and 5 who were not in hardship schools requested transfers to hardship posts. However, this is likely to be a viable option only where the teacher salaries are relatively low, and significant incentives are financially sustainable.

Monitoring of teacher attendance: There were strong indications that teacher absenteeism could be reduced with adequate monitoring. In Uganda, the absenteeism rate fell from 27 percent in 2004 to 19 percent in 2006, following increased measures to monitor attendance. In The Gambia, it was reported that church-run schools had higher teacher attendance than government schools, because managers routinely monitored attendance and deducted pay from teachers who were absent without permission. Also in The Gambia, teacher absenteeism decreased following the introduction of cluster monitors, who visited schools on a regular basis. Increased monitoring of teacher attendance is one of the low-cost interventions likely to have an immediate impact. Involvement of parents and community groups in monitoring attendance may also offer an efficient cross-check on school-reported data.

Decentralized monitoring: Systems of cluster-level supervision of schools allow supervision frequencies that are sufficient to have an impact on quality. In most countries, schools were inspected by external officials less than once per year, a frequency of inspection clearly insufficient to act as a quality assurance mechanism. Two countries had much more frequent external supervision of schools, and in both cases (The Gambia and Eritrea), this was achieved by having decentralized inspectors serving small clusters of schools, living in their cluster, and using low-cost transportation. In The Gambia, cluster monitors live at one of the ten schools in their cluster and are provided with a motorbike for transportation. In the context of the high cost of transportation, and the shortage of vehicles, supervision at the cluster level seems to be a viable method to ensure reasonable supervision frequencies.

Practical training for head teachers: No matter how frequent the external supervision, the daily supervision of teachers falls to school management. Despite the acknowledged importance of school leaders, too often head teachers were ill-prepared for this role. Most countries had no automatic training for head teachers. Instead, short courses were provided, frequently with external funds, and small numbers were drawn into long-term university-based courses. Provision of routine, practical training to all head teachers at the time when they take up their posts seems a promising measure to improve the quality of management and supervision of schools.

CHAPTER 1

Introduction

Enrollment in both primary and secondary schools in Sub-Saharan Africa has risen dramatically since Education for All was adopted as a global priority at the 1990 international conference at Jomtien, Thailand. Despite these successes, however, much remains to be done. Significant numbers of children never receive any schooling, and much larger numbers start school, but leave without achieving a reasonable standard of basic education.

Teachers are central to both the coverage and quality of education. Shortages of teachers and the inability to provide teachers in particular locations are major constraints to expansion. Teachers are also central to determining the quality of educational outcomes, and efforts to improve educational quality focus heavily on improving the capacity and management of teachers.

The scale of the challenges of teacher provision is daunting. For many countries there are simply not enough teachers. The number of primary teachers in Sub-Saharan Africa may have to rise by 68 percent, from 2.4 to four million in the period from 2006 to 2015 in order to meet the requirements of providing universal primary completion (UIS 2006). Even where there are sufficient teachers, they are not always employed where they are most needed, or specialized in the appropriate subjects. Often teachers are not well prepared to provide good quality education, lacking both sufficient understanding of the subject matter and appropriate pedagogical skills. Weak management and inadequate support for teachers have frequently resulted in a demoralized teaching force, poor professional standards, and high absenteeism.

In Sub-Saharan Africa, all of these challenges must be addressed in a context of severe resource constraints. Despite receiving a large proportion of government expenditure and assistance from external development partners, education systems frequently have inadequate funds. The combination of demographic factors, including growing young populations, and the pressures of expansion of coverage and retention, place heavy demands on these limited resources. Education is a labor-intensive activity, and teacher salaries typically account for the greatest part of the education budget. Teachers are often the single-largest group of public servants, and their remuneration has a significant impact on national budgets.

As countries seek to expand coverage, quality, and equity in their education systems, developing appropriate teacher policies is among the most important issues. Identifying the optimum policies is a complex issue, involving difficult choices and trade-offs. There is a need to achieve an adequate supply of suitable and trained teachers, at a cost that allows universal access. However, the simple equation of cost and quality is complicated by issues of deployment, utilization, retention, and the personal characteristics that impact on education.

This book is a synthesis of challenges and policy options emerging from a study of teacher issues in eight countries in Anglophone Africa conducted between August 2006 and January 2008. The inclusion of countries in the study was based largely on government interest in having a study of teacher issues. This selection of countries, therefore, is not intended to be statistically representative of the region, but rather to provide illuminating examples. Individual country studies were conducted mainly to support the development of teacher policies within each country. With that aim, the country studies were customized to the context and priorities in each country, while exploring a broadly comparable set of issues. Each country report involved collection of data from a spectrum of available sources, including official statistical data, existing analyses and reports, and opinions and insights gathered in school visits and interviews with a range of stakeholders, including teachers, head teachers, and education managers.

While the ultimate aim of any education system is the quality of student learning, these case studies do not attempt to study the impact of specific teacher characteristics on student outcomes. Instead, the study starts with the assumption that in order to achieve good quality education outcomes, a competent and committed teacher is required. Teacher policy is assessed through the lens of this basic aim.

The eight countries examined here, Eritrea, The Gambia, Lesotho, Liberia, Malawi, Uganda, Zambia, and Zanzibar[1] have some common traits. All are loosely described as part of Anglophone Africa, that is to say that English is the international language predominantly taught in schools, although not the mother tongue of the majority of the population. In all cases secondary schooling is taught mainly through the medium of English, at least officially. All eight countries have seen very significant expansion of participation in primary education in the last decade, and are now experiencing rapid expansion in secondary education. In the course of the expansion, all of the countries have experienced problems of teacher supply, which they have addressed in a variety of ways including increasing class size and recruiting untrained teachers.

The issues revealed by the studies are examined under five headings. The first part is concerned with the policies for teacher provision, and explores teacher supply, deployment, and utilization. Part two examines how teachers are prepared, looking at both pre-service and in-service training of teachers. The third part looks at the teachers' professional life after initial training, and examines the issues of teacher management and career structure. Part four is concerned with the financing of teachers. Finally, the last section provides an overview of these issues and highlights some of the promising policy options.

This book is intended to serve three purposes. First, as a report, it is intended to provide a **systematic comparative analysis** of a series of issues relating to teacher policy found in the eight case countries. Second as a **support for policy makers**, it is intended to identify promising practices and potential difficulties, and illustrate policy alternatives within the cases. Thirdly, as a **reference**, it is intended to provide easy access to comparative information on specific issues.

CONTEXT: TEACHERS AND TRENDS

The eight education systems examined in this study were organized in different ways, as shown in figure 1.1. The overall primary and secondary education cycle involved a total of 12 years in most cases, but Uganda had 13 years, and Zanzibar 14. The primary education phase, also called lower basic, or elementary, ranged from five years in Eritrea to eight years in Malawi, but was more frequently six or seven years.

In most cases, the phase of secondary education could be divided into two parts, which may be considered a junior and senior cycle of secondary education. However, the extent to which these are separated varied a good deal. In Eritrea, there were distinct middle school and secondary schools, with separate buildings and teachers. In Malawi, both phases of secondary education were normally offered in the same institutions and teachers frequently taught a mix of classes.

For all of the countries, the years from 2000 to 2006 were a period of growing enrollment. As table 1.1 illustrates, the numbers of students rose at all levels, but the fastest percentage growth was at the secondary level. In The Gambia, lower basic enrollment grew 18 percent in this six-year period, while secondary enrollment grew 92 percent.

Enrollment rates varied, but were significantly higher at the primary than at the secondary level. The gross enrollment rate (GER) for primary education ranged from 72 to 134, with four of the countries having GER over 100 (table 1.2). Secondary enrollment rates were much lower, particularly for upper secondary.

Table 1.3 shows that the pupil-teacher ratio (PTR) also varied widely. Liberia and Zanzibar had primary PTRs under 40, while Malawi had a PTR of 76. Generally, the PTR was higher in primary schools than at the secondary level. In Malawi the primary PTR was 76, but the secondary PTR was 21. In Lesotho the figures were 45 and 26, respectively.

Most countries had significant numbers of teachers who were not considered qualified by local standards (i.e., holding the certification required in the country to

Figure 1.1   Years of Schooling in Primary and Secondary Education

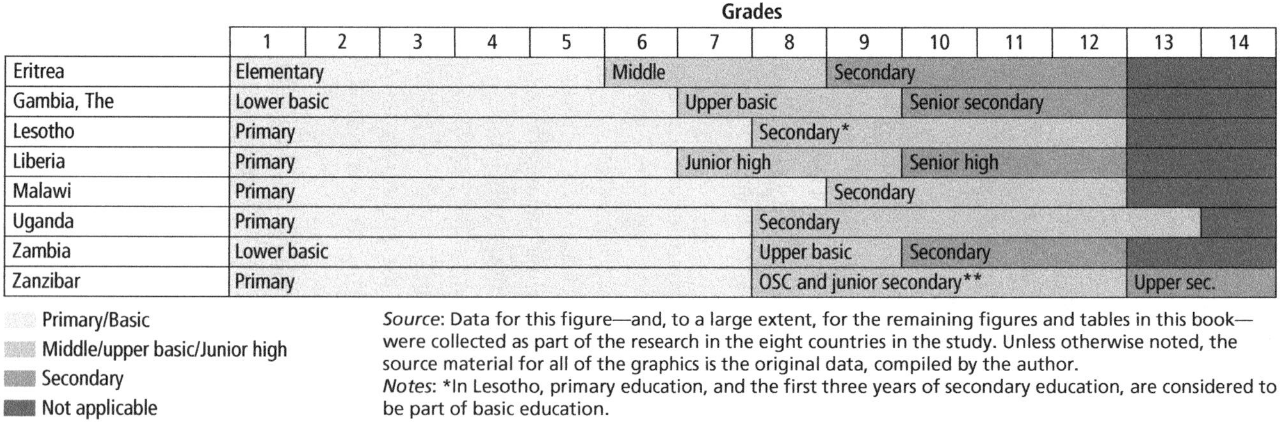

	Grades													
	1	2	3	4	5	6	7	8	9	10	11	12	13	14
Eritrea	Elementary					Middle			Secondary					
Gambia, The	Lower basic						Upper basic			Senior secondary				
Lesotho	Primary							Secondary*						
Liberia	Primary						Junior high			Senior high				
Malawi	Primary								Secondary					
Uganda	Primary							Secondary						
Zambia	Lower basic							Upper basic		Secondary				
Zanzibar	Primary						OSC and junior secondary**						Upper sec.	

Legend:
- Primary/Basic
- Middle/upper basic/Junior high
- Secondary
- Not applicable

Source: Data for this figure—and, to a large extent, for the remaining figures and tables in this book—were collected as part of the research in the eight countries in the study. Unless otherwise noted, the source material for all of the graphics is the original data, compiled by the author.

Notes: *In Lesotho, primary education, and the first three years of secondary education, are considered to be part of basic education.
**In Zanzibar, the first year of junior secondary, known as the Orientation Secondary Class (OSC), is being abolished, reducing the junior secondary cycle to four years.

Table 1.1   Growth in Student Enrollment, 2000–06

	2000	2006	Increase	% Increase
Gambia, The, lower basic	154,664	182,055	27,391	18
Gambia, The, upper basic	37,831	63,842	26,011	69
Gambia, The, secondary	14,857	28,535	13,678	92
Malawi primary	3,016,972	3,280,714	263,742	9
Malawi secondary	164,459	218,310	53,851	33
Uganda primary	6,559,013	7,224,761	665,748	10
Uganda secondary	518,931	814,087	295,156	57
Zambia lower basic	1,633,292	2,549,481	916,189	56
Zambia upper basic	173,462	298,475	125,013	72
Zambia secondary	102,839	193,726	90,887	88

Table 1.2   Gross Enrollment Rates in the Eight Countries Studied

	Year of data	Primary	Lower secondary/middle school	Upper secondary
Eritrea	2004–05	72	48	24
Gambia, The	2005–06	85	59	35
Lesotho	2006	127	40[a]	
Liberia	2006	87[b]	32[b]	11[b]
Malawi	2006	122	20[a]	
Uganda	2006	112	22[a]	
Zambia	2007	134	58	25
Zanzibar	2006	94	40	6

a. Secondary
b. Estimated

Table 1.3   Pupil-Teacher Ratio in the Eight Countries Studied

	Data year and notes	Primary	Lower secondary	Upper secondary
Eritrea	2004–05 (public schools)	53	63	50
Gambia, The	2005–06 (all schools)	41	27	32
Lesotho	2005 (all schools)	45	26[a]	
Liberia	2006 (all schools)	32	7.6	7
Malawi	2006 (all schools)	76	21[a]	
Uganda	2006 (all schools)	48	19[a]	
Zambia	2006 (all schools)	54[b]		20
Zanzibar	2006 (all schools)	35	29[a]	

a. Secondary
b. Primary/lower secondary

Table 1.4   Number of Teachers and the Proportion Who Were Qualified

	Primary, elementary		Lower secondary		Upper secondary	
	No. of teachers	% Qualified	No. of teachers	% Qualified	No. of teachers	% Qualified
Eritrea	7,154	85	2,198	25	1,510	82
Gambia, The	4,477	60	2,385	70	845	89
Lesotho	10,172	61	3,569	60	—	—
Liberia	26,188	38	12,357	48	4,536	56
Malawi	43,197	90	10,386	31	—	—
Uganda	150,135	67	42,673	76	—	—
Zambia	50,615	84	—	—	8,461	12
Zanzibar	5,781	85	2,480	58	—	—

Sources:
Eritrea, Education Management Information System (EMIS) 2004–05, public schools.
The Gambia, EMIS 2005–06, all schools.
Lesotho, EMIS 2005, all schools. Lesotho does not distinguish between lower and upper secondary teachers; the figures shown are for all secondary, Forms A–E.
Liberia, EMIS data 2006, all schools.
Malawi, EMIS data 2006, all schools. Data do not separate upper and lower secondary levels.
Uganda, EMIS data 2006, Data do not separate upper and lower secondary levels.
Zambia, EMIS 2006. Note that upper basic teachers are not distinguished from lower basic (primary) teachers.
Zanzibar, EMIS 2006, public schools. Note that while 58% of secondary teachers are qualified, only 9% have a degree, which is required to teach forms 3–6.
— Not applicable.

be considered a qualified teacher). In some cases, the greatest use of unqualified teachers was at the primary level. In The Gambia, Lesotho, and Uganda, at least one-third of primary teachers were unqualified (table 1.4). In others the problem was most acute at the secondary level. In Eritrea 75 percent of middle school teachers were unqualified, and in Malawi 69 percent of secondary teachers were unqualified.

Attendance of girls in Africa is generally lower than that of boys (GMR 2008). There are strong indications that the presence of female teachers is an important factor in encouraging enrollment by girls, both by providing a role model, and by making schools safer for girls (UNESCO-EFA 2003). In the eight case-study countries, the gender pattern varied. In Lesotho and Zanzibar, the majority of primary teachers were female (table 1.5), while in the other six countries the majority were male. In all cases, there were fewer female teachers in the secondary schools than in the primary schools, and only Lesotho had a majority of female teachers at the secondary level.

In addition, in some countries HIV infection rates are high, and present further challenges. Rates of infection vary widely, and data are elusive, as the nature of the disease and attitudes toward it prevent open reporting of infection. Table 1.6 summarizes the information the study was able to collect. In Lesotho, Zambia, and Malawi, the adult infection rates are high, exceeding 15 percent.

Table 1.5   Percentage of Teachers Who Were Female

	Data year and notes	Primary, elementary	Lower secondary	Upper secondary
Eritrea	2004–05 (public schools)	40	10	13
Gambia, The	2005–06 (all schools)	34	18	12
Lesotho	2005 (all schools)	78	56[a]	—
Liberia	2006 (all schools)	29	18	14
Malawi	2006 (all schools)	38	19[a]	—
Uganda	2006 (all schools)	39	22[a]	—
Zambia	2006 (all schools)	48[b]	—	40
Zanzibar	2006 (all schools)	70	36[a]	—

a. Secondary
b. Primary/lower secondary

Table 1.6   Summary of HIV Data Related to Teachers

Eritrea	No data on HIV status of teachers. National infection rate estimated at 2–3 percent.
Gambia, The	No data on HIV status of teachers. National infection rate estimated at 1.2 percent.
Lesotho	Estimates of HIV prevalence among teachers range from 22 percent to 27 percent. Anti Retroviral Treatment is provided free to all citizens through the health service.
Liberia	HIV prevalence rate for the 15–49 age group was estimated at 2–5 percent.
Malawi	Infection rate among teachers is estimated at 15–25 percent. Anti Retroviral Treatment is provided free through public hospitals.
Uganda	Infection rate estimated at 6.4 percent in the general population. There is no specific information on teacher infection rates.
Zambia	Adult infection rate estimated at 16 percent. In voluntary testing of teachers in 2005–06, 18 percent of those who were tested were found to be HIV positive. Teacher mortality (from all causes) has been rising. In 2006, 872 basic education teachers died, 1.7 percent of the workforce. In the same year 166 high school teachers died, 1.9 percent of the total.
Zanzibar	No data available on teacher infection rates.

These high infection rates are reflected in high levels of teacher deaths, and in absence resulting from illness.

These tables and data provide an illustration of the challenges of ensuring quality teaching in every classroom. While these countries have varied systems and structures, all are experiencing expansion of enrollment and are expecting to expand further, with the most rapid growth at the secondary level. In preparing for this expansion, they also face challenges arising from the existing situation, including large class sizes in some situations, large numbers of unqualified teachers in others, and additional challenges in addressing the gender imbalance and the HIV pandemic.

NOTE

1. Zanzibar is part of the United Republic of Tanzania. However, it retains considerable autonomy over its internal affairs. According to the Constitution of the United Republic of Tanzania, both primary and secondary education are the responsibility of the Zanzibar Government while tertiary education is a "union matter." For the sake of simplicity, Zanzibar is treated as a country case study throughout this report.

PART I

Teacher Provision

CHAPTER 2

Teacher Supply

Participation in education in Sub-Saharan Africa has increased dramatically in recent years, and the region has the fastest growth in school enrollment of any region (UIS 2006). There are now more children in school on the continent than at any other time in history. This rapid expansion is creating a requirement for increasing numbers of teachers, and in most countries the supply is not increasing rapidly enough to prevent shortages. In contrast to trends in other world regions, pupil-teacher ratios have been rising in Sub-Saharan Africa since 1991 (UIS 2006).

In all of the case-study countries there was a mismatch between the requirement for new teachers and the current output of newly qualified teachers. In most cases this has resulted in teacher shortages; in a few cases, however, there was a significant oversupply of teachers, but shortages in specific specializations. This reflects weak systems for planning and regulating teacher supply. None of the countries has a robust system for monitoring teacher attrition and wastage, forecasting teacher requirements, or using these data to adjust intake into training programs.

The inadequate supply of qualified teachers has resulted, in most cases, in large-scale use of unqualified primary teachers. In many cases the shortage of capacity in initial teacher training is such that there is little alternative to continued recruitment of unqualified teachers in the medium term.

In all of these cases, secondary education has been expanding more rapidly than primary education, with resulting pressure for additional secondary teachers. In a few cases, domestic secondary teacher supply was so limited that the country was dependant on expatriate teachers for some subjects. Secondary teacher supply is more problematic, as it involves training the required number of teachers in each subject of specialization. In most countries teachers train for two subjects, but often prefer to further specialize in an additional subject. While most countries expect a degree-level qualification at least for upper secondary teachers, few have an adequate supply of graduate teachers, and in practice most secondary teachers have diploma-level qualifications.

In almost all cases there was a more acute shortage of teachers of mathematics and the sciences. This appears to be a cyclical problem, with weak teaching of mathematics in primary school, and subsequently in secondary school, resulting in national shortages of mathematics and science skills, and consequent shortages of teachers of these subjects.

In some of the countries, the supply of new teachers was constrained by the limited number of school-leavers with the required entry qualifications. In these cases, there is little alternative to lowering the entry requirements to teacher training, at least in the short term. This has implications for both course content and focus.

TEACHER SHORTAGES

The problem of teacher supply has taken different forms in different countries, with impacts on the number of unqualified teachers and the pupil-teacher ratios in each system.

In Lesotho, with an initial surge in student numbers, the pupil-teacher ratio increased, accompanied by an increase in the number of unqualified teachers. More recently, the government has been able to recruit extra teachers, but the proportion of unqualified teachers is still rising. By 2007, the PTR had been reduced to 42, but only 60 percent of primary teachers were qualified.

In Malawi, the government policy was not to recruit unqualified teachers. The supply of qualified teachers was not sufficient even to replace the losses from attrition, and the overall number of primary teachers fell from 47,000 in 2000 to 43,000 in 2006, while the numbers of pupils in school continued to increase. As a result, by 2006, most primary teachers were qualified, but the pupil-teacher ratio had risen to 76 pupils per teacher.

In Uganda, there was an initial shortage of trained primary teachers following the introduction of universal primary education (UPE), leading to the recruiting of untrained teachers. However, the supply of trained teachers has subsequently increased, and by 2007, the main constraint was government funding to employ additional teachers. In 2006, there were 48 pupils per teacher, and 68 percent of teachers were qualified.

In Zambia, financial constraints prevented teacher recruitment in 2002–03, creating a large pool of unemployed qualified teachers. The stagnation in the number of government teachers resulted in a pupil-teacher ratio of 76 in grades 1–4.

MISMATCH OF OUTPUT AND REQUIREMENTS

Table 2.1 illustrates that, for many countries, the national output of trained teachers was poorly matched with the requirements of the system. In Zanzibar, the output of newly trained primary teachers in 2007 was roughly 33 percent of the total teaching force, resulting in a large oversupply and considerable frustration among

Table 2.1 Output of Primary Teachers as a Percentage of the Primary Teacher Numbers

	Number of primary teachers	Newly trained teachers each year	Teacher output as a percentage of the teaching force	Notes on teacher output data
Eritrea	7,154	644	9.0	2006–07
Gambia, The	4,477	256	5.7	2006
Lesotho	10,172	220	2.2	2006
Liberia	26,188	650	2.5	New course
Malawi	43,197	2,449	5.7	Intake 2006
Uganda	150,135	6,729	4.5	Intake 2006
Zambia	50,615	2,990	5.9	Output 2005
Zanzibar	5,781	1,907	33.0	Output 2007

the young teachers who were unable to find jobs. In contrast, in Lesotho and The Gambia, the output of newly trained primary teachers was equal to or less than the number of teachers lost each year to retirement and resignation, leaving an inadequate supply to meet current needs or expansion in the education system.

In Zambia, the picture was more complex. As a result of the hiring freeze, there was a substantial pool of qualified teachers who had not been employed in the teaching service. This created a perception of oversupply. However, analysis of the projected numbers indicated that supply was inadequate and even if all of the backlog of trained teachers were absorbed (assuming that they have not found more attractive work in the meantime), the country would experience teacher shortages within a few years.

SHORTAGES AT THE SECONDARY LEVEL

With the expansion of primary education over the last decade, the number of students completing primary school has increased, creating both an opportunity and pressure for expansion at the secondary level. For many of the countries in this study, and many others in the region (Mulkeen et al. 2007), secondary education is now the fastest-growing subsector. This expansion at the secondary level has resulted in teacher shortages at this level.

These teacher shortages have resulted in increasing class sizes in some countries. In Eritrea, the middle school population grew 400 percent between 1990 and 2006 and the pupil-teacher ratio increased from 47 to 63. In The Gambia, the pupil-teacher ratio at the secondary level grew from 23 to 31 between 1999 and 2006.

The shortage of secondary teachers has also resulted in the use of unqualified or underqualified teachers. In Lesotho only 60 percent of secondary teachers were qualified, and only half of the teachers recruited since 2000 were qualified. In Zanzibar only 59 percent of secondary teachers were qualified. Of these, most had a diploma qualification, which is intended only for teaching Forms 1 and 2; only

9 percent of the secondary teachers had a degree, which is the required qualification for teaching the upper secondary classes.

UPWARD MIGRATION

One of the consequences of this shortage has been the migration of teachers trained for the primary level into secondary schools. In some countries the scale of this migration is very significant. In Eritrea, 66 percent of the middle school teachers in government schools were only qualified at the elementary level. In Malawi, 61.5 percent of the teachers in secondary schools were actually qualified as primary teachers. These primary teachers were most often in the newly established Community Day Secondary Schools (CDSS), which in some cases had no qualified secondary teachers at all.

This large-scale migration from primary to secondary teaching without additional qualifications has a number of implications. First, it results in a loss of qualified teachers from the primary level, where they will often be replaced by untrained teachers. Secondly the teachers who migrate are poorly trained for secondary teaching, particularly in view of the pattern of subject specialization and in some cases the language of instruction. In Eritrea, for example, elementary teachers are trained to teach all of the subjects in the curriculum in the mother tongue, while middle school teachers are expected to teach one or two subjects, in English. In Malawi as well, primary teachers are expected to teach all subjects, while the secondary teachers are expected to be specialists.

The more abundant opportunities at the secondary level also lead primary teachers to seek to upgrade their qualifications with a view to moving to the secondary level. This can have a significant impact on the numbers in primary teaching. The annual intake to upgrading programs is equivalent to about a quarter of the number of primary teachers trained annually in Zambia, and almost half of the output of primary teacher training in The Gambia.

Upward migration through additional qualifications has both negative and positive consequences. It does draw some of the qualified teachers, probably the best educated, from primary schools. However, the opportunity for progression may act as an incentive for initial entry to the profession, and as a motivation for teachers to undertake further study. Where the upgrading courses are provided while teachers remain in the classroom, the availability of in-service opportunities may increase retention of teachers, at least for the period of study.

EXPATRIATE TEACHERS

In a few of the cases in the study, inadequate teacher supply had resulted in dependence on expatriate teachers. In Eritrea, expatriates were deliberately recruited to address skills shortages, and were paid significantly more than national teachers. The expatriates, mainly from India, were teaching in secondary schools, mainly in mathematics, sciences, and information and communications technology. The annual cost of each expatriate teacher was approximately U.S.$14,000, including salary and other benefits—more than 10 times the cost of an Eritrean secondary teacher.

For other countries, the expatriate teachers were paid at the same rate as nationals. In both The Gambia and Liberia, expatriates, mainly from other West African countries, were employed as secondary teachers, reflecting both the inadequacy of domestic teacher supply and the instability in some of the neighboring countries. Migration of teachers may help address temporary teacher shortages or surpluses in neighboring countries. Some Zambian teachers, unable to find jobs following a government hiring-freeze in 2002–2003, migrated to Botswana, addressing Botswana's immediate need for teachers (Appleton, Sives, and Morgan 2006). However, economic migration of teachers tends to cause shortages in lower-income countries nearby. Lesotho, for example, is vulnerable to loss of expertise to South Africa, where teacher pay is higher. Hence, teacher shortages in South Africa tend to result in migration of qualified teachers from Lesotho, with the burden of training replacement teachers falling on the lower-income neighbor. Dependence on expatriate teachers may also leave host countries vulnerable to fluctuations in supply. In The Gambia, at the time of this study, there had been high attrition as teachers from Sierra Leone returned home following the improvement of the security situation in that country.

SUBJECT-SPECIFIC SHORTAGES

Even when there were sufficient teachers in absolute numbers, there were frequently shortages of secondary teachers for specific subjects, particularly mathematics, science, and to some extent international languages. Similar shortages have been observed in Francophone African countries, with the result that subjects are sometimes not taught, or taught only by nonsubject specialists (Caillods 2001). These shortages may weaken student performance, as research has shown that assigning teachers to courses in which they are not trained to teach negatively affects student achievement (UIS 2006).

Typically, the greatest shortage was in teachers of mathematics and science. In The Gambia, the human resources database recorded that in 2007, 38 percent of upper basic teachers were qualified to teach social and environmental studies (SES), but only 17 percent were qualified to teach mathematics, despite the fact that both are core subjects. In Lesotho one secondary school reported that it had only one applicant for a recently advertised mathematics post, compared with approximately 30 applicants for a humanities post.

These shortages reflect subject imbalances in teacher training. In Lesotho, only 8 percent of the student teachers in 2006 were studying mathematics as one of their two teaching subjects, while 47 percent were studying English. In Uganda, only 15 percent of the student teachers taken in to the national teachers colleges (NTCs) in 2005–06 were studying mathematics as one of their two teaching subjects, although mathematics and sciences accounted for 40 percent of curriculum time.

The problem of poor teacher skills in mathematics and the sciences was not confined to the secondary level. In Zanzibar, where primary teachers specialize, mathematics teachers were in short supply. Nearly half of all primary teachers had a qualification to teach Kiswahili, but only 16 percent had a qualification to teach mathematics. In practice, mathematics was often taught by teachers without a mathematics qualification.

The impact of poor mathematics skill was also felt in countries where primary teachers do not specialize. In Lesotho, inspection reports suggested that some primary teachers were not teaching the required mathematics because they themselves did not have the required knowledge.

SCHOOL LEAVERS AS A CONSTRAINT ON TEACHER TRAINING

In a few of the case-study countries, teacher supply was constrained by the shortage of school leavers qualified to take up the places in teacher training courses. Typically the best-qualified school leavers took up places in the universities, and the entrants to teacher training were drawn from those with sufficient qualifications for teacher training, but without grades good enough to earn a university place. In Lesotho and The Gambia, the relatively small output from secondary school, and relatively large university intake left insufficient candidates for teacher training, while the teacher training colleges were unable to fill the available places in primary teacher training.

In Lesotho, only 3,500 students passed the COSC (school leaving examination) in 2005, and only 1,450 achieved a division 1 or 2, the normal requirement for entry to higher education. The National University of Lesotho had expanded its intake to 1,440, absorbing almost all of those with the expected qualifications. The teacher training college, the Lesotho College of Education, accepted those with a division 3 pass, provided they had passed English, but was unable to fill all of the available places. In The Gambia, the one national teacher training college, Gambia College, was unable to fill the places in its primary teacher course in any year between 2001 and 2006 because of insufficient qualified applicants (table 2.2).

In Eritrea, the expansion of the Eritrea Institute of Technology had resulted in a reduction of the examination scores required to enter an institution of higher education. This in turn resulted in a reduction in the entry requirement to the training for elementary schools teachers at the Asmara Teacher Education Institute

Table 2.2 Intake to the Lower Basic, Primary Teachers Certificate Course in
Gambia College, 2001–06

	2001	2002	2003	2004	2005	2006
Target	374	403	425	350	350	350
Actual students registered	331	386	170	340	237	256
%	89	96	40	97	68	73

(ATEI). New entrants to ATEI in 2007 typically had GPA scores of only 0.6 or 0.8 (out of a maximum of 5). In effect, this means that some of the newly enrolled student teachers may have failed two of their best five subjects and achieved only the lowest passing grade in the other three.

This constraint to intake and quality was not found in every case. Some countries had substantially greater numbers leaving secondary school than could be absorbed in post-secondary education and teacher training. In Zambia in 2005, 23,000 students passed the grade 12 examination with 5 credits including English, while the total intake into the university was approximately 2,000 and the entry into pre-service teacher training was under 7,000. As a result, there were more applicants than places, and entry was competitive.

Uganda also had adequate numbers of qualified applicants, and there was competitive entry to places in both universities and in teacher training. In 2006, 45,539 students achieved two or more principal passes in the Uganda Advanced Certificate of Education (UACE), the required standard for entry to the national teachers colleges (NTC) to train as a secondary teacher. This was far in excess of the intake into universities and NTCs. Entry to the primary teacher colleges (PTCs) was based mainly on performance in the O-level (junior secondary) examination, where there were even larger numbers of qualified applicants.

SHORTAGE OF STUDENT TEACHERS IN MATHEMATICS AND SCIENCE: THE VICIOUS CYCLE

The supply of school leavers with the appropriate qualifications is often an even more serious constraint on the training of mathematics and science teachers. In Zanzibar the teacher training colleges are restricted in their ability to train mathematics teachers because of the shortage of entrants with even a pass in mathematics. Nine hundred and seventy students passed the A-level examination in 2006, but only 53 of these passed mathematics.

Despite a lower admission requirement, Uganda found it difficult to fill the places for secondary mathematics and science teacher training in the national teachers colleges (NTCs). Entrants to science courses are expected to have one principal pass in a science subject, while entrants to other courses are required to have two principal passes. This reflects the imbalance in examination results. In the 2006 UACE examination, 25,836 students passed history, but only 5,776 passed mathematics and only 3,235 passed chemistry.

This weakness in mathematics and science can be seen as a vicious cycle. The shortage of good mathematics teachers leads to poor teaching of mathematics at the primary and secondary levels. This results in poor performance in mathematics in examinations, which in turn restricts the supply of entrants to teacher training, and the supply of qualified mathematics teachers.

The shortage of teachers in mathematics and the sciences has other negative consequences as well. If there is a national shortage of mathematical and scientific expertise, then people with these skills tend to command greater salaries in the labor market. This can lead to losses of teachers of mathematics to other jobs. Further, if there is a shortage, then the available mathematics and science teachers tend to be able to avoid working in the least desirable schools, leaving an even greater shortage in the most remote rural areas.

PLANNING FOR TEACHER SUPPLY

Ensuring an adequate supply of trained teachers requires some planning and management. Some, mainly high-income, countries are able to avoid planning teacher supply by allowing autonomous universities to train teachers and thus allowing the labor market to regulate supply. This is not a viable option for low-income countries in Africa, for a number of reasons. First, in many countries the labor market of teachers does not function normally, as there are school leavers so eager for any form of free further education that entry to teacher training does not necessarily reflect either perceived availability of a teaching job, or the desire to work as a teacher. Second, planning of the requirements for newly trained teachers is needed to avoid wasting the public funds that are used to train teachers. In these case studies, poor planning frequently resulted in training too many of some kinds of teachers, wasting both public resources and opportunities for training additional students in areas of need. Third, teacher training output is slow to respond to labor market signals, as there is typically a lag of several years between the decision about how many student teachers to enroll in training and the emergence of trained teachers. Where education enrollment is expanding rapidly the labor market will tend to lag behind the trend, resulting in shortages. Fourth, the intake to teacher training is often used to address equity issues. Governments may wish to increase the proportion of female teachers, or teachers from particular geographic regions, or ethnic or language groups. These issues of the composition of the teaching force may not be addressed by a poorly functioning labor market.

Managing teacher supply calls for monitoring of two main parameters, **teacher requirements** and **teacher attrition**, and adjusting the intake into teacher training to appropriate levels. Both the requirement and attrition are fluid, and respond to both external factors and to policy. The number of teachers needed changes over time in response to changes in population, admission policy, promotion and repetition policy, and teacher allocation policy. The attrition rate is also in flux, and reflects *inter alia* the teacher age profile, retirement policy, deployment policy, teacher pay and benefits, and competing opportunities in the labor market.

In a sense, teacher supply is analogous to managing a pool of water with a leak. If both the volume of water in the pool and the size of the leak change constantly, there is a need for constant adjustment of the flow into the pool, to maintain the desired level.

Box 2.1 offers a method for calculating how many teachers are needed in a specific country in a given year.

Ministries of Education typically have educational planning units, responsible for preparing projections of school enrollment and teacher requirements. However planning units tend to focus on the finance needed for teachers, rather than the supply implications. Planning for teacher finance requires a calculation of the total number of publicly-funded teachers needed, and the cost per teacher.

Planning for supply requires a more complex calculation. First needed is a calculation of the number of new teachers who need to be trained, taking into consideration both the number of additional teaching positions and the number of replacement teachers. Second, both public and private schools need to be taken into account, because if the national supply is inadequate, the public and private schools will simply compete for the available teachers. Thirdly, numbers need to be disaggregated into teachers for specific subjects, and in some cases teachers from specific regions, or language groups. Among the eight countries studied, none had projections of the number of newly trained teachers that would be needed for each subject.

Even if projections of teacher requirements were available, many of the ministries have weak mechanisms to regulate teacher supply. In some cases teacher training institutions are semi-autonomous and can control their own intake. In Zanzibar the main source of secondary teachers, the State University of Zanzibar (SUZA), is a semi autonomous body. In other cases teacher training is controlled by the Ministry of Education (MoE), but not very responsive to the projected needs. In Zambia teacher training colleges are controlled by the MoE, but intake to each college and each subject is determined by historical patterns, rather than as a response to projected requirements.

BOX 2.1   HOW MANY TEACHERS ARE NEEDED?

The number of teachers needed in any year can be calculated from the population in the school-age group, the expected gross enrollment rate (GER), and the average pupil-teacher ratio.

As primary education expands, the GER tends to rise above 100 for a period, and then gradually reduce to close to 100. During the period of expansion, the number of new teachers needed increases sharply. However, once enrollment stabilizes, the number of new teachers required each year should fall to the number required to replace teachers lost to attrition.

For long-term planning of major infrastructure items such as teacher training colleges, each country should have an estimate of the number of teachers that will be required in the long term.

As a rough approximation, it can be assumed that a country with six years of primary education will require between 3,400 and 4,700 teachers per million of population. This estimate is calculated as follows: An African country with slow population growth, such as Lesotho, has approximately 23,000 children per million of population in each one-year age cohort. A country with fast population growth, like Zanzibar, has approximately 31,000 children per million of population in each age cohort. Based on these population figures, and a PTR of 40:1, the number of teachers required can be calculated.

General Calculation for Teachers per Million of Population

Population	Children in each year	Teachers for each year of primary school	Teachers for 5 years of primary school	Teachers for 6 years of primary school	Teachers for 7 years of primary school
Slow-growing population	23,000	575	2,875	3,450	4,025
Fast-growing population	31,000	775	3,875	4,650	5,425

Note: Calculations assuming a pupil-teacher ratio of 40:1. All numbers are per million of population.

ATTRITION

One of the keys to managing teacher supply is an understanding of teacher attrition. Teacher attrition is the number of teachers leaving their teaching jobs for any reason, including retirement, illness, death, movement to nonteaching posts, and resignation. This information is not always recorded in detail. Where it is available, attrition data are usually drawn from one of two sources, both of which have potential for error. One source of data is the department responsible for managing human resources. This should capture all employees who leave the public service, but does not always distinguish between teaching and nonteaching staff, or capture data on moves from teaching to nonteaching posts. The second main source of data is the annual survey conducted for the EMIS. This survey often includes a question asking each school to record the number of teachers who have left the service in the previous year, and the reason for departure. Unfortunately, this does not allow analysis of the subject specialization of the teachers who have left. In some cases the wording is not sufficiently clear to ensure that teachers leaving the school, but moving to another teaching post, are not considered as attrition. In Zambia, for example, the 2005 and 2006 EMIS surveys asked schools about "teachers leaving in the previous year," and it was unclear whether this was interpreted consistently by schools as referring only to those leaving the profession.

Reported teacher attrition rates in the countries studied ranged from 2 percent to 10 percent per annum, as shown in table 2.3. In those countries where the attrition rates for primary and secondary teachers were recorded separately, the attrition rates for secondary teachers were in all cases higher. In Lesotho, for example, the attrition rate for primary teachers was 3 percent, while the attrition rate for secondary teachers was up to 10 percent.

Some of these teacher attrition rates are unusually low, and likely to increase. In a stable system there is an inverse relationship between teacher attrition rates and the average time in service of each teacher. If each teacher recruited works for 50 years, then one in 50 would retire each year, resulting in an annual attrition of 2 percent. An average length of service of 33 years would result in an annual attrition of 3 percent. In reality it seems likely that many teachers will teach for much shorter periods than 33 years, especially in countries with low life expectancy. An attrition rate of 6 percent, reflecting an average length of service of 16 years, is probably the lowest attrition rate that could be achieved in the long term, and many will probably be higher.

Rapid changes in the scale of education systems tend to cause unusual patterns in teacher

Table 2.3 Annual Teacher Attrition Rates

Eritrea	2%
Gambia, The	3%
Lesotho	3% primary, up to 10% for secondary
Liberia	Estimated at 1.6%
Malawi	5% primary, 10% for secondary
Uganda	5% primary, 6% secondary
Zambia	9%, though may be overestimated by inter-school movement
Zanzibar	5% primary, 6–7% secondary

Table 2.4   Teacher Attrition in Lesotho, 2004: Reasons for Leaving

Reason for leaving	Number	Percent
Resigned	362	55
Retired	140	21
Deaths	131	20
Desertion	17	3
Medical retirement	4	1
Total	654	100

Source: Teaching Service Commission records.

attrition. In times of expansion large numbers of new teachers are recruited at the same time, which can result in an unusually young age profile, and lower attrition than could be sustained in a stable system. In Zanzibar, for example, only 12 percent of teachers are over the age of 50 (2006 data). When the teacher requirement stabilizes after an expansion, this can result in a "bulge" in the age profile, as the unusually large number of teachers recruited in the expansion gradually gets older. this can result in unusually high attrition some years later, of course, as this cohort of teachers reaches retirement age.

In the cases where the cause of departure is known, most teacher attrition is not a result of retirement or death, but of resignation (table 2.4). In Lesotho, 55 percent of the teachers who left the public service in 2004 left through resignation. Involuntary causes of attrition, including death, illness and retirement, accounted for less than half of the teacher departures. Most teacher resignation is likely to be for the purposes of taking up another job, so resignation rates are likely to be highly related to the alternative opportunities available to teachers in the labor market.

As attrition is partly a reflection of alternative opportunities in the labor market, it should be expected that the attrition rates will vary for different types of teacher. As stated, in all the cases where information was available there was a higher rate of attrition for secondary teachers than for primary teachers. In addition, there were anecdotal reports in Lesotho and Malawi of higher attrition rates for teachers with degrees than for those with diploma qualifications, and higher rates for mathematics and science teachers than for teachers of other subjects. Unfortunately, the recorded data were not sufficiently detailed to permit further examination.

These patterns of attrition have important implications for the planning of teacher supply. First, if the current attrition rates are relatively low, and reflect an unusual age distribution resulting from recent expansion, teacher attrition rates can be expected to rise over the medium term. Second, if a significant portion of teacher attrition is a result of voluntary movement to alternative employment, it should be expected that attrition rates will vary with the labor market demand, and will be highest for the best educated teachers and those whose skills are in greatest demand. In responding to labor market demand, attrition rates are likely to fluctuate with market conditions and be highest in times of rapid economic growth.

"WASTAGE"

Unfortunately, in some countries, many of the teachers who are trained never actually enter the teaching profession, a phenomenon often known as "wastage."

Accurate information on wastage is rarely available, but there are indications that it is a significant problem in some cases. In Zambia in 2005 there were 1,017 teachers with degrees working in schools, but the University of Zambia had an output of over 400 graduate teachers each year (431 in 2006). Clearly most of the graduates were either not entering the teaching profession, or not staying in it very long.

In Liberia the University of Liberia graduated 13 teachers with degrees in primary education and 23 with degrees in secondary education, in 2007. Most of these were existing teachers who had undertaken the degree course on study leave from their posts. However, despite a system of bonding, where students were required to sign a bond committing them to work in schools after completing their training, very few returned to the public service once their degrees were completed.

GUIDELINES FOR PLANNING TEACHER SUPPLY

The number of each type of teacher required can be projected relatively easily, given a small number of key pieces of information:

- The projected student enrollment
- The policy on pupil-teacher ratio
- The existing number of teachers, broken into their subject specialties, where applicable
- The annual teacher attrition rate
- The annual output of newly trained teachers
- The wastage rate (the percentage of newly qualified teachers who do not take a teaching job).

Ideally, these calculations should include both public and private schools, and public and private teacher training, unless there are particular restrictions in the teacher labor market.

A model used to project the number of primary school teachers needed in The Gambia in 2005 is presented in box 2.2.

Calculation of the number of teachers required for particular subjects (as is the usual case in secondary schools) is a little more complex, because (i) some subjects are optional, (ii) not all subjects have the same expected teaching time, and (iii) some teachers teach more than one subject.

For optional subjects, the number of teachers should be reduced in proportion to the number of students who study that subject. This assumes efficient teacher deployment and utilization.

For a compulsory subject, the calculation can be based on curriculum load. Consider the example of a country where each secondary school hosts 40 periods

BOX 2.2   RAPID TEACHER REQUIREMENT PROJECTION MODEL

The table below shows a projection for the number of primary teachers that was needed in The Gambia in 2005. In this projection, the primary school enrollment was expanding steadily, raising teacher requirements. However, the number of new teachers trained was only marginally greater than the numbers lost through attrition and movement to upper basic (lower secondary) schools. As a result, the shortage of teachers was projected to increase to 30 percent of the teacher requirement by year 7. A model such as this highlights to policymakers the need to adjust the numbers of teachers being trained to meet national needs.

		Year 1	Year 2	Year 3	Year 4	Year 5	Year 6	Year 7
A	Projected enrollment	193,801	205,001	215,273	224,085	235,659	248,562	264,891
B	Pupil-teacher ratio	41	41	41	41	41	41	41
C	Teachers required (A/B)	4,727	5,000	5,251	5,465	5,748	6,062	6,461
D	Number of teachers	4,428	4,510	4,407	4,413	4,418	4,423	4,428
E	Attrition rate (percent)	3	3	3	3	3	3	3
F	Attrition (D*E/100)	133	135	132	132	133	133	133
G	Movement to upper basic teaching	100	100	100	100	100	100	100
H	Teachers, after attrition (D − F − G)	4,195	4,274	4,175	4,180	4,185	4,190	4,195
I	Newly trained teachers	331	140	250	250	250	250	250
J	Wastage rate	5	5	5	5	5	5	5
K	Wastage (I*J/100)	17	7	13	13	13	13	13
L	New teachers taking up jobs (L − K)	314	133	238	238	238	238	238
M	Teachers, minus attrition, plus new entrants (H + L)	4,510	4,407	4,413	4,418	4,423	4,428	4,432
N	Balance of requirements and actual, minus values indicate a teacher shortage (M − C)	−217	−593	−838	−1,048	−1,325	−1,635	−2,029

Source: Calculations based on Department of State for Education data, collected in 2007.
Notes: In row D, the first year shows the actual number of teachers. Subsequent years are calculated numbers, based on the starting year, minus attrition, plus new entrants.

per week. If mathematics is a compulsory subject, and each student is supposed to receive eight periods of mathematics per week, then eight of every 40 periods taught will be mathematics (20 percent). If 20 percent of teaching time is spent on teaching mathematics, then 20 percent of the teachers should be mathematics teachers, if each teacher teaches only one subject.

If each teacher teaches two subjects, the calculation is less precise, as the balance of the workload between the two subjects can vary. If it is assumed that each teacher spends half of his or her time on each subject, and if 20 percent of teaching time is to be spent on mathematics teaching, then 40 percent of teachers would need to have mathematics as one of their teaching subjects. In countries where teachers have a major and minor teaching subject, a less even balance may be assumed.

Box 2.3 presents a method for calculating the number of teacher needed in a secondary school where each teacher specializes in two subjects.

BOX 2.3 CALCULATING TEACHER REQUIREMENTS WHERE TEACHERS SPECIALIZE

The table below illustrates how to calculate the number of teachers needed in a secondary school system where each teacher specializes in two subjects. For the purposes of planning and teacher allocation, there are 100,000 secondary students and there is a student-teacher ratio of 35:1.

Mathematics is compulsory for all students, and has eight periods per week, out of a total of 40. As a result, 20 percent of the teaching time is spent teaching of mathematics, and the requirement for mathematics teachers is 20 percent of the full-time teachers (571 teachers in this case). However as each teacher specializes in two subjects, the number of teachers who should be qualified to teach mathematics is doubled, assuming that each teacher may only teach the subject for half of the time.

For history, the picture is different, as only 40 percent of the students take history, and it requires only four periods per week. As a result, the total number of history teachers required is less than one-quarter of the required number of mathematics teachers.

A	Number of students	100,000		
B	Student-teacher ratio	35		
C	Teachers required	2,857		
	Subject	Mathematics	Chemistry	History
D	Percent of students who take this subject	100	30	40
E	Number of students who take this subject (A*D/100)	100,000	30,000	40,000
F	Number of periods per week (all subjects)	40		
G	Number of periods per week (this subject)	8	5	4
H	Percent of curriculum time for this subject (G*100/F)	20	13	10
I	Full-time equivalent teachers required (C*(H/100)*(D/100))	571	107	114
J	Number of subjects each teacher teaches	2		
K	Number of teachers who should have this as *one* of their teaching subjects (I*J)	1,143	214	229

DIRECTIONS FOR POLICY MAKERS

These case studies highlight the need for better planning of teacher supply. Effective planning both anticipates requirements and adjusts systems of teacher training to provide the required numbers. Countries with rapidly expanding education systems often experience teacher shortages, as teacher supply lags behind the increased demand. Unless requirements are projected and supply adjusted accordingly, countries will likely experience periods of teacher shortage during expansion, and oversupply when demand stabilizes.

Clear lines of responsibility within government departments are necessary to effectively plan and regulate teacher supply. In the countries studied, planning units normally produced projections of teacher requirements. However, these were poorly linked with the policies and actions of the institutions with responsibility for training teachers. The increasing autonomy of universities also appeared to make it more difficult for ministries to regulate supply, even when these universities were state funded.

Constant monitoring of data from a variety of sources, disaggregated by different types of teacher, is key to planning for teacher supply. Without monitoring, it is difficult to either identify problem areas or assess where the limited funds would be best used to address shortages. Chief data sources are likely to be student enrollment and projections, teacher numbers and qualifications, and the rates of attrition and wastage. Teacher attrition and wastage rates, in particular, require annual monitoring, as they are likely to respond to prevailing labor market conditions, and may fluctuate rapidly.

RESPONSES TO A TEACHER SHORTAGE

Many of the countries in this study face shortages of qualified teachers. While the obvious long-term solution is to increase the supply of trained teachers, there is a considerable delay before such an increase has an impact. In response to the shortage of qualified teachers, most of the countries studied had little option but to allow recruitment of unqualified teachers.

Recruitment of unqualified teachers, and subsequent provision of in-service training to bring them to a qualified status, presents some benefits for policy makers facing a teacher shortage. First, it provides an immediate solution to the shortage. Second, it can reduce wastage, as this approach is less likely to involve those who will not actually take up teaching posts. Even if teachers leave the profession after a few years, they have at least been teaching for that period of time. Third, recruitment of untrained teachers may help in recruiting teachers from rural communities, and may contribute to reducing the inequities in deployment.

However, there is legitimate concern that the use of untrained teachers may reduce the quality of teaching, at least for the period before they complete their in-service training. The empirical evidence of the quality of untrained teachers is limited, and presents mixed findings (UIS 2006). Part of the reason for the mixed research findings may lie in the diverse nature of unqualified teachers. The category of unqualified teachers can range from people who are poorly educated and have a very weak comprehension of the material they are expected to teach to highly educated people with a high level of understanding of the content, who lack the formal certification required to be qualified teachers.

The Gambia provides a good example of this diversity. In the periurban region 2, education managers reported satisfaction with the performance of unqualified teachers, while in the more remote region 5, management's perception was that the unqualified teachers were noticeably inferior to the qualified teachers. These reports may reflect the differences in background and motivation of the unqualified teachers. In region 2, the typical unqualified teachers were well-educated school leavers, often teaching while repeating their secondary school-leaving exams in order to improve their chances of university entry. As a result, many of them had better grades in their school-leaving examinations than those who were admitted to teacher training. In region 5, the unqualified teachers typically had a much lower level of education, and most would not have been eligible for teacher training. However, there is little objective evidence, as yet, of the impact of this difference on student learning.

RESPONSES TO A SHORTAGE OF QUALIFIED SCHOOL LEAVERS

In some of the case-study countries, a shortage of suitably qualified school leavers limited teacher supply. This presents a difficult challenge for policy makers, and one that cannot be solved simply by increasing the capacity of teacher training. In the long term, the shortage of qualified applicants is likely to be resolved through improved secondary completion, but in the interim, the countries experiencing this problem cannot afford to wait an entire generation for a sufficient supply of school leavers.

In most of the case studies where this problem was apparent, the response was to lower the requirements for entry to teacher training. In Lesotho, The Gambia, and Eritrea, the entry requirements were lowered in response to the inability to fill teacher training places. In Uganda, the entry requirement for school leavers entering the national teacher colleges with mathematics or sciences was lowered to increase the intake in these subject areas.

Ideally, compensatory measures should be put in place to help less-well-qualified school leavers to succeed in teacher training. In The Gambia, additional courses in

English and mathematics have been introduced into The Gambia College Primary Teachers Certificate to compensate for falling entry requirements. In Lesotho, the Ministry of Education and Training (MoET) was planning to introduce a booster course in mathematics and science that school leavers with poor mathematics and science scores would take before entry to teacher training.

There may also be a need for compensatory measures at the secondary school level. In Zanzibar, for example, there were plans to introduce science camps for secondary students, to help raise the quality of mathematics and the sciences at the secondary level.

RESPONSES TO HIGH WASTAGE OR ATTRITION

Both attrition and wastage are, at least in part, the result of alternative opportunities available in the labor market. Clearly, that part of attrition resulting from death, illness, or retirement for reasons of age is not amenable to change. However, the data suggest that the bulk of attrition and wastage are a response to more attractive options in the labor market.

Voluntary attrition in response to more attractive employment could be addressed through three different strategies. First, the teacher remuneration and conditions of employment could be improved to increase the attractiveness of teaching. While this is the most obvious solution, it is unlikely to be affordable in many of the countries studied, particularly in areas of skill shortage, where private sector salaries are highest. Second, teachers could be required to stay in the profession for a period of time through a bonding scheme. None of the countries included in the study had effective bonding schemes, and where bonding had been tried, poor enforcement had undermined its impact. Third, the targeting of those recruited into teacher training, and subsequently into teaching, could be refocused to include the teachers most likely to remain in the profession. At the secondary level, where data were available, the attrition rate for teachers with degrees was higher than for teachers with diploma-level qualifications. This suggests that, in the medium term, increasing the number of graduates trained for teaching may have little impact, while preparing more and better-quality diploma students might be more productive.

CHAPTER 3

Teacher Deployment: Getting Teachers to the Right Places

The challenges of teacher supply are compounded by difficulties with teacher distribution. Almost all countries in Sub-Saharan Africa find it difficult to achieve an equitable deployment of teachers, with the poorest and least developed areas experiencing the greatest difficulty in teacher supply (UIS 2006). Uneven deployment also results in inefficient utilization of some teachers, increasing the cost of provision (Verspoor and SEIA team 2008). In general, the best qualified teachers tend to be even more inequitably distributed (UIS 2006). Further, there tends to be a gender pattern in teacher distribution, with fewer female teachers in the more remote areas (Bennell and Akyeampong 2007). As these geographical patterns of teacher distribution tend to amplify existing inequities in education attainment, addressing the inequity of deployment is essential to ensuring greater educational opportunities in the difficult areas.

These general patterns were reflected in the case study countries. In almost all of the cases, there were unemployed teachers seeking work, and vacancies that could not be filled, because of unwillingness to move to undesired locations. Deployment systems were not generally successfully in achieving equitable distribution of teachers. Frequently the greatest differences were between schools within the same district, reflecting the importance of micro-geographical factors such as access to roads or other facilities. Some schools had ten times the pupil-teacher ratio of other schools in the same district. The qualified teachers were normally distributed even more unequally, as were teachers of mathematics and science, and female teachers.

In response, the case study countries had different strategies to increase the supply of teachers to rural schools. Most countries had some financial incentives to encourage teachers to rural areas, but these were hampered by poor targeting, and appeared to have a limited impact. One exception was in The Gambia, where a new incentive that was both very substantial (up to 40 percent of basic salary) and carefully targeted was resulting in experienced teachers requesting transfers to remote schools. Other promising approaches included location-specific recruitment, which allowed teachers some choice of location, and tended to result in teachers from rural areas taking posts in local schools. Lesotho was using a local recruitment system, Zambia allowed some choice of location, and Uganda was introducing local recruitment for secondary teachers in difficult schools. There were some indications that there were people who were willing to teach in rural areas, and that it could be beneficial to target these people more specifically for entry into teacher training.

UNEVEN TEACHER DISTRIBUTION

The reluctance to work in hardship areas was often reflected in higher pupil-teacher ratios in rural districts. In Malawi in 2006, the average pupil-teacher ratio in urban primary schools was 46:1, while in rural schools the average was 81:1. In Uganda in 2006, the average pupil-teacher ratio in primary schools in the capital city, Kampala, was 40:1, while in rural Kitgum district the ratio was 93:1 (figure 3.1).

District pupil-teacher ratios tell only part of the story, however. *Within districts*, there were also very significant variations in teacher distribution, often much greater than the variations *between districts*. This intra-district variation in teacher deployment is often invisible in statistical bulletins, which usually report district averages. These micro-level variations in teacher distribution may reflect variations in the attractiveness of specific schools, such as the availability of housing, or the proximity to roads and access to centers of population.

Figure 3.1   Variation in District Average Pupil-Teacher Ratio (PTR) in Primary Schools

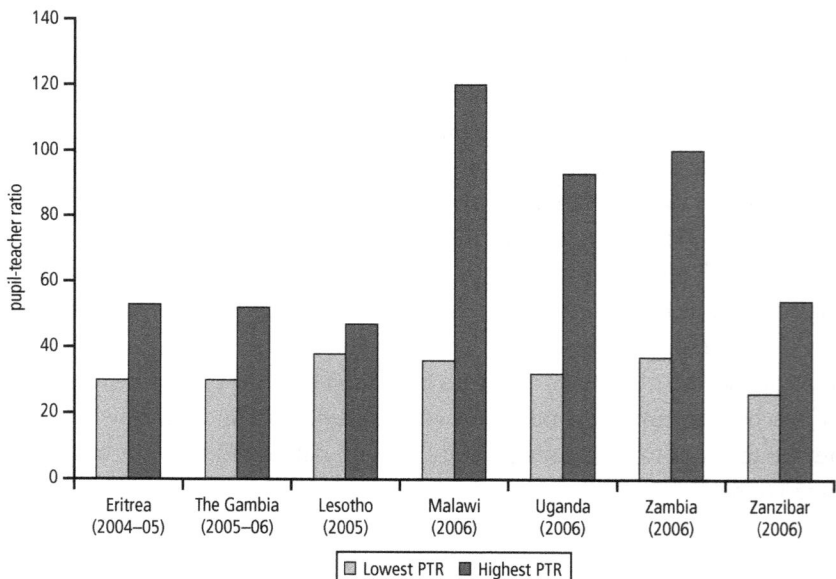

Table 3.1 illustrates the extent of this variation in Malawi, showing the highest and lowest pupil-teacher ratios in schools within the same district. Similarly, in Zambia, there was wide intradistrict variation. Pupil-teacher ratios in the 115 government schools of the Chibombo district ranged from 22:1 to 210:1.

DISTRIBUTION OF QUALIFIED TEACHERS

In most cases, the best-qualified teachers were even more unevenly distributed and overconcentrated in urban areas. In Lesotho, 80 percent of the primary teachers in lowland schools were qualified, while in the mountain schools only 52 percent were qualified. In Zanzibar, in the relatively rural Micheweni district, there were only two qualified mathematics teachers in 2006, serving a district with 3,800 secondary school students.

Table 3.1 Malawi: Schools and Pupil-Teacher Ratio in Dziwe Zone, Blantyre Rural District

School names replaced with letters	Pupils	Teachers	PTR
A	191	1	191
B	762	4	191
C	567	3	189
D	906	5	181
E	665	5	133
F	742	6	124
G	320	3	107
H	194	2	97
I	668	7	95
J	435	6	73
K	676	10	68
L	309	7	44
M	46	3	15
Total	6,481	62	
Average	499	4.8	105

Teachers with degree-level qualifications seem particularly reluctant to work in hardship schools. In Uganda in 2006, 60 percent of the secondary teachers in Kampala district were graduates, while in the rural Yumbe district only 11 percent were graduates. In Malawi, it was reported that 20 graduate teachers were deployed to rural schools in Kusungu district, but only two or three of these stayed in the jobs for even one year. In 2006, Zambia's Shangombo district, in a rural location in Southern province, did not have a single applicant with a degree.

GENDER

There was also, in most countries, a gender pattern in teacher distribution, with a smaller proportion of female teachers in rural areas. In Uganda, 57 percent of primary teachers in Kampala district were female, but only 15 percent of teachers in the rural Kaabong district were female. In Zambia, 60 percent of teachers in government schools connected to the main power grid were female. In schools without a power connection, a proxy for a rural location, only 35 percent of teachers were female. Table 3.2 presents data on the percentage of secondary teachers who are female in selected rural and urban areas of the case-study countries.

Table 3.2 Percentage of Secondary Teachers Who Are Female in Selected Rural and Urban Areas

	Urban/well developed region	% Female	Rural/ less developed region	% Female
Gambia, The	Region 1	12	Region 6	8
Lesotho	Maseru	62	Thaba-Tseka	50
Malawi	Urban	36	Rural	13
Uganda	Central	28	Northern	16
Zanzibar	Urban	53	North A	21

Both community and personal factors can deter female teachers from accepting jobs in rural areas. In some countries, rural communities may not accept the arrival of an unmarried female teacher. In The Gambia, it is reported that rural communities will often refuse to provide a house for an unmarried female teacher. In Zambia and Malawi, in some cases rural communities have attempted to drive out unmarried female teachers posted from outside the area. The reluctance to accept unmarried young females into a community is attributed to a variety of dynamics, including religious and cultural factors. In some cases the women of a village are particularly reluctant to accept the arrival of a female teacher in the belief that a relatively well-paid and educated young woman could either attract the attention of the most eligible single men in the village, or even begin a relationship with a married man.

Single women may be unwilling to accept postings to rural areas, as is often the case in Malawi (Kadzamira 2006). A relatively well-educated single woman from an urban background may feel that moving to a rural area will restrict her opportunity to find a husband with a similar or higher level of education and income. In such contexts, the decision to accept a post in a rural school can have major impacts on life chances for a young teacher.

Moving to a rural area is also reported to be difficult for married female teachers. In countries where husbands do not traditionally move to follow their wives' employment, this can mean separating a couple, with the resultant social and health risks. Some countries, such as Malawi, Zambia, and Eritrea, have policies and informal practices that allow a female teacher to request a transfer to locate near to her husband's employment. However, these policies tend to result in migration of female teachers to urban areas, as they are often married to other educated professionals who are mainly employed in urban locations. These policies are also open to abuse. In both Malawi and Zambia there were reports of female teachers producing faked marriage documents to support a claim for a transfer.

LANGUAGE OF INSTRUCTION

For countries where multiple languages are used, deployment of teachers to areas of linguistic minorities seems particularly difficult. Increasingly, mother-tongue instruction is used, particularly in the early years of primary schooling. Even where the mother tongue is not used as the language of instruction, teachers may be reluctant to locate in areas where they do not speak the local language comfortably. Ability to speak the main language of the community is likely to assist a teacher in integrating into a community, and in overcoming student difficulties in understanding the formal language of instruction. Studies in Tanzania and South Africa suggest that at both primary and secondary levels, teachers frequently use the mother tongue to help students understand the lessons conducted in English (Brock-Utne 2007).

Despite the importance of familiarity with the local language, the mother tongue of a teacher is not always a factor in deployment. In The Gambia, teachers are assigned to districts on a somewhat random basis, and no allowance is made for languages spoken. On the other hand, in Zambia teachers are able to apply to the district in which they wish to work, and are more likely to apply to districts where their own language is spoken. A summary of the practices of the case-study countries regarding language of instruction is presented as table 3.3.

HIV AND DEPLOYMENT

In some cases medical conditions are also a factor in teacher location. Recognizing the greater access to medical services in urban areas, Eritrea, Malawi, Uganda, and Zambia allow teachers who are ill to be transferred to a school near to medical facilities. Teachers already located near medical facilities are allowed to avoid redeployment to more remote locations. Ill teachers are often given some flexibility in teaching hours when treatments are necessary. Table 3.4 summarizes the practices of the eight countries vis-à-vis HIV and deployment.

DEPLOYMENT SYSTEMS

In principle, there are two main approaches to teacher deployment. The first is planned deployment, where the education authorities assign teachers in response to an assessment of needs. The second involves allowing teachers to apply for jobs in specific locations, thus deploying themselves in a labor market. In the case-study countries, a variety of different teacher distribution systems were used; the majority involved some form of planned deployment, most commonly arranged in a two-level manner, where central authorities deployed teachers to a region or district, and the district authorities deployed teachers to specific schools.

Table 3.3 Language of Instruction, Summary of Practices

Eritrea: Elementary schools use the mother tongue, comprising a variety of different languages of instruction, principally Tigrinia (53 percent of schools), Tigre (19 percent), and Arabic (10 percent). There is a relative shortage of teachers from the minority language groups. Middle and secondary schools teach in English.

Gambia, The: There is some use of local languages in grade 1, but older classes are officially taught in English. Mother tongue is not considered in deciding on teacher posting.

Lesotho: Primary teaching is in Sesotho up to grade 4, and in English in later years and in secondary schools. Older classes are sometimes taught in Sesotho, as the standard of English of both pupils and teachers is sometimes poor.

Liberia: All teaching is done in English.

Malawi: Junior primary grades (1–4) are expected to use local languages. Older primary classes, and secondary classes, are taught in English. Although there are a number of local languages, only Chichewa was used in the older classes, as materials in other languages have not been produced. Teacher training colleges take in a quota of students from each district, thus ensuring a supply of teachers from each language background.

Uganda: Local languages are used in junior classes in primary schools. Older classes and secondary schools use English. The policy of local languages in lower primary is relatively new and is causing some difficulties, as more than 40 different local languages are used in the country. In some cases, teachers can speak the local language but are not able to write in it.

Zambia: Local languages are used in grade 1, and English is used in the later years. There are 72 local languages, but only seven of these are used as languages of instruction. The current deployment system facilitates the use of local languages in the early grades, as most teachers apply only to districts where the local language is familiar.

Zanzibar: The language of instruction in primary schools is Kiswahili, while secondary schools teach in English. English is not a requirement for entry to teacher training, although the teacher training is done in English. It is reported that student teachers frequently find it difficult to work in English. In practice, the teachers' poor facility with English is a barrier to quality, and a mixture of Swahili and English is often used in secondary schools and in teacher training. There are some reports of difficulties arising from the language policy, as teachers who were trained in English struggle to translate some concepts, particularly in mathematics, into Kiswahili.

Table 3.4 HIV and Deployment, Summary of Practices

Eritrea: Teachers with health problems are not posted to the schools with the most difficult conditions.

Malawi: Teachers with HIV are frequently transferred to urban schools to be nearer to medical facilities. As a result, the percentage of sick teachers in urban areas is higher, contributing to higher absenteeism in these areas as the teachers receive treatment.

Uganda: Efforts are made to facilitate teachers infected with HIV who wish to either (i) move to a school with better health facilities in the vicinity or (ii) avoid redeployment and thereby maintain their linkage with medical facilities familiar with their medical history.

Zambia: Teachers who are ill are allowed to transfer to schools near a health clinic if there isn't one near their post. Many of the sick teachers are referred to the University Teaching Hospital in Lusaka, and as a result, there have been some transfers of ill teachers to the area. However, some of the most seriously ill teachers are nursed at home.

Five of the cases, summarized below, illustrate a range of deployment options. The first three (Eritrea, Malawi, and The Gambia) all used planned deployment systems, but with varying results. Eritrea had a very even distribution of teachers, while in Malawi the central system failed to ensure equitable deployment, particularly to the most remote schools. The introduction of a very substantial financial incentive for teachers in hardship schools in The Gambia seemed to be effective in attracting teachers to difficult locations.

Lesotho and **Zambia** allowed an element of teacher preference in deployment. Lesotho allowed each school to advertise posts and select its own teachers. This resulted in very few unfilled posts and a high level of local recruitment of teachers, but an uneven distribution of the best-qualified teachers. In Zambia the system provided some choice of posting. Teachers were allowed to apply to the district where they wished to work, but not to specific schools. While this achieved some equity in interdistrict deployment, there remained difficulties in intradistrict teacher allocation.

Eritrea uses a planned deployment system at two levels. At the national level, teachers are assigned to one of the six zobas (regions). The management at the zoba level then allocates the teacher to a specific school. Teachers are not given a choice of location, and deployment is strictly enforced. As a result, Eritrea has a very even teacher deployment, as shown in figure 3.2. Within zobas, teacher numbers are very highly correlated with student numbers. There is some variation between zobas, ranging from 30 to 53 PTR, but this is biased in favor of the most rural areas, with the lowest pupil-teacher ratios in the North and South Red Sea zobas (41 and 30 PTR, respectively) reflecting the smaller schools in those zobas.

Figure 3.2 Eritrea, Plot of Teacher and Pupil Number in Each School, by Zoba, Showing the Very Even Distribution Pattern (EMIS data 2004–05)

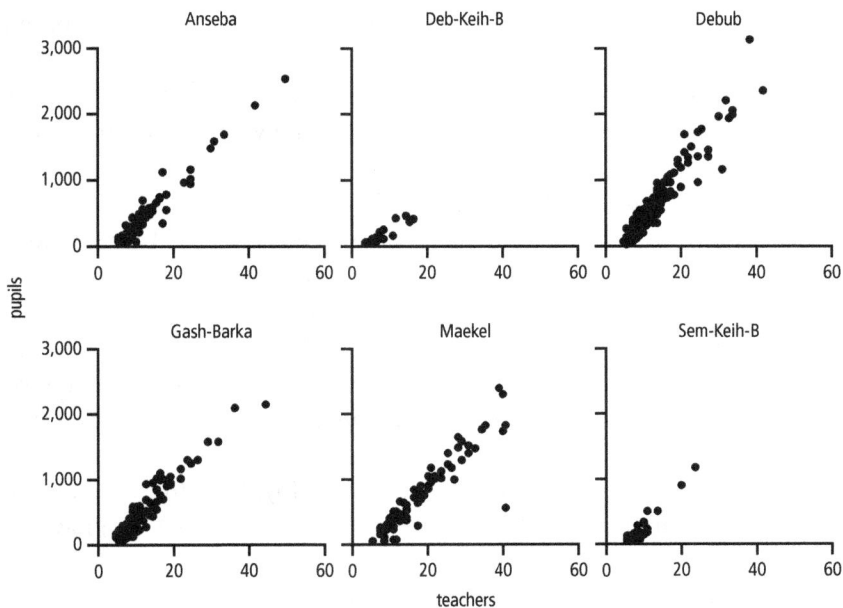

This very systematic deployment in Eritrea is facilitated by the presence of large numbers of teachers who enter teaching as part of their period of national service and have little expectation of a choice of post. These national service teachers are often posted to the most difficult schools, allowing the zoba management some flexibility in transferring the more experienced teachers.

Teacher deployment in **Malawi** is done through a planned deployment system at two levels. The MoEVT assigns teachers to districts, and the district education management deploys them to schools. However, the rational deployment of teachers is weakened because many teachers refuse to accept the posts they are offered, often citing inadequate housing as the reason. In rural Malawi, there are few houses available for rent. Teachers accustomed to brick houses frequently refuse to live in local housing with mud walls and grass-thatch roofs. Teachers also tend to have expectations of electricity and running water, which are frequently not available in rural houses. However, housing alone may not be sufficient to attract teachers; urban areas are also seen as offering a better lifestyle, greater social opportunities, better education and health services, and some additional economic opportunities. There are even greater difficulties at the secondary level, where graduates have higher expectations for housing and lifestyle. As a result, in 2006 only 27 percent of the secondary teachers in rural areas in Malawi were qualified.

> *"if you send one where there is no house, they come back and you are forced to put them somewhere"* (District officer, Malawi, 2007)

Teacher deployment is also weakened because it is not always based on vacancies or needs of schools. When unable to deploy teachers to the schools where they are most needed, district officials normally assign them to other schools in the district, even if there is no immediate vacancy, in order to retain them in the district. Teachers are also allowed to transfer, regardless of vacancies, in the case of marriage or illness. This ability to transfer teachers, even where there is no vacancy, is also rumored to allow transfers based on friendships, influence, and political connections. There is little evidence of effective redeployment of these teachers to schools where they are needed at a later time. High teacher mobility also contributes to weakening of the deployment system in Malawi. Almost 10 percent of teachers move schools each year. Many of the teachers who take up positions in rural schools quickly begin to seek a transfer back to an urban area.

The result of these practices is very uneven deployment. In 2006, urban primary schools had an average PTR of 46:1, while rural schools had an average of 81:1 (table 3.5). In 2006, there were ten districts where the average PTR for the district exceeded 90, and four districts where the average was less than 55.

Table 3.5 Malawi: Teacher Numbers and PTR in Primary and Secondary Schools (EMIS 2006)

National data	Primary teachers	Primary PTR	Secondary teachers	Secondary PTR	Secondary qualified teachers	Secondary qualified PTR
Rural	36,974	81:1	8,008	21.3	2,225	76.8
Urban	6,223	46:1	2,360	20.1	943	50.4
Total	43,197	76:1	10,368	21.1	3,168	68.9

Table 3.6 Comparison of Two Schools in Malawi

Lumbadzi school (periurban)	Mbengwe School (rural)
1,706 pupils in 17 classes	192 pupils in 5 classes
29 teachers	1 teacher
As there are more classes than teachers, each teacher works only part of the school day.	The teacher moves among the 5 classes, and uses 2 local unqualified volunteers as part-time assistants.

Table 3.6 provides data on the numbers of teachers and students in two schools in Malawi—one peri-urban and one rural—to illustrate the wide variations in PTRs that occur in case-study schools.

The Gambia has a two-level deployment system. At the central level, teachers are deployed to the six regions and the regional management takes responsibility for deployment to individual schools. The number of qualified teachers to be deployed to each region is determined centrally, based on pupil and teacher numbers, and the allocation of teachers is done on a random basis, with some adjustments made to distribute female teachers evenly, and to accommodate married couples and ill teachers. Regional authorities are allowed to post the teachers to specific schools, and to recruit unqualified teachers to fill the remaining posts.

This system has resulted in relatively even deployment of teachers, but uneven deployment of qualified teachers. In region 2, 82 percent of the teachers were qualified, compared with only 42 percent of those in the more remote region 5 (2005–06). Qualified teachers have often refused to accept a posting to a rural school, and particularly to the most isolated schools. These qualified teachers have been able to get posts in the more attractive locations, and the places in the most remote schools were often filled by unqualified teachers.

The introduction of a special allowance for teachers in hardship schools has done much to encourage teachers to take up posts in remote areas (box 3.1). This carefully targeted incentive has resulted in large numbers of rural teachers requesting transfer to a hardship school, and a reduction in teachers requesting transfers away from hardship schools.

BOX 3.1   THE GAMBIA'S SPECIAL ALLOWANCE FOR HARDSHIP SCHOOLS

To address the reluctance of qualified teachers to accept hardship posts, The Gambia introduced a special allowance in 2006 to attract and retain teachers located in schools classified as hardship schools. Only schools more than 3 km from a main road are eligible to be considered as hardship schools. This hardship allowance is equivalent to 30 percent of salary for teachers in hardship schools in regions 3 and 4, and 35 percent and 40 percent in regions 5 and 6, respectively.

The hardship allowance is reported to be having the desired effect of encouraging teachers to take up posts in schools in difficult areas. There were reports of teachers requesting transfers to regions 5 and 6 (the most remote from the capital) and teachers within these regions requesting transfers to hardship schools. In a survey of student teachers in The Gambia College in 2007, 24 percent reported that they would choose to work in a hardship position where the additional payment was available, and 65 percent said that if posted to a hardship school, they would take up the post. By 2007, 24 percent of the existing teachers in regions 3, 4, 5, and 6 had requested transfers to hardship posts, with negligible numbers requesting transfers in the opposite direction.

Lesotho uses a local hiring system for teacher deployment. The ministry "grants" teaching posts to schools in response to school population and budget considerations.

Once the school is granted a teaching post, the school management committee can advertise the post and select a teacher to fill the position. Once the teacher is identified, the papers are sent to the Teaching Service Commission (TSC) and the teacher receives a salary from the Ministry.

This local hire system allows most schools to fill the available posts and there is relatively little variation in pupil-teacher ratio between rural and urban areas. As teachers only apply to those schools where they are willing to teach, the problem of teachers failing to accept a post is minimized. However, qualified teachers can more easily compete for the jobs in urban areas, so many of the rural schools recruit unqualified teachers. In 2005, 80 percent of teachers in lowland schools were qualified, compared to only 52 percent of those in mountain schools (table 3.7).

One of the results of this local hire system is that schools are more likely to select an applicant from the area, either in the belief that this will result in better

Table 3.7 Lesotho: Distribution of Qualified Primary Teachers (EMIS data 2005)

	Qualified	Unqualified	Total	% Qualified
Foothills	1,383	692	2,075	66.7
Lowlands	4065	1016	5,081	80.0
Mountain	1420	1329	2,749	51.7
Senqu River Valley	160	107	267	59.9
Total	7,028	3,144	10,172	69.1

attendance and retention, or because of pressure from influential people in the area. In Lesotho it is quite common for rural teachers to work in schools within walking distance of their family homes. This local bias in selection may be a contributing factor to the high proportion of female teachers in Lesotho.

While reducing the number of vacant positions and encouraging local recruitment, this system has some drawbacks. The ministry has little ability to move teachers from schools that are overstaffed, a situation that occurs frequently when new schools are constructed, reducing overcrowding in existing schools. Transfers between schools are sometimes complicated by the pattern of church affiliation of schools, as church authorities seek to hold as many teaching posts as possible in their schools.

Zambia uses a planned deployment system that incorporates some elements of individual choice. Each year the availability of posts is advertised nationally in newspapers, radio, and television, with an indication of the number of posts available at each district. Candidates are asked to apply directly to the district (or districts) in which they are willing to work. The advertising encourages candidates to apply to rural districts, pointing out the higher probability of gaining employment in these districts.

All of the applications are brought together for a meeting of district officers (which can take up to two weeks) at which candidates are selected and deployed. This meeting is monitored by a panel of observers, including representatives of a teachers union and the Zambian president's office, to ensure that the process is fair. Each district first draws from the teachers who applied to their district. If there are insufficient applicants for one district, some applicants from other districts can be offered places. Nevertheless, some remote rural districts are unable to attract sufficient applicants and are left with vacant positions, as many of the teachers transferred to fill the shortages do not take up their appointments.

There are indications that teachers are more likely to accept posts in the districts to which they applied. In Eastern province in 2006, 1,116 teachers were recruited in the first round, and only 83 of these failed to report. In a second round of recruitment, many of those who were appointed had not applied to the district in which they were appointed, and while 869 were appointed, 232 failed to report.

Table 3.8   Zambia: Provincial Differences in Average PTR for Basic Schools (EMIS 2006)

Province	Community	Grant-aided	Public	Private/church	Overall
Central	56	60	72	29	64
Copperbelt	67	66	58	21	55
Eastern	54	62	70	33	63
Luapula	65	77	71	36	69
Lusaka	51	43	52	18	46
North Western	74	78	60	25	65
Northern	69	81	86	19	79
Southern	63	59	68	20	64
Western	58	86	58	34	58
Total	62	68	69	23	64

This deployment system is weakened by a pattern of transfers that allows teachers to leave rural schools after two years. District Education Board Secretaries (DEBS) are often inundated with requests for transfers, and one described them as making up the greatest proportion of her mail. The DEBS usually prioritize those who need a transfer for humanitarian reasons, including illness or marriage. Transfers can only be made once a vacancy exists, but due to district shortages of teachers, it is often possible for teachers to transfer even before they have completed two years in their initial post. This pattern of deployment and transfer may make it more palatable for young teachers to accept a rural posting (as they can see that it is temporary), but it also results in a higher proportion of both inexperienced teachers and vacancies in the most remote schools.

The deployment of teachers remains uneven. Given the demand for the more urban positions, this system tends to fill all the desirable posts as soon as they become vacant, leaving all of the vacancies in remote schools. There were substantial differences both within provinces and within districts. Central province had a PTR of 72 pupils per teacher in government schools, compared with Lusaka province, which had a PTR of 52 (table 3.8). Within Central province, Kabwe district (relatively urbanized) had an average PTR of 37 in government schools, while the rural Chibombo district had an average PTR of 73. Taking government basic schools in the country as a whole, in 2006, one-quarter of districts had an average PTR of 46 or less, while another quarter had a PTR of 83 or more.

DIRECTIONS FOR POLICY MAKERS

In seeking to address the problems of teacher deployment, three main types of strategies were used in the case-study countries. First, some countries provided incentives to attract teachers to difficult locations, using either direct financial incentives or indirect incentives such as housing or a promise of more rapid promotion. Second, in some cases location-specific recruitment systems were used, providing teachers with some choice of location. Third, there were some attempts to target student teachers, who were more likely to accept posts in the areas of greatest need.

HOUSING

"Teachers won't go to a grass thatch house" (District officer, Malawi, 2007)

Provision of teacher housing was one of the strategies used to address the inequity of teacher deployment. In the absence of available housing, teachers posted to a school often refused to accept the post. In areas of subsistence farming, the teachers might be the only salaried employees in the area, and in such a context there was little to support a private market for housing. The absence of housing was a particular obstacle for female teachers, who might be less safe without adequate accommodation. It was also reported that qualified teachers had expectations of a certain standard of accommodation and, as a result, may have been less willing to accept the basic facilities available in rural areas.

While lack of housing is certainly a barrier, public provision of housing is expensive, both in initial and maintenance costs, and none of the countries in this study were able to provide housing for all teachers. In The Gambia, Malawi, and Zambia, teacher housing provision was sufficient for only one-quarter or less of teachers (table 3.9), and even this was often "temporary" housing, sometimes in poor condition.

Where housing is not available, rural communities sometimes provide some accommodation to attract a teacher to the area. Where this is done with community resources, the housing is typically built to local standards, and seen as poor quality by teachers from urban areas. In The Gambia, teacher housing provided by the community was often constructed from mud bricks with thatched roofs (see figure 3.3). In other countries, communities were able to access funds to provide teacher housing, either through social action funds or funds from NGOs. Community provision of housing may have other effects. In The Gambia, it was reported that rural communities would not normally provide accommodation for an unmarried female teacher, believing that she would be a destabilizing influence in the community.

Table 3.9   Zambia: Availability of Staff Houses (EMIS 2006)

	Permanent houses	Temporary houses	Teachers	Permanent houses as a percent of teachers
Basic schools	12,835	5,942	52,317	25
High schools	5,091	300	13,537	38

Figure 3.3   The Gambia: A Head Teacher's House

Mr. Peter Gomez, headmaster of Bassaras lower basic school, outside the house built by the community for his use. The school had 250 students and five teachers, of whom three were qualified.

In addition to housing, teachers might expect access to facilities such as electricity, a clean water supply, and mobile telephone coverage. In Zambia, individual districts are implementing innovative schemes to attract and retain teachers. For example, in Gwembe district a loan is given to female teachers in the most rural schools to purchase solar panels. A summary of the practices surrounding housing in the case-study countries is provided in table 3.10.

FINANCIAL INCENTIVES

Financial incentives are widely used to attract and retain teachers in rural schools, but in most cases have limited impact. A recent example from The Gambia suggests that incentives, if large, well targeted, and well managed, can have a very significant impact.

Four of the eight countries included in this study provided some financial incentive for teachers working in rural schools. Zambia paid an incentive of 20 percent of salary for teachers in rural schools. Uganda had a bonus of 30 percent of salary, recently increased from 15 percent. In Lesotho, the incentive was a fixed amount of 275 maloti (LSL) per month, the equivalent of 20 percent of the starting salary for a qualified teacher.

Table 3.10   Summary of Housing Practices in the Case Study Countries

Eritrea: Teacher housing is not normally provided, although some recently built schools in rural areas have included some teacher quarters.

Gambia, The: Housing is provided in some schools, but not all. It is estimated that about 25 percent of teachers have some form of school housing. Where housing is not provided, communities may provide some form of accommodation, but this is often of poor quality, and a deterrent to teachers accepting rural postings. The government is currently using donor funds to provide permanent teacher housing in rural schools. Where this is provided, there is no charge to the teachers, and they continue to receive their housing allowance. In the absence of housing, many teachers find it difficult to find a place to rent and live in the school, in storerooms, or in other poor conditions.

Lesotho: Teacher housing is provided for some teachers in secondary schools, but rarely in primary schools. Teacher housing, when it is provided, is usually free to the teachers.

Liberia: Teacher housing is not normally provided at schools, although a few NGOs have constructed teacher housing. It is reported that rural communities often provide some basic accommodation for teachers.

Malawi: Some schools provide houses for teachers. In 2006, there were 11,812 permanent teachers' houses and 5,594 temporary ones (EMIS 2006), providing one house for every 4.2 teachers in the public schools. In other areas, the communities are asked to provide a house in order to attract a teacher. Where a teacher house is provided, the teacher is expected to pay a rent, typically about 4,500 Malawi kwacha (MWK) per month for secondary teachers and a little less for primary teachers. This money is retained by the school, and can be used for maintenance and other school activities at the discretion of school management. Nevertheless, district officials report that lack of housing is one of the main reasons why teachers refuse to take offered posts.

Uganda: School housing is not normally provided, although teacher accommodation is provided in a few places. Accommodation for teachers is reported to be a major issue, as it can be difficult to find a place to rent in some areas.

Zambia: The absence of suitable housing is a major barrier to location in rural areas. Housing is provided for some, but not all, teachers. In basic schools, there are 18,777 teacher houses, of which 31 percent are temporary structures (typically huts); permanent (i.e., brick) housing is available for approximately 25 percent of teachers. In high schools, there are permanent houses for approximately 38 percent of teachers.

Zanzibar: Teacher housing is not normally provided.

Despite these incentives, Lesotho, The Gambia, and Uganda all had difficulty in getting teachers to rural schools. The limited impact of the incentives may be related to their size. In Lesotho, it was argued that the incentive did not outweigh the additional costs of living in a rural area, and that the entire incentive might be used in paying for one trip to town to buy supplies, plus the additional cost of using paraffin rather than electricity for heating and cooking.

Urban schools may also offer alternative sources of additional income. In Zambia, teachers in more crowded schools could teach two shifts, and receive a double shift allowance of 20 percent of salary, equivalent to the incentive payment for location in a rural school. In Uganda, secondary schools raise funds from fees and other sources and are able to use part of this money to supplement teachers' salaries. One study found that these could be up to one-quarter of the regular salary (Shinyekwa 2006). Schools in more relatively affluent areas are able to make greater payments, further enhancing their ability to attract and retain the most experienced and qualified teachers.

In some cases the impact of the incentives was weakened by poor targeting. In Lesotho, the incentive was paid to all teachers (and other government employees) in mountain areas. As a result, teachers in schools in small towns in the mountain districts received the allowance, while teachers in remote and difficult locations in lowland districts did not. As noted earlier, much of the challenge of deployment is within districts, as teachers are often unwilling to work in a specific school but willing to work in another school within the same district, typically citing availability of housing or accessibility by public transportation as the reason. In this context, offering the same incentive for teaching at relatively comfortable schools and at the most difficult school within the same district is likely to seriously weaken the impact of the incentives.

Further, the incentives were not always targeted at the types of teachers most needed in rural schools. In Uganda, incentives were paid to primary teachers, but not to secondary teachers. In Lesotho, a fixed allowance of 275 LSL per month was paid to teachers in mountain areas, whether qualified or unqualified, and was a greater proportion of salary for the unqualified teachers. In both cases the incentive to accept a rural position was lower for the higher-skilled teachers, although it is the highest-skilled teachers that are in short supply in rural areas.

Recognizing the difficulties of scale and targeting, both Zambia and Lesotho were considering adding a further and more tightly targeted incentive. In Lesotho, the existing incentive applied to all public employees, and the Ministry of Education and Training was considering an additional incentive for teachers, targeted only at the most difficult locations. In Zambia, the Ministry of Education was considering introducing a two-tier system. The existing rural allowance was paid to teachers in schools more than 15 miles from the administrative center. An additional allowance for *remote rural schools* was proposed, targeted at the most inaccessible of these rural schools. The criteria for establishing which schools would be considered remote were yet to be determined, but might include a basket of indicators such as distance from a main road, post office, bank, or clinic.

The experience in The Gambia provides a very different picture, and suggests that incentives, if sufficiently large and well targeted, can have a significant impact. In The Gambia there was a system of allowances ranging up to 17.5 percent of salary, based on the region to which a teacher was posted (table 3.11). In addition, a special hardship allowance was introduced in 2006, based initially on the distance of a school from a main road. This hardship allowance ranged from 30 percent to 40 percent of salary, depending on the region. As both of these allowances were paid simultaneously, the salary for a teacher in a hardship school in region 6 could be more than 57 percent greater than the salary of the same teacher in region 1.

Table 3.11   The Gambia: Scale of Additional Allowances Based on Geographical Location

Region	Regional allowance, % of salary	Hardship allowance introduced 2006, % of salary
Region 1	0	Not applicable
Region 2	Urban areas – 0 Rural areas 7.5%	Not applicable
Region 3	9%	30% only in designated hardship schools
Region 4	12%	30% only in designated hardship schools
Region 5	15%	35% only in designated hardship schools
Region 6	17.5%	40% only in designated hardship schools

Table 3.12   Summary of Practices: Incentives for Teachers in Rural Areas

Eritrea: No special incentives.

Gambia, The: Regional bonus of up to 17.5 percent for all teachers in a region. An additional hardship allowance for teachers in difficult posts, ranging from 30–40 percent of salary.

Lesotho: Fixed bonus of 275 Maluti per month (20 percent of starting salary for a qualified primary teacher).

Liberia: No specific incentives.

Malawi: No specific incentives.

Uganda: 30 percent bonus (recently increased from 15 percent) in hard to reach areas. For primary teachers only.

Zambia: 20 percent bonus for rural areas.

Zanzibar: No special incentives.

This incentive seems to be successful in encouraging teachers to locate in hardship schools. In 2008, 42 percent of the teachers in regions 3, 4, 5, and 6 were already in hardship schools, and 24 percent of the teachers in these four regions had requested a transfer from a nonhardship school to a hardship school. Thus, more than one-third of the teachers who were not in hardship schools were actively requesting transfers to hardship schools in order to receive the allowance.

It is noteworthy that these figures are for intraregional transfer requests. Thus, this incentive seems to have been effective in encouraging teachers already in rural regions to transfer to hardship schools within the same region. There is no indication that teachers in urban schools were requesting transfers to hardship schools.

Table 3.12 describes the incentives for teachers in rural areas offered by each of the eight countries.

LOCATION-SPECIFIC RECRUITMENT

Mechanisms that allow some choice of location seem to offer a promising way of improving deployment outcomes. When jobs in specific locations are advertised, it allows teachers some influence in their posting, and those who are unable to find an urban post may be able to choose the rural area in which they will teach, thus increasing the likelihood of retention in the post. There were indications in the case studies that teacher choice of location increased the likelihood of teachers taking up a post.

Location-specific recruitment systems were in use in different forms in a number of the case-study countries. In Lesotho, schools were involved in the selection of teachers, and posts in specific schools were advertised. Teachers applied only for posts they were prepared to accept, and school managers tended to prefer candidates who they believed would stay in the area. As a result, many of the recruited teachers were from the local area, and most posts were filled.

In Zambia, teachers were able to choose the district to which they applied, and teachers assigned to their district of choice were much more likely to take up the offered post than those sent to another district. In Uganda, a system of location-specific recruitment for difficult secondary schools was introduced in response to high wastage. In 2006, an additional 2,000 secondary teachers were recruited, but almost half failed to take up their posts, particularly in the rural areas. In light of this experience, the Ministry of Education and Sports (MoES) began advertising for vacancies in specific districts, to attract only applicants willing to work in those districts.

Where teachers are offered a choice of location, many of course will choose to work in urban schools. However, once those posts are filled, the remaining teachers are likely to choose their home areas or areas where they have relatives or friends, rather than completely unfamiliar areas. In The Gambia College, the student teachers seemed to feel that location near home was more important than location in an urban area. Of 200 student teachers who responded to a survey, 25 percent said they wanted to work near home, and a further 37 percent said they wanted to work in their home district. Only 9 percent said they specifically wanted to work in Banjul (the capital city) or region 1.

LOCAL RECRUITMENT OF UNQUALIFIED TEACHERS

Where no qualified teachers are available, recruitment of local people as unqualified teachers, combined with appropriate in-service training opportunities, may be a promising way to develop capacity in rural areas. Even in remote schools where governments are unable to deploy teachers, there are often people already in the area with sufficient education to contribute to the teaching within the school. Systems that build on that capacity, and provide unqualified teachers with a pathway into a professional career, seem likely to help in addressing the short-term problem of teacher provision, and the long-term challenge of retaining educated people in isolated communities.

In The Gambia, regional education management is able to recruit unqualified teachers, who earn less than half of the starting salary of a qualified teacher, to fill vacancies. In Lesotho, schools that are unable to find qualified teachers recruit unqualified teachers. These unqualified teachers earn about three-quarters of the salary of a qualified teacher, and accounted for 39 percent of primary teachers in 2005. In both Lesotho and The Gambia, there are programs that will allow some unqualified teachers to gain the full teaching qualification while they remain in school. In both cases, the courses are organized by the teacher training college and are equivalent to the traditional pre-service teacher training. Both are delivered using a mix of self-study materials and compressed courses offered outside school hours.

The opportunity to work in local schools is attractive to young people in rural areas, giving them some status within the community, and in some cases the possibility of a long-term career; in other cases it has resulted in the emergence of unpaid volunteer teachers. In Lesotho many rural schools have volunteer teachers, typically local school leavers, mostly female, who have passed the school leaving examination (Cambridge Overseas School Certificate), but have not achieved sufficient grades to enter teacher training. They may teach without pay for a number of years in local schools, in the hopes of getting a position as an unqualified teacher once a vacancy appears. While this free labor has been very helpful to schools, the expectation of a post may cause tensions if a job does not materialize or is awarded to an external candidate. In rural areas in Malawi, volunteer teachers are also common (see figure 3.4). In Ntchisi district, for example, there were

Figure 3.4   Malawi: Mbengwe Primary School, Blantyre Rural District

Mbengwe Primary School has 192 pupils in five grades, but only one government teacher. He is supported by two volunteers, both young men from the local village who have completed a junior secondary education, and are studying at home to complete senior secondary examinations.

90 volunteer teachers in 2007, adding 12 percent to the total number of teachers in the district. These are typically local people educated to the high-school or to at the least middle-school level who are encouraged by the community to work as teachers to make up for the shortages. They may receive some payment in kind from the community.

The combination of local recruitment and in-service training provides a pathway for people in rural areas to gain access to a teaching career. This approach may assist in enabling provision of female teachers to rural schools. In Lesotho, most of the unqualified teachers who are recruited are young women, some of whom would not be able to leave the area for family reasons. Studies in other regions have also noted the importance of developing local capacity. In Pakistan, for example, rural areas that have secondary schools are more easily able to find primary teachers, as there are people from the community with a secondary education (Andrabi, Dans, and Khwaja 2006).

ATTRACTING THE RIGHT STUDENT TEACHERS

Some NGOs have been successful in targeting and training people specifically to teach in rural communities. In Malawi an NGO-supported teacher-training college operates for the sole purpose of training teachers for rural schools. This college, the Development Aid from People to People College at Chilangoma, only enrolls young people with a commitment to return to rural areas, and provides the regular state-recognized teacher training, along with training in community work and leadership. Students engage in community development initiatives as an integral part of the school practice period and are expected to return to a rural area on completion of the course and take up a teaching post. The college reports that most of their graduates return to rural areas on completion of their training. While this may not be practical in all teacher training, it does illustrate that there is a body of people who can be motivated and prepared specifically to work in rural schools. Similar colleges are in operation in Mozambique and Angola.

The availability of people willing to enter a teacher college specifically oriented to work in a rural area and the availability of volunteer teachers in rural areas both demonstrate that there are people for whom teaching in a rural area is an attractive career. However, selection into teacher training on the basis of academic performance alone is unlikely to make the best selections in cases like these, and may favor those from urban and periurban areas with access to the better secondary schools.

CHAPTER 4

Teacher Utilization

Ensuring an appropriate and equitable utilization of teachers is important in the expansion of education systems. Where countries struggle with a shortage of skilled teachers, ensuring that the available teachers are productively employed is an obvious priority. In cases where resources are constrained, improvements in teacher utilization provide an opportunity to improve efficiency and reduce cost per student. Getting the right teacher utilization is particularly important in education systems that are expanding, as poor utilization may create cost structures that impede expansion (Lewin 2008).

Two factors are central to teacher utilization, the teaching load expected of each teacher, and the way in which schools are organized into classes. The expected teaching load has a direct impact on teacher requirements. In primary schools, teachers are often expected to teach all subjects to one class, and so the teaching hours are the same as the student hours, and the teacher requirement is one teacher per class. Once teachers begin to specialize in particular subjects, normally at secondary level but in some places at upper primary level, teacher working hours become independent of student contact time, and a staffing of more than one teacher per class may be required. In Zanzibar, for example, primary teachers are expected to specialize, and to teach about two-thirds of the student contact hours. As a result, an allocation of three teachers for every two classes is required.

Teacher requirements are also influenced by the organization of schools and classes. Wherever there are classes with very small student numbers, the overall teacher requirement and the cost per student are increased. This typically occurs in small primary schools, where there are insufficient pupils to make full classes, and in small secondary schools where multiple subject options result in small classes. Options to increase teacher utilization include use of multigrade teaching, and regulation of the range of optional subjects that can be offered. In some overcrowded schools, double-shift teaching systems are used, which also impact on teacher utilization.

This chapter examines teacher utilization patterns and policies in the case-study countries. Official teacher workloads varied widely, from 12 to 32 hours per week, with secondary teachers generally having lower workloads than primary teachers.

Actual utilization was often lower, particularly in schools with excess staff, either as a result of failures of deployment systems or because of recruitment of additional staff paid by the community. Teacher utilization was generally poorly regulated, and in some countries the expected working hours were not well known.

There were large numbers of very small primary schools, with very small classes, particularly in the older grades. Multigrade teaching was widely used in some countries as a practical measure to compensate for missing teachers, but was poorly integrated into teacher deployment policy and teacher training. Double-shift teaching was used in some of the countries to address overcrowding in schools. A mix of double-shift policies was in use, in some cases resulting in reduced teaching hours for teachers. At the secondary level, some countries allowed small schools to offer a multiplicity of subject options, resulting in small class sizes for some of the least popular subjects.

TEACHER WORKLOADS

The expected teaching hours[1] varied both by country and by level of education. In most cases the teaching hours for secondary teachers were lower than those for primary teachers. In Lesotho, for example, primary teachers were expected to teach 25 hours per week, while secondary teachers taught 20 hours (table 4.1). The exceptions were in Eritrea, where the teaching load was greater at the secondary level, and Malawi, where lower secondary teachers were expected to teach more hours than either primary or upper secondary teachers.

In primary schools, teaching hours ranged from 12.5 hours per week in the early grades in Malawi to 32.5 hours per week in the upper primary grades in Uganda.

Table 4.1 Official Weekly Teaching Hours for Teachers in Primary and Secondary Schools

	Primary	Lower secondary/upper basic/middle	Upper secondary
Eritrea	16–20	22.5	22.5
Gambia, The	25	16–19	16–19
Liberia	20–25	17.4	Varied
Lesotho	25	20	20
Malawi	12.5 (Std 1–2) 22.5 (Std 3–5)	30	15–22.5
Uganda	20 (P1–P2) 32.5 (P3–P7)	16 (Sec O) 13.3 (Sec O–A)	12
Zambia	17.5 (Gr 1–4) 27.5 (Gr 5–7)	16.5	16.5
Zanzibar	16 hours, 2/3 of school contact hours	16	16

Teacher working hours were normally determined by the amount of student contact time, as teachers were normally expected to teach all subjects to one class. As a result, in Malawi, Uganda, and Zambia, teachers in the lower grades had shorter working hours than teachers working with the older primary classes. The exception to the normal pattern was in Zanzibar, where primary teachers were expected to specialize in one of three subject groups. In this case teaching hours were only two-thirds of the school contact hours, as three teachers were allocated for every two classes.

In secondary schools, teachers were expected to specialize. In all of the case-study countries, secondary teachers normally specialized in two teaching subjects, but there were some single-subject teachers. The official teaching hours in the lower secondary schools ranged from 30 hours per week in Malawi to 16 hours per week in Uganda. In Malawi and Uganda, there were variations within secondary schools, with lower teaching hours for the teachers teaching the upper secondary classes. In Uganda teachers teaching only lower secondary classes (O-level) were expected to teach 16 hours per week. Teachers teaching both lower and upper secondary classes were expected to teacher 13.3 hours per week, and teachers with only the upper classes (A-level) were expected to teach 12 hours per week. Teaching loads at the secondary level were less than half of the student contact time in some countries. Ugandan secondary teachers worked 12 to 16 hours per week, while the student contact time was about 33 hours (Liang 2002); in Zambia, teachers taught 15 to 20 periods per week out of 36 timetabled periods for students (Lewin 2008).

These teaching requirements resulted in annual teaching workloads ranging from 488 hours per year to 1,599 hours per year (table 4.2). Compared to the 17 mainly middle-income countries in the World Education Indicators Survey

Table 4.2 Official Annual Teaching Hours for Teachers in Primary and Secondary Schools

	Primary	Lower secondary/upper basic/middle	Upper secondary
Eritrea	667–810	810	810
Gambia, The	975	624–741	624–741
Liberia	700–875	525	Varied
Lesotho	900	720	720
Malawi	488–878	1,170	585–877
Uganda	984–1,599	787–654	590
Zambia	668–1050	630	630
WEI average*	868	848	860

*Average of the 17 countries in the World Education Indicators Survey; Argentina, Brazil, Chile, Egypt, India, Indonesia, Jamaica, Jordan, Malaysia, Paraguay, Peru, Philippines, Russian Federation, Sri Lanka, Thailand, Tunisia, and Uruguay.
Source: Education Counts: World Education Indicators 2007, UIS 2007, p. 141.

(UIS 2007), the teaching load expected of primary teachers was similar to the average of case-study countries. However, at both the lower and upper secondary levels, most of the case-study countries had expected teaching loads below the WEI average.

In reality, teaching hours were sometimes shorter than the official figures. Teaching hours were eroded by unrecorded events, including late starts to term and unscheduled school closures. Two other factors, overstaffing and teacher specialization, were also associated with lower teacher utilization.

OVERSTAFFING

Where schools had more staff than classes, or more staff than classrooms, the result tended to be lower teacher utilization. In Malawi, poor deployment practices had resulted in overstaffing in some urban and periurban schools, leading to a practice of "shared teaching," or allocating more than one teacher to a class (see box 4.1 for an example). In some cases this was driven by a shortage of classrooms, but in other cases teachers had even amalgamated classes to allow reduced workloads. Where shared teaching occurred, it did not normally mean two teachers present in the class at a time, but rather two or more teachers taking turns teaching the class. In Lesotho, teachers were allocated by formula, but there were schools where a shortage of classrooms resulted in very large classes, with two teachers assigned to some classes. As in Malawi, this resulted in shorter teaching hours, as the workload was shared between the two teachers.

Teacher workloads were also reduced by the presence of additional teachers paid from school funds. In Uganda, secondary schools charged fees and used part of these funds to hire additional "off-payroll" teachers. While these were intended to supplement the teaching staff, they also allowed some teachers to have reduced workloads.

TEACHER SPECIALIZATION

Teacher specialization was associated with reduced working hours. In Zanzibar, primary teachers were expected to specialize, and teacher allocation was on the basis of three teachers for every two classes, reducing teacher workload to two-thirds of the school hours. There was a minor specialization in The Gambia, where religious instruction was provided by specialist Koranic teachers. These additional Koranic teachers reduced the workload of the class teachers, who normally had free time while their class was taking religious instruction. Specialization often carried with it the expectation of shorter working hours. In Liberia, for example, when teachers specialized they normally expected to have some "free periods" during the day.

BOX 4.1   MALAWI: TEACHER UTILIZATION IN LUMBADZI PRIMARY SCHOOL (PERIURBAN)

Lumbadzi Primary School had 1,706 pupils in 17 classes and 29 teachers (a PTR of 59:1). The school used a double-shift system, where the younger classes started early in the morning, and the older classes used the same classrooms once the younger ones were finished. In standard 1, the pupils were broken into five classes, with one teacher for each. In standards 2–8, two teachers were assigned to each class. As a result of this pattern of utilization, class sizes averaged 100, despite an overall pupil-teacher ratio of 59:1.

Standard	Pupils	Classes	Average class size	Teachers
1	323	5	65	5
2	238	2	119	4
3	251	2	126	4
4	222	2	111	4
5	225	2	113	4
6	230	2	115	4
7	137	1	137	2
8	80	1	80	2
Total	1,706	17	100	29

Unofficial teacher specialization was widely reported, particularly in the upper grades of primary school. In The Gambia, Liberia, Lesotho, Malawi, and Uganda, schools frequently had informal arrangements to share classes. This was particularly common for mathematics and English teachers, and seemed to arise mainly from concern that not all teachers were able to teach these subjects to a high enough standard at this level. Teacher specialization also seemed to be encouraged in some cases by the structure of teacher training courses. In Uganda, for example, teachers doing a diploma course in primary education have the option of specialization in (i) English and one of the humanities/arts subjects, or (ii) mathematics and one of the science subjects.

At the secondary level, teacher utilization was reduced by teacher specialization and the provision of a multiplicity of optional subjects. The number of periods per week to be taught in each subject was determined by the curriculum and the number of classes taking the subject. Where teachers specialized in only one subject, allocating a full workload to each teacher became increasingly

Table 4.3   Teacher Utilization in Three Lesotho Secondary Schools

	School A	School B	School C
Pupils	424	200	180
Teachers	21	17	10
Students per teacher	20	12	18
Classes taught as a percentage of the expected workload of 30 periods (20 hours) per week	90	67	87
Average class size	36	28	36

difficult, particularly in smaller schools. Teachers of the less-popular optional subjects were likely to have both the smallest classes and the lightest work-loads. In Lesotho, for example, visits to three secondary schools revealed class sizes as small as ten students in some optional subjects, and in one school, teachers were teaching only two-thirds of the expected number of periods each week (table 4.3).

Secondary teacher utilization was also uneven, typically with higher workloads for the teachers where there was a shortage, and for those in the core subjects. In Uganda, Lesotho, Zambia, and Zanzibar, it was reported that mathematics and science teachers usually had heavier workloads, sometimes teaching even more than the official requirement. Similarly, in Ghana, 20 percent of teachers were overextended, teaching 25–35 periods while 40 percent taught less than 18 periods (Mulkeen et al. 2007).

DOUBLE-SHIFT TEACHING

Double-shift teaching, where two separate groups of students are taught in the school at different times of the day, is often proposed as a solution to a shortage of classrooms in crowded schools. Approaches to the double shift vary, with some models using two separate teams of teachers, while other approaches involve one teacher teaching both shifts. Some approaches to double shifting result in a compression of teaching hours for each shift, with potential detrimental effects on quality. It is perhaps not surprising that the research findings are mixed, with some studies showing a strong negative impact on student performance (Michaelowa 2001) and others showing that pupils do no worse in double-shift schools (Bray 2008).

Double-shift teaching was used in some cases in most of the countries. In Liberia and Malawi, double shifting was done to optimize use of classrooms, and separate teams of teachers were provided for each of the shifts. In Eritrea, teachers were sometimes assigned to teach classes in both shifts, but retained the same overall teaching hours. Two countries had systems where individual teachers could be asked to work in both shifts, and receive additional pay. In The Gambia, teachers teaching two shifts received a double-shift allowance of 50 percent of their salary. In Zambia, the double shift allowance was 20 percent of salary.

Where double-shift teaching occurred, it often resulted in an unofficial reduction in the time allocated to each shift. In Zambia, it was reported that the student contact time was often reduced to as little as two-and-a-half hours per day in double-shift systems. The second shift was often seen as less desirable, both by parents and teachers. In The Gambia, the perception was that in the afternoon both students and teachers were tired and performance was poorer. In response, some schools tried to operate rotation systems, where the first and second shifts exchanged regularly.

A summary of the eight countries' practices in double-shift teaching is presented in table 4.4.

Table 4.4   Summary of Practices: Double-shift Teaching

	Teacher utilization in the double shift
Eritrea	Teachers can be assigned to work in both shifts, but with the same overall working hours.
Gambia, The	Teachers teaching two shifts receive a 50 percent double-shift allowance.
	Parents often see the second shift as inferior, and in some of the regions, management encourages schools to use a rotational system, where the first and second shifts exchange regularly (perhaps monthly).
	In practice, the second shift is often slightly shorter than the first. In one school visited, the first shift ran from 8:30 a.m. to 1:45 p.m. (five and one-quarter hours), while the second shift ran from 2:00 p.m. to 6.30 p.m. (four and a half hours).
Liberia	Two shifts with separate teachers. Double shift is most common in Monrovia.
Lesotho	No double shift.
Malawi	Double shift with separate teachers.
	In primary schools, there is often "overlapping." This means that one of the older classes may begin at 10.00 a.m. and use the classroom vacated by a younger class.
	Many secondary schools use multishift teaching, especially in urban areas. Where multishift teaching is practiced, the duration of teaching periods is usually reduced (typically to 30 minutes).
Uganda	Double shift in primary schools is rare. A pilot of double shift in secondary school is underway, using separate teams of teachers.
Zambia	Teachers teaching two shifts receive a 20-percent double-shift allowance.
	Where double-shift systems are used, the student contact time is frequently compressed to as little as 2.5 hours per day.

MULTIGRADE TEACHING

Multigrade teaching, the practice of a teacher teaching more than one grade at the same time, was used in most countries, mainly in the small rural schools and where there was a shortage of teachers. Although multigrade teaching is widely used in areas of low population density in high-income countries and seems to produce results comparable to those in more conventional schools (Little 2006), it was often perceived as an unfortunate necessity in the case-study countries.

Despite the widespread usage of multigrade teaching, it was rarely well integrated into policies or teacher education systems. In Malawi, Uganda, and Zambia, where multigrade teaching was widely used, there was no formal training for multigrade in initial teacher training. Some work was underway in Uganda, Lesotho, and Zambia to provide training in multigrade techniques, but this was at an early stage.

The countries' multigrade teaching practices are described in table 4.5.

DIRECTIONS FOR POLICY MAKERS

Improving teacher utilization provides an opportunity to make the best use of available expertise, increase efficiency, and reduce costs, and as such is an important focus for policy makers. Improvement of utilization may be particularly important at the secondary level, where utilization tended to be lower as a result of shorter teaching hours and a greater use of optional subjects, which was associated with smaller class sizes for some options. As a result, in most countries the cost of teachers on a per-student basis was a multiple of the cost at the primary level, constraining the expansion of enrollment.

The experiences of the case-study countries suggest a series of actions that could help to improve the efficiency and equity of teacher utilization:

- The expected teaching workload could be clearly articulated, thus enabling school managers to redistribute work to the teachers who have less than the minimum expected load.
- A clear policy on the number of optional subjects could enable schools to ensure minimum class sizes in optional subjects.
- Teacher allocations to schools could be based on these policies, so that schools would be unable to acquire excess teachers paid from government sources.
- Student teachers could be encouraged or required to study at least two teaching subjects, and to choose at least one of the core subjects, to increase their employability.
- A clear policy on multigrade teaching could be developed and included in the formula for teacher allocation.

Table 4.5   Summary of Practices: Multigrade Teaching

	Use of multigrade	Multigrade in teacher training
Eritrea	Used in remote schools with low enrollment. Normally one teacher for two classes, with class sizes below 15.	No specific training for multigrade teachers, but supervisors are expected to give them some orientation.
Gambia, The	Used in schools where there is a teacher shortage, normally when the combined class size is less than 40. Used relatively rarely.	Not included in teacher training, but a module on multigrade is planned.
Liberia	Used where there is a shortage of teachers.	Teacher training includes some preparation for multigrade teaching.
Lesotho	Used in small schools. Teacher allocation is based on a formula assuming more than 40 pupils per teacher, making multigrade a necessity where numbers are low.	Not included in initial teacher training.
Malawi	Widely used. Over 1,500 primary schools (30 percent of all schools) had fewer teachers than classes. These are mainly located in rural areas, and are often the smallest schools. Where numbers are large, teachers sometimes move between classrooms assigning work to the different grades.	Not included in initial teacher training.
Uganda	Widely used. Approximately 22 percent of primary schools (over 3,000 schools) have less than 300 pupils. The MoES supported a pilot of multigrade teaching in Kalangala district, and is currently producing multigrade resource materials for primary teachers.	Not included in initial teacher training, although there is a plan to have one teacher college specialize in multigrade teachers.
Zambia	Widely used, particularly in community schools.	Not included in initial teacher training, but a draft manual has been prepared.

Multigrade teaching is likely to become increasingly important as primary education expands to include the most marginalized communities. However, despite the widespread use of multigrade in practice, multigrade techniques were rarely well integrated into initial teacher training. This is particularly unfortunate, as all classrooms are to some extent "multi-ability," and all teachers can benefit from the skills of working with different abilities in the same classroom (Little 2006).

In considering teacher utilization, some thought could be given to the use of part-time teachers. While the dominant model at present is full-time employment based at one school, the ability to employ teachers on a part-time basis could give schools greater flexibility in staffing and allow some teachers specializing in one subject to share their time between two schools.

NOTE

1. Teacher workload is made up of both the direct teaching time and the work of preparation, marking, and associated administration. As the preparation time is difficult to measure, and likely to vary between individual teachers, the teacher workload is normally described in terms of the teaching hours.

PART **II**

Teacher Training

CHAPTER 5

Pre-service Teacher Training

Throughout Sub-Saharan Africa, there are concerns that the quality of instruction is suffering as a result of teachers who have inadequate preparation for
their task. Teaching can be impeded by poor understanding of the subject
matter or inadequate pedagogical skills. One of the obvious responses to this
problem is to improve the quality of teacher preparation, either through
increased training or through selection of better-educated candidates into teacher
training. Finding the most effective teacher preparation involves balancing the
duration of the training with the available capacity and requirements, balancing
the teaching of subject matter with the development of practical skills, and balancing the desire to teach to the highest international standards with the real
level of education of the entrants to teacher training.

Improving the quality of teacher training is a complex task, as is shown in all
case countries. In struggling to find the optimal compromises, teacher training
has been subject to frequent adjustment. Some programs have been compressed,
while in other cases the duration has been extended. Blends of campus-based and
school-based periods have been developed, and the subject content has been
adjusted. The eight case studies showed a variety of structures and compromises
in their teacher training.

STRUCTURE AND DURATION OF INITIAL TEACHER TRAINING

PRIMARY PRE-SERVICE TRAINING

Pre-service primary teacher training systems varied in terms of entry requirements,
duration, and the balance of campus-based and school-based components. Nevertheless, some common trends emerged. In most cases, students completed 13 years
of full-time study (including both schooling and full-time teacher training) before
beginning to teach primary classes on a full-time basis (table 5.1).

In six of the eight cases, students entering primary teacher training were expected
to have completed upper secondary education. The other two, Uganda and
Zanzibar, had entry following lower secondary education, which in both cases
normally implied 11 years of schooling. This represented a change from earlier

Table 5.1   Pre-service Training for Primary Teachers, Entry Level and Duration

Country	Entry (years of school)	Training
Eritrea	Upper secondary, 12 years	One-year certificate
Gambia, The	Upper secondary, 12 years	Three-year certificate One in college, two in school
Lesotho	Upper secondary, 12 years	Three-year diploma Three years in college, since reorganized as a sandwich model—three years, but middle year in school
Liberia	Upper secondary, 12 years	12-week emergency course, but one-year certificate being introduced
Malawi	Upper secondary, 12 years	Two-year certificate One in college, one in school Formerly MIITEP, as in school
Uganda	Lower secondary (O level), 11 years	Two-year certificate
Zambia	Upper secondary, 12 years	Two-year certificate, one in college, one in school
Zanzibar	After lower secondary, 11 years	Two-year certificate

practices, where entry to primary teacher training commonly followed completion of lower secondary education.

The duration of courses ranged from one year to three years, but the three-year courses normally included one or two years based at a school. Two of the countries had one-year teacher training courses, four had two-year courses, and a further two had three-year courses. Liberia also had a very short 12-week course, but this was a short-term measure in response to an emergency situation.

In four of the countries, the course was divided, with some years of college-based instruction and other years of full-time school-based work. In The Gambia, the teacher training course takes three years, with one year of full-time training on campus, followed by two years of full-time work in a school, while completing coursework. Lesotho had the longest period of full-time campus-based study, with a three-year campus-based diploma course. However, since the case study, this has been changed to a sandwich program, with one year of campus-based training followed by one year of full-time teaching in a school, and then a further year of full-time campus-based training.

Despite this apparent diversity, there was a remarkable consistency in the overall duration of study. The total years of study to become a teacher (including primary and secondary school and teacher training) ranged from 13 to 15 years (table 5.2). If only college-based training is included (assuming that while placed full time in a school, the student teachers are taking responsibility for classes and effectively working as teachers while studying), the consistency is even greater. In all cases, 13 years of study were required before taking responsibility for teaching for a full year.

Table 5.2   Total Years of Study (School and Training College) for Primary Teachers

Country	Total years (school and teacher training)	Total years (school and teacher training) excluding full years of school placement
Eritrea	12 + 1 = 13	12 + 1 = 13
Gambia, The	12 + 3 = 15	12 + 1 = 13
Lesotho	12 + 3 = 15	12 + 2 = 14 years in total, but teaching full time after 13
Liberia	12 + 1 = 13	12 + 1 = 13
Malawi	12 + 2 = 14	12 + 1 = 13
Uganda	11 + 2 = 13	11 + 2 = 13
Zambia	12 + 2 = 14	12 + 1 = 13
Zanzibar	11 + 2 = 13	11 + 2 = 13

The duration and structure of teacher training programs were quite fluid, and most countries made recent changes. In some cases, courses were upgraded from certificate to diploma courses. In Lesotho, for example, the certificate-level teacher training course had been replaced by a three-year diploma-level course, subsequently reorganized as a sandwich course with one year of school-based training between two years based at the teacher training college. In Zanzibar, the major teacher training institution, Nkrumah Teacher Training College, had been absorbed by the State University of Zanzibar (SUZA), which had ended certificate courses and was focusing on diploma and degree courses. In both Lesotho and Zanzibar, the move to diploma courses was associated with higher entry requirements and increased academic requirements for lecturers.

In other cases teacher training had been shortened in response to emergency teacher shortages, resulting either from conflict (Eritrea and Liberia) or the rapid expansion of enrollment (Malawi). In Malawi, a two-year pre-service course was abolished with the introduction of MIITEP (Malawi Integrated In-Service Teacher Education Programme, a system of employment and in-service training for untrained teachers). In 2004, MIITEP was closed and replaced with a new two-year pre-service certificate, based on one year on campus and one year of school-based study. In Eritrea, when there was an acute shortage of teachers in the early 1990s, a short course of a few months' duration was provided. This was later replaced with a one-year certificate course. In Liberia, the same trend was apparent, as the 12-week emergency course was being replaced by a one-year course.

Entry to teacher training was primarily based on academic performance either in state examinations or in dedicated entry tests. In six of the cases, state examinations were used as the prime mechanism for selection of students. In The Gambia, the state examinations were supplemented by a special entrance examination and an interview, both used mainly to ensure the validity of the state examination results, which were reported to suffer from high levels of impersonation. In Liberia, the

Table 5.3 Entry Requirements for Primary Teacher Training

Eritrea	Eritrean School Leaving Certificate (Grade 12) with a Grade Point Average of 0.6 or higher, on a four-point scale
Gambia, The	West African Senior School Certificate Examination (Grade 12) with one credit and three pass grades, including a pass in English
Lesotho	Cambridge Overseas School Certificate (Grade 12) with four credits and one pass grade, including at least a pass grade in English
Liberia	The selection system was under development, and seemed likely to involve an entrance examination, testing competence in English and mathematics
Malawi	Malawi School Certificate of Education (Grade 12) with a credit in English and a pass grade in mathematics and two sciences
Uganda	O-level (junior secondary, grade 11) examination with six passes including English, mathematics, and one science subject
Zambia	Grade 12 certificate with at least three credits and two passes, including at least a pass mark in English and mathematics
Zanzibar	Varies by institution

selection mechanism was under development, but the intention was to have some kind of dedicated entrance test, again in response to concerns about the validity of other credentials.

The academic performance required to enter teacher training was quite low, and in some cases declining (table 5.3). In The Gambia, the requirement was a credit in one subject and a pass grade in three. This requirement, increased from a previous level, resulted in an enrollment rate that was 32 percent lower than expected between 1999 and 2006. In response, The Gambia College was forced to accept students with marks of only 25 percent in the entrance examination. In Eritrea, the requirement for entry to primary teaching had fallen in response to greater intake to higher education courses, and in 2007, students with grade point averages[1] (GPA) of 0.6 and 0.8 were admitted. In effect, this means that a student who had a grade D (the lowest passing grade) in three subjects and failed another two could gain admittance to primary teacher training. In Lesotho, the college of education was forced to lower its entry requirements in 2008 because of a lack of qualified applicants.

In most countries, entrants to teacher training were required to have achieved some competence in English, which was the official medium of instruction in teacher training in all cases. A pass in mathematics was a requirement in only half of the countries, despite the importance of mathematics in the primary school curriculum. The ability to require minimum competence levels in key subjects was constrained by the limited number of qualified applicants.

In Lesotho, following the introduction of a requirement that new entrants have at least a pass grade in English, the Lesotho College of Education had found it difficult to fill all of the available places. The college reported that it considered a pass in mathematics to be desirable, but was unable to make this a requirement because it would be unable to find sufficient students to fill the available places. This inability to find sufficient applicants with at least a passing grade in mathematics makes the task of teacher training much more difficult and contributes to the poor standard of mathematics teaching in primary schools.

There were some nonacademic selection criteria, mainly affirmative actions to increase participation of female teachers or linguistic or ethnic minorities. Selection on the basis of academic performance alone is likely to favor those from the groups with greater participation in education, which may include students from urban areas, male students, and those from the linguistic and ethnic majorities.

To improve the equity of access, some of the countries had systems of affirmative action to increase the proportion of particular groups in teacher training. Both Malawi and Zambia reserved places for female student teachers, 40 percent of places in Malawi and 50 percent in Zambia. However, in Malawi, the colleges were often unable to reach this target, because there was no reduction in the entry requirements, and there were insufficient applicants with the required credits in mathematics and the sciences. The Gambia had an externally funded Remedial Initiative for Female Teachers (RIFT) running from 1999–2002. Under this scheme, a quota of female students was enrolled, even with lower academic qualifications, and provided with additional classes to help boost quality. This scheme seemed to be successful and the proportion of female student teachers rose to 41 percent, but later fell to only 22 percent following the end of the program. Lesotho used a quota system to ensure geographical balance, with a fixed proportion of students drawn from each district. In practice this had little impact, as the college at the time of the study found it difficult to fill the available spaces, and accepted all qualified applicants. Eritrea had also used quota systems in some years, to admit more students from the minority language groups.

SECONDARY PRE-SERVICE TRAINING

Systems for secondary teacher training were more complex, as most countries had dual systems with both diploma/certificate and degree-level qualifications. Diploma courses were normally of two years' duration, offered in teacher training colleges, and in some cases qualified teachers to teach only junior secondary classes. Degree-level courses usually required higher academic qualifications at entry, and typically took three or four years in a university (table 5.4).

In most cases the university courses involved degrees in education, where students studied their chosen subjects and the professional education content concurrently. However, there were some indications of emerging options for graduates from noneducation degrees to gain a qualification in teaching. In Uganda, some private universities had systems to enable graduates from general degrees to convert to teaching through a one-year postgraduate course. A similar course was under

Table 5.4 Training of Secondary Teachers, Duration

	Diploma level	Degree level
Eritrea	Two-year diploma for middle school teachers	Four-year degree for secondary school teachers
Gambia, The	Higher Teachers Certificate (HTC), three-year course, of two years in college followed by one year of teaching in a school	Four-year degree, normally an upgrade for an existing teacher, two years for an HTC holder, three years for a primary teacher
Lesotho	Diploma in Education (Secondary), a three-year diploma	National university, four-year degree
Liberia	Two-year certificate, no longer in operation	Four-year degree
Malawi	Three-year diploma	Four-year degree
Uganda	Two-year diploma	Three-year degree
Zambia	Two-year diploma, increased to three years in 2005	Four-year degree
Zanzibar	Two-year diploma	Three-year degree

discussion in Lesotho, while in Eritrea a two-to-three month conversion course was being planned.

In addition, some of the countries had a separate provision for primary teachers to upgrade their qualifications to teach at the secondary level. In The Gambia, qualified primary teachers could return to The Gambia College for the three-year Higher Teachers Certificate and upgrade to teaching in upper-basic schools. In Malawi, qualified primary teachers could upgrade to secondary school teachers through a three-year full-time diploma course.

In some of the cases, the public teacher training was supplemented by a significant private provision of training for secondary teachers. In Liberia, Malawi, Uganda, Zambia, and Zanzibar, there were private or faith-based teacher training colleges. These differed in their motivation and structure. In Zanzibar, an international university had established a private university college, financed by a charitable foundation, with a large and well-equipped campus. In Zambia, the commercial Zambia Open University (ZAOU) had established a distance-teaching system with two-week courses each semester, along with self-study materials.

In most cases, student teachers at both the diploma and the degree level were prepared to teach two subjects (table 5.5).

For students with sufficient academic qualifications to enter a university course, teaching was often not considered an attractive option. In Eritrea, it was reported that the best students admitted to the Eritrea Institute of Technology tended not to select education courses, so the education courses tended to be filled with students with relatively low scores, for whom education was not their first preference. In Liberia, fewer than 5 percent of the students who gained access to the

Table 5.5   Number of Teaching Subjects

	Diploma courses	Degree courses
Eritrea	Two subjects	One or two subjects
Gambia, The	Two subjects	Two subjects
Lesotho	Two subjects	Two subjects
Liberia		Two subjects
Malawi	Two subjects	Two subjects
Uganda	Two subjects	Two subjects
Zambia	Mostly two subjects, but some take one	Mostly two subjects, but some take one
Zanzibar	Two subjects	Two subjects

university chose to enter the education course, and in the private faith-based Stella Maris College, only 6 of the 8,000 applicants in 2007 chose education.

The education courses had particular difficulty in attracting sufficient students with qualifications in mathematics and science. Inability to find sufficient students with mathematics and science was a problem in Eritrea, The Gambia, Lesotho, Malawi, Uganda, and Zanzibar. In Malawi, only 21 percent of the new student teachers enrolled in 2007 took mathematics or science courses. In Uganda, only 14 percent of the student teachers in the national teachers colleges were studying mathematics or science in 2007, despite a lower entry requirement for any student with a "principal pass" in mathematics or science.

There were indications that many of the graduates from university degree-level courses in education were not retained in the teaching profession. In Zambia and Malawi, it was reported that most of the graduates from degree-level courses in education did not go on to teach. In Zambia, the total number of teachers with university degrees was less than 2.5 times the annual output of graduates with education degrees from the university. In Liberia, of the 23 education students who graduated in 2007, it was believed that none were teaching in public schools, although some may have been teaching in private schools.

BALANCING DURATION, SELECTION, AND NATIONAL NEEDS

Finding the optimal balance of course duration, entry requirements, and structure is problematic and involves difficult trade-offs. As Schwille and Dembele (2007) point out, the dilemma for policy makers is that "the longer, the more expensive; and the shorter, the more difficult to do anything worthwhile."

In almost all cases, countries faced difficult trade-offs between duration and capacity. In the context of expanding systems, there were pressing national needs for increased output of teachers. Yet almost universally, teacher training institutions preferred to increase the duration of pre-service training. Longer periods of training offer the possibility of improved quality of both content knowledge and pedagogy. However, in most of these cases, this was not practical in the short term, as the capacity of the colleges was limited by bed capacity, teaching space, and personnel. At the primary level, most countries provided one or two years of campus-based training. The only country that provided a three-year campus-based pre-service training (Lesotho) subsequently modified this to two years on campus and one year in school, partly in response to the need to increase output. On the other hand, courses of less than one year's duration were normally seen as emergency measures and were being replaced by longer courses.

There were also trade-offs between campus-based and school-based components of teacher training courses. Placing student teachers in a school for full academic years allows them to take responsibility for teaching classes over an extended period, getting to know the students and the operation of the school, helping to develop pedagogic skills, and making the theoretical parts of the course more meaningful. However, school-based work supported by either occasional courses or self-study materials is less likely to improve the quality of content knowledge in key areas, particularly mathematics, science, and international languages, which may be better taught in a college context. Finding the right balance is difficult and controversial. In Malawi the MIITEP system, which was entirely school-based, was abolished following strong opposition from the teacher training colleges, who considered it inadequate to maintain standards. In other cases, the school-based component was increased to improve both capacity and the development of pedagogical skills. In Lesotho, the full-time three-year campus-based diploma was changed into a sandwich model with one year of full-time teaching in a school sandwiched between two years on campus. In The Gambia, a two-year campus-based training course was changed to a three-year program with two years based in a school.

There were concerns that the quality of student teachers entering the teacher training courses fell below the standards expected. In Eritrea, Lesotho, and The Gambia, there were difficulties in finding sufficient qualified applicants to fill the places in teacher training courses. In other countries, applicants who seemed to meet the required standards were struggling to deal with the course material. In Zambia, for example, only 51 percent of the students in primary teacher training were passing the examination at the end of the first year. There were a few cases where course content had been adjusted to match the real level of competence of the entrants. One exception was in The Gambia, where additional courses in basic English and mathematics had been provided to help students build their skills in these crucial areas in the early part of the course.

Selection into teacher training based primarily on academic performance had unintended effects detrimental to motivation, geographical distribution, and in some cases gender balance. Using examination results as the primary method of selection provided little opportunity to select the students with the greatest interest in teaching or the personality and behavioral characteristics desirable in teachers. As teaching was often perceived as less attractive than other professions with similar entry requirements, the teaching courses tended to absorb those with the lowest eligible qualifications, for many of whom it was a last resort, rather than a first choice.

In this context, efforts to increase quality by raising entry standards could decrease the pool of eligible potential applicants and increase the geographical selectivity of intake. With a relatively small number of people completing secondary school and a disproportionate number of secondary school completers coming from urban areas and wealthier families, selection based on academic performance tended to result in fewer entrants from remote rural areas, from disadvantaged minorities, and in some cases fewer female students. It is noteworthy that, while many of the countries where entry to primary teacher training required an upper secondary education had difficulty in filling the available places, the two cases with entry after lower secondary education (Uganda and Zanzibar) had no shortage of applicants, and had applicants from a broad spread of geographical and social backgrounds.

CONTENT OF INITIAL TEACHER TRAINING

The teacher-training curriculum was not always well aligned with the needs of the classroom. Three major observations emerge. First, training in pedagogical methods was often theoretical, making it less likely to have an impact on classroom practices. Second, the teaching of the content knowledge (that is, the subjects that a teacher would be expected to teach) was often not closely aligned to the school curriculum. Third, these difficulties were often compounded by students' poor proficiency in the language of instruction.

PEDAGOGICAL TRAINING OF TEACHERS

Traditionally, the pedagogical training of teachers has centered on the teaching of theoretical foundation disciplines, usually psychology, philosophy, history, and sociology. Some of the teacher education programs, particularly at the primary level, were moving away from this model and toward greater alignment with the skills required in the classroom. Typically this involved more concentration on specific pedagogic skills and the pedagogy of individual curriculum subjects. Other teacher education programs, most notably at the secondary level, were moving toward more theoretical content, driven by the requirements of the academic awards.

In The Gambia, the primary teacher-training program had been moving toward a more practice-oriented format. Prior to 2005 the theoretical foundation disciplines of psychology, philosophy, and sociology of education had each been taught as separate subjects, and teaching methodology had received about 15–20 percent of total contact time. Following a restructuring in 2005, the foundation disciplines ceased to be discrete subjects and instead the core concepts from them were integrated into the study of methodology in order to increase the relevance of the material. Total time devoted to methodology rose to up to 40 percent of contact time. In addition, specific training for multigrade teaching was introduced as part of the pre-service curriculum. In the secondary program, the theoretical component has also been significantly reduced, with separate theory modules (philosophy, psychology, sociology and history of education, and comparative education) replaced by one module on learning theories and another entitled "Introduction to the Sociology of Education." The time previously used for theory was instead used to teach methodologies related to the teaching of academic subject-areas in upper basic schools.

Similarly in Eritrea, a revised teacher-training curriculum has been developed, designed to encourage more learner-centered teaching and placing greater emphasis on skills development. The student teachers study the subjects of the elementary school curriculum and the methodology for use of each is integrated with the study of the subject content. To accompany the new teacher-training curriculum, a teacher-training manual has been designed. Teacher trainers have also been asked to keep reflective diaries, which can be used in evaluation of the teacher-training curriculum. Despite these practice-oriented curricula, the delivered teacher training often remains dominated by memorization of material. One methodology class observed in Eritrea was used to transcribe and memorize a long list of ways to introduce a new topic, including options likely to be of little relevance for most Eritrean teachers, such as "introduce a guest speaker" or "announce a field trip."

In other cases, the teacher-training curriculum seemed to be becoming more theoretical. In Zanzibar for example, the absorption of Nkrumah Teacher Training College into the State University of Zanzibar resulted in a greater emphasis on the academic content of the pre-service diploma course, at the expense of some of the more practical skills.

SUBJECT CONTENT IN TEACHER TRAINING

Ensuring the mastery of teachers' knowledge of subject content has increasingly been a key focus of global teacher training in the last few years. Research has shown a positive correlation between teachers' content knowledge and their students' learning (Villegas-Reimers 2003, UIS 2006). Despite the importance of adequate content knowledge, there are concerns that some teachers in sub-Saharan Africa do not reach the level of knowledge required. SAQMEQ data shows that in several countries the average teacher did not perform significantly better on reading and mathematics tests than the highest performing sixth-grade students (UIS 2006).

In the case-study countries, the academic content of teacher training courses was often not closely aligned with the curriculum in the classroom. Teacher training curricula all included some component of development of the subject-content knowledge of the student teachers. In provision of these courses, there is a natural tension between teaching more advanced material and ensuring mastery of the school-level material. Traditionally, teacher-training courses have tended to build on the *expected* entry level of the students, teaching more advanced material than was delivered at secondary school. Where student teachers have weak understanding of the secondary school content, this can lead to teaching of inappropriately advanced material in teacher training colleges. This is particularly problematic in mathematics and the sciences, where poor understanding of basic material makes comprehension of more advanced material extremely difficult. In Zambia, for example, 51 percent of the student teachers failed the examinations at the end of the first year of teacher training, a problem attributed by the lecturers to poor prior learning, especially in mathematics and science.

The difficulty of alignment of content was exacerbated by the poor academic standards of the students entering teacher training. The shortage of qualified applicants, leading to falling entry thresholds in The Gambia, Eritrea, Lesotho, and Malawi, has resulted in teachers with poorer academic performance entering teacher training. Measures to attract specific groups into teaching, such as women and people from linguistic and ethnic minorities, often also involve lowering entry standards. Further, in some cases the expansion of access to education was reported to have been accompanied by "grade inflation," where the performance required to get a particular examination grade had fallen. The level of prior learning of students entering teacher education was a particular concern in mathematics. In Lesotho, Eritrea, and The Gambia, passing mathematics was not a requirement for entry to teacher training, although all primary teachers are expected to teach mathematics.

At the secondary level, there was also often a mismatch between the school curriculum and the content taught in teacher training, particularly in university courses. Student teachers in universities often followed standard university courses in their chosen subjects. The National University of Lesotho personnel noted that these courses were designed to prepare students for university examinations, and were quite different from the secondary school curriculum. In Malawi about 70 percent of the content of the B.Ed. program for teachers was made up of standard university courses not adapted to the school curriculum. The potential for mismatch between the taught content and the school curriculum also arises where students are expected to undergo a general degree and later undergo pedagogical training. This model of consecutive training is attractive because of the greater flexibility it provides, and was being adopted in Eritrea and The Gambia at the time of the studies.

In some countries there were positive reforms to ensure greater alignment between the taught content and the school content. In Eritrea at the elementary level, and in The Gambia at the lower and upper basic level, the teacher training curricula had been adapted to ensure a stronger match between the content and school curriculum. In The Gambia it was estimated that about 90 percent of the content covered in the primary and higher teaching certificate programs reflected the school curriculum.

LANGUAGE OF INSTRUCTION IN TEACHER TRAINING

A further challenge to the quality of teacher training came from the language of instruction. In all of the case-study countries, the language of instruction in the teacher training colleges was, at least officially, English. Yet in almost every case, the inability of some student teachers to communicate in English was reported to be a major barrier. In practice, there was some informal use of other languages to assist students with weak English-speaking skills, but examinations and resource materials were provided in English. The low level of English fluency makes it harder to move from a system of transcription and memorization to one of more meaningful engagement with the material.

English was used as a medium of instruction in teacher training, even in places where primary teachers were expected to teach in local languages. In Zanzibar, for example, it was reported that primary teachers faced additional difficulties in explaining primary mathematics in Swahili because they themselves had been taught in English and were not familiar with the Swahili words for mathematical terms.

The use of English as a medium may also make it more difficult for students from the most remote areas to successfully participate in teacher training. Two of the countries had specific actions to address this challenge. In Eritrea, the government had provided a separate college where teacher training was done in minority languages. This was later closed, but replaced with a system where courses at the Asmara Teacher Education Institute (ATEI) were provided in local languages in parallel with the English language syllabus, so that students could have some instruction in their mother tongue. In The Gambia, as part of a special initiative to encourage more female teachers (Remedial Initiative for Female Teachers (RIFT)), teachers enrolling with poor academic qualifications were provided with additional courses in English and other subjects.

TEACHING PRACTICE

Learning how to teach emerges not only from textbooks but also from experience, and teacher training programs normally include some component of hands-on teaching practice. These practical experiences offer student teachers an opportunity to develop their skills and are also likely to make the theoretical material more relevant and meaningful for the student teachers. In almost all of the case-study

Table 5.6   Length of In-school Teaching Practice

	Primary certificate or diploma	Secondary diploma	Degree (usually secondary)
Gambia, The	2 years	1 year	12 weeks
Malawi	1 year	12 weeks	n/a
Zambia	1 year	1 term	5 weeks
Lesotho	2 × 6 months	2 × 6 months	8 weeks
Eritrea	2 weeks + 6 weeks	4 hrs/week for 1 term	n/a
Uganda	6 weeks	n/a	n/a

countries, pre-service teacher training included a period of teaching practice. The duration of the period of practice teaching varied widely, from six weeks in Uganda to two years in The Gambia (table 5.6). At the secondary level, teaching practice was generally more limited and in Malawi, Eritrea, and Uganda, there was no formal teaching placement for students in degree-level courses.

Where student teachers were sent to schools for periods of practice teaching, they were normally expected to work with a mentor teacher in the school, but in the context of teacher shortages, in practice they usually ended up teaching a full workload. In The Gambia and Zambia, student teachers were routinely teaching full classes for a full year at a time. Malawi had tried to avoid this through a system of posting two student teachers together, with the expectation that they would each teach half-time, and retain some time for study and reflection.

On the other hand, when student teachers were sent to schools for short periods, they often received less teaching experience than might be imagined. In Uganda and Eritrea, it was the usual practice to send groups of students to each teaching practice school, where they would share the work with the existing teachers. In these cases some students taught only a small number of classes, despite spending weeks in the school.

The geographical distribution of students in teaching practice also presented difficulties. Where transportation was limited, students were often placed in schools close to their colleges. This tended to increase the density of student teachers in each school, and reduce the teaching time for each. Further, it often meant a concentration of student teachers in less remote schools, and in schools of particular language groups. In Eritrea, for example, the practice of placing student teachers in nearby schools meant that all student teachers were placed in Tigrinia-speaking schools. By contrast, in Zambia student teachers are deliberately sent to remote rural schools, both to fill vacant positions in these schools, and to make them accustomed to working in a rural area. While this may assist in teacher distribution, it increased the logistical difficulties of supervision, and in effect reduced the frequency of external supervision.

The integration of the period of teaching practice with the campus-based part of the teacher training was often poor, and weakened by issues of timing, supervision, and assessment. In many cases, for logistical convenience, students first completed the campus-based part of the year's work, and then spent a period in a school. This arrangement reduced the opportunities to bring the classroom experience into the taught course. Recognizing this limitation, in both Zambia and The Gambia, additional "wrap-up" courses have been added, where students return to the training college for a period after their teaching practice. In Zambia, students returned to college for a short one- or two-week course following their school-based year. In The Gambia, a more extensive four or five week *face-to-face* course focused on content-related teaching methodologies, allowing students to integrate their experiences during their teaching practice with what they had learned during teacher training.

The supervision of student teachers by tutors from the training institutions was limited. In Malawi, for example, tutors were expected to visit each student six times during the year of teaching practice, but this was prevented by difficulties of transportation and the availability of vehicles. The impact of the teaching practice was also diminished by the limited role it played in the final assessment of student teachers. In some cases, performance in teaching practice had no impact at all on the final grade of the student. In Zambia, for example, there was no assessment of teaching practice in the student's overall grade.

In addition, it should be acknowledged that there are risks involved in teaching practice. Placement away from the training colleges, often to unfamiliar areas and sometimes even to areas of different language and culture, may involve particular risks for female students. For female students, teaching practice may even carry a greater risk of becoming pregnant, as has been reported in Zambia where the resulting children had been nicknamed "ZATEC babies" in reference to the pre-service teacher training course (Zambia Teacher Education Course).

MENTORS

Logically, the easiest source of support and supervision for student teachers is the presence of experienced teachers in the school who can act as mentors. In Eritrea, The Gambia, Malawi, and Zambia, there were designated mentors in the teaching-practice schools who were expected to provide support for the student teachers. However, it was reported that the quality and quantity of support from the mentors varied widely. In both Zambia and The Gambia, student teachers were expected to be assigned to an experienced qualified teacher, but in reality many were assigned to work with unqualified teachers or given complete responsibility for classes with no cooperating teacher.

Mentors were normally not paid or provided with any incentive to provide support for student teachers, although in some cases the presence of student teachers may have reduced the teaching load of the experienced teacher. In Malawi, a plan to pay mentor teachers a bonus of approximately $10 per month, or the equivalent of an increase of about 20 percent of salary, was under discussion but not agreed upon. In Eritrea, the role and motivation of the mentors was strengthened by giving them a role in grading the student teachers. Tutors from the training college assigned 80 percent of the marks, and the remaining 20 percent were awarded by the mentor.

There was also limited training provided to prepare mentors for this role. In some countries there was no training or support for the mentors at all, while others were beginning to provide support for mentor teachers. In The Gambia an annual mentor training course was offered to support new mentors. In Eritrea the Ministry of Education had developed a guide for mentors, to be printed and distributed to all mentor teachers.

TEACHER TRAINERS

The key to the quality of the teacher training is the quality of the tutors (teacher trainers) in the teacher training colleges. The impact of teacher trainers goes beyond the knowledge they impart, as it has been widely observed that teachers often teach in the manner in which they were taught (Schwille Dembélé, and Schubert 2007), placing teacher-trainers in an ideal position to provide models of appropriate teaching methods by demonstrating good practice in their own teaching.

In most cases, colleges were reasonably well staffed, with student-tutor ratios as low as 13:1 in some cases (table 5.7). However, tutors did not always have the skills and experience to provide the best guidance to future teachers.

The selection of tutors for primary teacher training colleges was usually based on academic qualifications. As a result, most of the tutors were formerly secondary teachers, and some had never been primary teachers. Consequently, their training for, and experience of, teaching young children may be very limited. In The Gambia, for example, 77 percent of the tutors teaching on the primary teacher certificate course had never been primary teachers themselves. In Eritrea and Zambia, most of the tutors in primary teacher training institutions were drawn from secondary schools, although some had primary teaching experience earlier in their careers. In Zanzibar, the academic requirements were resulting in a loss of teaching

Table 5.7 Students per Teacher in Primary Teacher Training Colleges

Country	Institution	Students	Tutors	Student-teacher ratio
Eritrea	ATEI	644	25	26
Malawi	Lilongwe TTC	540	29	19
Zambia	10 colleges	5,018	389	13

expertise from the system. With the absorption of the Nkrumah Teacher Training College into the State University of Zanzibar, the university requirements for masters-level qualifications meant that most of the tutors, including some with the greatest classroom experience, could not be employed in the new structure.

Most tutors received little specialist training in teacher development. In Uganda, Kyambogo University had a special program to prepare experienced teachers to become tutors. In other countries, training of tutors was sporadic, and often provided by external projects and for short periods. The lack of training for teacher trainers affects the consistency in what is taught and how it is taught. Indeed, any consistency is likely to come from the common experiences as learners. Poorly prepared teacher trainers are likely to teach the way that they themselves were taught, and are slow to incorporate new methods into their teaching (Avalos 2000, Lewin and Stuart 2003).

Some of the countries were also experiencing a shortage of sufficiently qualified tutors, and were reliant on external expertise. In Eritrea, one-fifth of the tutors in ATEI were expatriates, mostly from India. In The Gambia, volunteers from Voluntary Services Overseas (VSO) were delivering some of the primary teacher training at The Gambia College. In Zanzibar, lecturers from Dar Es Salaam regularly traveled to Zanzibar to teach in the teacher training course, a process that was costly in both time and money.

DIRECTIONS FOR POLICY MAKERS

The pre-service training of teachers presents a series of difficult challenges in the case-study countries. The requirement for more teachers creates a demand for shorter courses and lower entry requirements. The concern for quality of teaching creates opposite demands for higher entry standards and longer periods of training. Further, the geographical and social patterns mean that raising entry standards is likely to make it more difficult to recruit teachers from remote and disadvantaged communities and thus increase the inequity of educational provision. In some cases the entry qualifications were falling in response to a shortage of qualified applicants, and in many cases the students entered teacher training because they did not get places in the courses they wanted, rather than from a real desire to become teachers.

In this context of low quality and motivation at entry, teacher training is expected to build both a solid foundation of subject-content knowledge and a repertoire of practical and appropriate classroom teaching skills. It cannot be assumed that new entrants to teaching already have sufficient content knowledge to ensure mastery of the primary school curriculum, and as a result, some of the initial teacher training must focus on building foundations of content knowledge. At the same time, pedagogical practices in schools are often poor and overly reliant on transcription and rote learning. Newly qualified teachers cannot be assured of finding examples of good pedagogical practice either in their own experiences of schooling or in the performance of their colleagues when they begin to teach.

While teacher training must provide instruction in both content knowledge and pedagogy, there are concerns about the quality and relevance in the provision of both. For content knowledge, the risk is that the content may be too advanced and designed with the assumption of greater prior knowledge than is really the case. Teaching content that is too advanced is likely to encourage rote memorization rather than real understanding of the material. On the pedagogy side, too, there is cause for concern about the relevance of the material taught. Where it is too theoretical and too distant from the reality of the classroom, it is unlikely to have an impact on teacher performance in practice. In both cases, there may be a need to review the content and approach, to ensure that the teacher training is compatible with both the level of entry of student-teachers and the practical needs of the classroom. There are ways in which teacher training could be more closely aligned with classroom needs.

First, the subject content could be matched with the content of the school curriculum, ensuring that teachers have a deep understanding of the content they are supposed to teach. To support this, school textbooks could be provided to teacher colleges, to ensure that teachers are familiar with the books and their contents. Assessment of student teachers could be adjusted to include a stronger focus on testing for mastery of the content that teachers will be expected to teach.

Second, the impact of teacher training on pedagogy could be strengthened. The mismatch between the methods taught in teacher training and those used in practice is well known (Dembélé and Miaro 2003), and the challenge is to find successful ways to change teaching practices. These cases suggest that pedagogy is often taught in a theoretical manner, and that the teaching methods and assessments used in training colleges do little to provide models of good pedagogical practice. A reduction of theoretical content and a stronger focus on practical and context-relevant classroom skills could make better use of the available time. Teacher training could model the desired teaching methods consistently during the period of training, in order to provide practical examples for student teachers. Achieving this, however, would involve ensuring a high level of pedagogical skills in the teacher trainers. The impact of teaching practice could be improved by ensuring that practice is monitored and supported at the school level, and that the messages conveyed during teaching practice are consistent with those conveyed during the period of training. This could be achieved through a system of mentors at the school level, and training and orientation of those mentors.

Third, teacher training could be better aligned to the needs of teachers by matching the language of instruction. Where teachers are expected to teach in the mother tongue, it may be appropriate to have all or part of their teacher training delivered in the mother tongue. This involves logistical and curricular difficulties, but is likely to increase the relevance and impact of teacher training.

Finally, it should be recognized that teacher trainers are central to all developments in teacher training. Selection of teacher trainers on the basis of purely academic criteria does not always guarantee the most appropriate selections, and in some cases teacher trainers in primary teacher colleges had little or no primary teaching experience. Developing the capacity of teacher trainers is an obvious step in improving the quality and relevance of initial teacher education.

NOTE

1. Students at the end of grade 12 sit the Eritrean School Leaving Certificate, a national examination used for matriculation purposes. Examination results are translated into grade points, where an A is worth 4 points, a B gets 3 points, a C gets 2 points, and a D earns 1 point. For each student, the top five results are averaged to give an overall grade point average.

CHAPTER **6**

In-service Training for Unqualified and Upgrading Teachers

I n addition to the pre-service training of teachers, all of the countries had some provision of in-service teacher training. The term "in-service teacher training" was used to cover a variety of different types of training, which can be classified into three main groups:

1. In-service initial training for unqualified teachers, designed to allow unqualified teachers to obtain a recognized teaching qualification while they continue to teach.
2. In-service upgrading for qualified teachers, enabling teachers to upgrade to a higher level qualification, usually associated with higher pay.
3. Continuous professional development, usually in the form of short courses not linked to a specific qualification.

This chapter examines the provision of all three types of in-service in the case-study countries.

IN-SERVICE TRAINING FOR UNQUALIFIED TEACHERS

With the rapid expansion of enrollment in schools, many countries in the region experienced teacher shortages, and recruited unqualified teachers. In response, many countries have provided in-service courses, allowing unqualified teachers to gain their initial teaching qualification while they worked. For unqualified teachers, these courses offer a pathway to a professional career. For countries with expanding systems and inadequate teacher supply, they offer the potential to upgrade the quality of untrained teachers, while retaining them in the workforce. Unqualified teachers often fill the places in the schools where the government has difficulty in deploying trained teachers, thus contributing to redressing the

Table 6.1   In-service Programs for Unqualified Primary Teachers

Country	Description
Eritrea	Two-year course, with 36 weeks face-to-face contact
Gambia, The	Three-year course with 27 weeks face-to-face contact
Lesotho	Four years total. Two-week residential course every semester, three short workshops (one weekend) every semester (in 42 locations) (approximately 24 weeks contact time in total), plus printed self-study materials.
Liberia	12 weeks total. Teachers withdrawn from school.
Malawi	No in-service for primary teachers at present. Previously, the in-service MIITEP system (1994–2002) was offered. It was responsible for training many of the teachers in schools, but was terminated in 2002, partly because of concerns about the quality of the teachers emerging.
Uganda	Three years total. Short residential sessions during school holidays. Bi-monthly workshops at coordinating centers. Peer group meetings at intervals. Direct supervision in schools by coordinating center tutors.
Zambia	Two years total. Uses self-study modules and a face-to-face component during each school holiday.
Zanzibar	Four-year course provided in local teacher resource centers two days per week, one day at the weekend and one day of school time.

deployment problems. However, the provision of in-service courses is challenging. The level of academic achievement of the untrained teachers is sometimes lower than would be expected of new entrants to teacher training colleges, yet their time for study and their contact with tutors is often more limited than it is for their colleagues in teacher colleges.

Most of the case-study countries had some system for training and accreditation of unqualified teachers already employed in the system (table 6.1). These in-service training courses varied in duration and structure, but typically involved between two and four years of part-time study, supported by some combination of residential training at a teacher training college, short courses provided at local centers, and printed self-study materials.

Lesotho, The Gambia, and Uganda had similar models, with delivery managed by teacher training colleges, and implemented through residential courses, short workshops, and printed self-study materials. In Lesotho, the Distance Teacher Education Program (DTEP), operated by the Lesotho College of Education, provided a four-year path to a diploma-level qualification either for unqualified teachers or for teachers with the now-defunct certificate qualification. Teachers with no teaching qualification started at the first year, while teachers with a certificate qualification began the course in the second year. The course was delivered through a combination of two-week face-to-face courses every semester, three short (usually weekend) workshops every semester delivered in a network of outreach centers, and printed self-study materials. There was high demand for places in the course, but the attrition rate was high. In 2005, 42 percent of the year-one students dropped out before reaching the second year.

In The Gambia, the in-service teacher training had been recently introduced and was initially offered only in region 5. The course was managed by The Gambia College, and used the same curriculum content as the campus-based pre-service course. The course enrolled all of the untrained teachers in region 5 who had at least two years of teaching experience. This three-year program involved nine weeks of residential training each year during school vacations. During the school term, the teachers were provided with self-study modules, and supported by a network of cluster monitors who visited the schools regularly to observe teaching.

In Uganda the in-service training was done by designated primary teacher colleges (called core-PTCs), each of which managed a network of coordinating centers. Uganda had 539 coordinating centers, typically a one-classroom building with an office and a nearby house for the coordinating center tutor. The training was provided through short residential courses during the school vacations, bimonthly workshops at the coordinating centers, and direct supervision by coordinating center tutors who visited teachers at their schools. As in other countries, attrition was reported to be high, but had declined over time with the number of failures dropping from 46.9 percent in 2001/2002, to 19 percent in 2004/2005.

Eritrea followed a different pattern. Unqualified teachers were provided with three months of face-to-face training before they began to teach, followed by two blocks of three-month training during the school vacation over the following two years. The course was modeled on the pre-service training course, compressed for delivery in a shorter time. Standards were perceived to be comparable, because the classroom experience was seen to help students to absorb the content, and over 90 percent passed the final examination.

In Liberia, an emergency training course of 12 weeks' duration was introduced to address the large number of unqualified teachers. Training colleges were asked to run three courses per year, and teachers were withdrawn from their schools to attend the course.

The in-service training courses were usually managed by teacher training institutions already involved in pre-service provision, but the delivery of the training, particularly the training delivered at local level, was done by a variety of different groups. In Uganda, the local training was done by coordinating center tutors, full-time support workers based at local coordinating centers. In Lesotho, the local training was delivered by a mix of lecturers from the teacher training college and local secondary school teachers. In The Gambia, both college lecturers and the locally based cluster monitors delivered the training. In Zanzibar, the training was sometimes delivered by staff from the teacher resource centers, but often provided by local secondary school teachers.

Table 6.2   Entry Requirements for Pre-service and In-service Courses in Selected Countries

Country	Pre-service	In-service
Eritrea	Eritrean School Leaving Certificate (grade 12) with a grade point average of 0.6 or higher (on a 5-point scale)	Mostly grades 11 or 12; Grade 10 for minority languages
Gambia, The	West African Senior School Certificate Examination (grade 12) with one credit and three pass grades, including a pass in English	No academic requirements, two years of teaching
Lesotho	Cambridge Overseas School Certificate (grade 12) with four credits and one pass grade, including at least a pass grade in English	Two years of teaching + five passes (no credits required)
Zambia	O-level (junior secondary, grade 11) examination with six passes, including English, mathematics, and one science subject	Same qualification as for pre-service program

The in-service teacher training courses usually required lower entry qualifications than the campus-based courses (table 6.2). In Lesotho, for example a student would require four credits and one pass to begin the pre-service course, but only five passes to enter the in-service course. This made the in-service course an attractive pathway into the teaching career for many who would not have reached the higher standards required for entry to the pre-service course. This possibility encouraged the growth of volunteer teachers, who worked at schools without pay in the hope of later getting a paid post and gaining access to the distance teacher-education program.

Despite the lower entry requirements, some teachers were unable to gain entry into the in-service courses. In Lesotho, approximately 9 percent of primary teachers had qualifications too poor to be accepted in the in-service training. Yet because of the shortage, these unqualified teachers continued to teach in schools. Similar trends were reported in Liberia and Zanzibar. In Lesotho, a bridging course designed to help poorly educated teachers upgrade to the point where they could enter the in-service course was proposed but had not been implemented. In The Gambia, the teachers union provided summer courses for teachers aimed at assisting teachers to improve their educational qualifications, usually by helping unqualified teachers gain access to the Primary Teaching Certificate.

No formal data on the relative quality of different programs are available, but generally anecdotal evidence suggested that the quality of the teachers with in-service and pre-service training was comparable, with some reports that the teachers from the in-service courses were more skilled in the classroom, while those from the pre-service courses had better understanding of the academic content, particularly in mathematics and English. In Lesotho, the students in both pre-service and in-service courses sat comparable final examinations and the pass rates were similar.

The scale of the in-service teacher training courses makes it unlikely that all of the unqualified teachers can be trained quickly. In The Gambia, in-service training has begun with a two-year course, operating in only one region. In Lesotho, the annual output from the in-service training course of about 450 students is approximately 10 percent of the number of unqualified teachers. Even if no new unqualified teachers were recruited, it would take at least ten years to train all the existing unqualified teachers. In Uganda, the annual output of approximately 1,000 teachers from the in-service program was approximately 2 percent of the 48,000 untrained primary teachers. These figures illustrate the need to scale up and sustain these in-service teacher-training courses until all of the untrained teachers can be reached.

UPGRADING QUALIFICATIONS

In-service courses were also provided to allow teachers to upgrade their qualifications, either from certificate to diploma, or diploma to degree. In Lesotho, the normal pre-service teacher qualification had been changed from a certificate to a diploma, and the pay for a diploma holder was considerably more attractive (83 percent higher starting salary) than for a certificate holder (table 6.3). This created an enormous demand for upgrading courses, and the in-service distance teacher education program (DTEP) was forced to limit the number of certificate holders enrolled in order to preserve places for the unqualified teachers.

Table 6.3 Duration and Delivery of In-service Upgrading Courses for Qualified Primary Teachers

Eritrea	Open and Distance Learning Program, aimed at elementary teachers working in middle schools. A three-year course based on self-study text materials and four or five tutorials per year.
Lesotho	The Distance Teacher Education Program (DTEP) enrolls teachers with an existing certificate qualification into the second year of the program, allowing them to upgrade to a diploma in three years. Delivery is through a two-week residential course every semester, plus three short workshops (one weekend) every semester, and printed self-study materials.
Malawi	A three-year part-time course is provided for primary teachers who are teaching in secondary schools. Delivery is through an eight-week initial residential course, then two further three-week blocks of training each year, supplemented by printed modules that students are expected to study.
Zambia	A three-year upgrading course, delivered through a two-week residential training each term for three years (a total of 11 residential blocks), supplemented by printed text modules.

In Eritrea, Malawi, and Zambia, the upgrading was primarily to address the needs of primary teachers teaching secondary-level classes. Typically these were three-year courses, using a mix of residential training and self-study modules. In Malawi and Zambia, the content was matched to the content of the pre-service diploma, and the self-study materials were based largely on the lecture notes from the pre-service course. These upgrading courses could have a significant impact on teacher supply. In Zambia, for example, there was an annual output of 4,300 newly trained primary teachers from the pre-service training, but annual losses of 1,100 primary teachers upgrading to secondary level.

In parallel, most countries also provided opportunities for upgrading through paid study leave, allowing teachers to study full time. In most cases the number of teachers involved in full-time upgrading course was small, but in The Gambia, the number of lower-basic teachers leaving the classroom to enter the Higher Teachers Certificate (HTC) course and upgrade to teach in upper-basic schools was approximately 40 percent of the annual output of new teachers for lower basic education.

IN-SERVICE CONTINUING PROFESSIONAL DEVELOPMENT AND SUPPORT SYSTEMS

Internationally, professional development is increasingly seen as a continuum throughout the career of a teacher (OECD 2005, UIS, 2006). In this view, teachers do not emerge from their initial training with a full range of skills, but develop and refresh their skills throughout their careers. Provision of continuous professional development (CPD) opportunities for in-service teachers plays an important role in improving teacher quality by providing opportunities to refresh knowledge, to update on new curricula, and to reflect on professional experiences. In low-income countries where the quality of entry may be lower than desirable, the value of such CPD supports for teachers may be even greater.

Although most of the case-study countries had some form of CPD provision, the scale and coverage of CPD provision was quite limited, as much of the focus of in-service training was on provision of initial qualifications to unqualified teachers. In most of the countries, government provision of CPD was supplemented by a significant volume of short courses provided through donor projects and NGOs, often with limited geographical coverage. In Liberia, almost all of the CPD was provided by NGOs, resulting in very uneven coverage. In most countries the uncoordinated provision of short courses by multiple providers meant that some teachers were exposed to multiple opportunities for training, while others received none. Where teachers were paid a per diem when attending courses, opportunities to attend courses could be valuable sources of additional income, and hence become a form of patronage distributed by officials to favored teachers.

Where short courses were held during school time, the uneven distribution of access to courses resulted in multiple absences by some teachers.

Government provision of CPD often involved a combination of short training inputs at local centers, and support visits to individual schools. In Zambia, Malawi, and Uganda, the support service used a network of local centers and much of the CPD was provided at these centers. In Malawi, the primary education advisers (PEA) seemed to spend much of their time at the teacher development centers, and although they had only 12–15 schools each, many were visited only once a year. In The Gambia and Lesotho, the provision of support centered on more mobile support staff (called cluster monitors in The Gambia and district resource teachers (DRTs) in Lesotho) and most of the support, including observation of lessons and provision of feedback and support to individual teachers, was provided at the school level. Both approaches have some merits. Provision of CPD at local centers allows greater coverage, and allows teachers from local schools to meet and share experiences. Support at the level of individual schools provides greater opportunities to observe individual teachers and provide one-on-one support.

In most cases the provision of support for teachers was separate from the inspection or monitoring of teachers. In Lesotho, for example, there was a network of district resource teachers with a mandate to provide support, and a separate network of district inspectors, who were expected to monitor quality. Uganda and Zanzibar had similar separate inspection and support systems. In two of the cases, the inspection and support functions were integrated. In Malawi, the inspectorate had been renamed the Education Methods Advisory Service (EMAS) and inspectors had been renamed primary education advisers to reflect their role in providing support. In The Gambia, the inspectorate had been replaced in 2005 with a system of cluster monitors, who were expected to visit schools frequently and to identify difficulties and provide support at a local level. Both arrangements seem to offer some advantages. Combining the supervision and support functions should reduce the risk of teachers receiving inconsistent messages and reduce the cost of travel, allowing increased coverage. On the other hand, having two separate systems may enable the support personnel to have a more open dialogue with the teachers and to concentrate on their supportive function.

Much of the CPD provision was centrally designed and planned in a top-down manner, but there were some examples of demand-driven provision with needs identified by school leaders or by teachers. In the typical "cascade" model the training needs were determined centrally, standard courses (and sometimes training materials) were designed, trainers were provided with training, and then expected to deliver this training in their districts.

There were a few cases of demand-driven provision, where school leaders were able to determine the training needs. In Eritrea school directors were expected to determine the training needs of their teachers, and to either provide the required training or see to it that it was provided. In Zanzibar the management of each training center was empowered to identify training needs locally, and organize events to meet those needs, often drawing on expertise within the area from secondary teachers.

In a few cases, teachers were able to have a strong voice in the identification of their CPD needs. In Malawi, under an externally funded project, groups of secondary schools were combined into clusters and given a budget (of about U.S.$100) per term to facilitate meetings between schools to consider matters such as HIV, gender, management, and curriculum issues. The level of activity of clusters varied, but some worked very well, and even developed and marked in-house examinations together.

Zambia had a particularly sophisticated three-tier hierarchy of support structures, with school level in-service education and training (INSET) committees, zonal centers with volunteer staff, and district centers with full-time staff and more facilities. It also had a unique credit system to motivate teachers to participate in in-service activities, although credits were of limited value.

A summary of practices of the case-study countries in provision of CPD is presented in table 6.4.

Table 6.4 Continuing Professional Development (CPD) Provision, Summary of Practices

Eritrea: School directors were expected to arrange in-school support for teachers. This was delivered, depending on expertise, by school directors, experienced teachers in the school, or members of the community or the Parent Teacher Association (PTA). The Ministry of Education also provided booster courses in English during the summer vacations, delivered as four months of residential training spread over two years.

The Gambia: Combined supervision and pedagogical support provided through mobile cluster monitors. Cluster monitors typically visited schools twice a month, and were expected to observe classes and provide individual feedback to teachers.

Lesotho: Inspection and support functions were separate. Support was provided by district resource teachers assigned to a cluster of schools. These DRTs were a legacy from an externally funded project supporting poorly qualified multigrade teachers in rural schools. Although they were ministry staff, the project had ended, and coverage was incomplete. Very few schools received more than two visits per year.

Liberia: A network of curriculum material centers had been destroyed in the war. Most CPD was provided by NGOs. Coverage was uneven, with some areas receiving too much training, resulting in loss of teaching time, while others received almost none.

Malawi: Combined inspection and support functions provided by a network of primary education advisers. These PEAs were given a small teacher development center (TDC) and a motorbike, and responsibility for 12–15 schools. Many schools received visits only once a year.

Uganda: Inspection and support functions were separate. A network of coordinating center tutors (CCTs) provided support through coordinating centers serving a cluster of schools. However, the CCTs mainly concentrated on training unqualified teachers.

Zambia: A multilevel system. At the lowest level, volunteer zonal INSET coordinators (ZICs) served small clusters of schools (see box 6.1).

Zanzibar: Inspection and support functions were separate. A network of ten teacher resource centers each had a full-time coordinator who was guided by a management committee made up of the head teachers in the zone.

BOX 6.1 ZAMBIA'S HIERARCHY OF CPD SUPPORT STRUCTURES

Support was provided at three levels, the school, zonal centers, and district centers. Each school had a school INSET coordinator (SIC) who worked with the head teacher to identify training needs within the school. Teachers were formed into teachers' groups of up to ten members. These groups met bi-weekly for one hour to discuss issues of relevance to their professional development. Based on these meetings, schools could arrange in-house training or request assistance from the zonal or district level.

Within each zone (cluster of schools) there was a zonal resource center, usually a classroom in a school, and a zone INSET coordinator (ZIC), usually a teacher who took the post as a voluntary part-time activity. These local centers housed some resource materials, and served as a center for training activities and meetings. For example, Nkwashi Zone in Kabwe district had five government schools and five community schools, the furthest being 18 kilometers away. In one term in 2007, the zone monitored mathematics and science teaching, and coordinated an HIV/AIDS quiz for students, a science fair, and a workshop for senior teachers on management skills.

At the district level, there were district resource centers (DRC), often equipped with libraries, photocopying facilities, computers, printers. and sometimes Internet access. Each DRC had a full-time district INSET coordinator (DIC). Teachers met informally in study groups for distance learning courses and had more formal training sessions led by college lecturers. The DRC was also a local hub for information from the Ministry of Education about the latest initiatives and directives, and housed copies of materials that should be available to schools.

Motivation to participate in in-service activities was provided by a credit system. Teachers were awarded one credit for every in-service activity they attended, whether it was a teachers' group meeting within the school or a training course at one of the resource centers. In addition to their symbolic value, the credits accumulated could be considered when selecting teachers for promotion or study leave. Teachers were required to have 50 credits before they could enroll in The Primary Teacher Diploma by Distance Learning (PTDDL). However, credits were not considered for all courses and had limited value.

THE IMPACT OF CPD

The governments in the eight countries in the study had very little research to evaluate the impact of this CPD work on teacher behavior. This is perhaps not surprising, given the methodological difficulty of such research and the range of competing priorities in African countries. One of the few cases where an attempt was made to assess the impact of CPD was Lesotho, where an evaluation showed an increase in learning performance in the schools visited by DRTs (box 6.2).

BOX 6.2   LESOTHO: DISTRICT RESOURCE TEACHERS

In Lesotho, district resource teachers (DRTs) were established in the 1980s with support from USAID. Teams of district resource teachers were to regularly visit teachers in remote schools to bring instructional materials and develop further resources, help teachers improve their classroom and instructional skills, and provide supportive contact and training.

The first efforts to prepare a group of DRTs who would visit teachers in the remote schools were quite random. Experienced teachers proposed by the district education officers were appointed. The second group of DRTs were recruited in a more systematic way. They needed to be qualified, experienced teachers, to have had head teacher or deputy head teacher experience, be willing to travel frequently, and to ride horseback where necessary. Efforts were made to try to have a gender balance as well as distribution by district and religion. Potential participants needed to write about why they wanted to be a DRT; interviews were conducted and were followed by training.

Activities undertaken by the DRTs with classroom teachers included individual consultations, group workshops for clusters, and dissemination of new curricula produced by the National Curriculum Development Center. DRTs sat down with teachers, discussed their perceived difficulties, offered suggestions to help them, gave demonstration lessons, team taught, and developed learning and other materials. Typical difficulties encountered by the teachers included classroom organization and management for multigrade schools, group work, learning centers, peer learning, and mobilizing community members to help with children's learning activities. DRTs usually visited four times a year for two to three days at a time. Additional workshops were organized a few times a year for all the teachers in the schools under the DRT's care (typically between 10 and 15 schools). These workshops were usually held on weekends.

BOX 6.2 (continued)

About 700 of the 1,200 schools were covered by DRT visits by the year 1996, accounting for 2,000 of the country's 6,000 teachers. Examination results of students in the case schools from school year 1988–1989 improved by 17 percent, compared with 6 percent in other schools throughout the country.

Source: "Lesotho: Teacher Support Networks—District Resource Teachers' Program," in World Bank 2000.

It seems likely that the quality of CPD depends heavily on the skills of the CPD staff, particularly in cases where support workers visit schools to assist teachers. In these cases, the CPD personnel are not in a position to deliver a prepackaged course, but must rely on their own expertise to provide relevant support. In most cases the people asked to give support were experienced teachers (in Lesotho and Malawi) or even head teachers (in The Gambia). However, they were often given relatively little training in their role, typically short courses of one or two weeks' duration. This combination of experience and brief training may provide adequate preparation to upgrade the skills of unqualified teachers, but it may not be adequate preparation to provide support for experienced teachers who are having difficulties.

One of the risks with support services is that they can become the mechanism for delivering other kinds of training, thus distracting from the role of pedagogical support. In The Gambia the cluster monitors were expected to provide both monitoring and support functions, but were also drawn into administrative tasks, including checking on textbook delivery, verifying statistical returns, and recording the quality of buildings and latrines. In Malawi, the primary education advisers (PEAs) and their teacher development centers were also used for training by NGOs and by noneducation ministries. These training activities, often associated with opportunities to earn additional income for the center, tended to distract the PEAs from visiting schools, and although each PEA had only 12–15 schools to support, many schools received only one visit a year.

DIRECTIONS FOR POLICY MAKERS

IN-SERVICE TRAINING OF UNQUALIFIED TEACHERS

In the context of teacher shortages, systems to provide unqualified teachers with an opportunity to train while in-service are attractive policy options. For the teachers, they offer a path to a professional career. For the system, they offer a mechanism to retain and up-skill the existing unqualified teachers. If sustained over a sufficient period, these have the potential to bring most of the unqualified teachers to a professional qualification.

Systems of in-service teacher training may help to address deployment difficulties. Unqualified teachers are most often found in the places where there is most difficulty in deploying teachers, and in-service training is likely to retain them in their current positions at least for the duration of the training. There are also potential longer-term beneficial impacts. Unqualified teachers are often recruited from the local area, and are often (though not always) people with insufficient qualifications to enter teacher training colleges. By providing a pathway to a qualification, in-service training can help to build capacity in the educationally disadvantaged communities, providing a longer-term response to the deployment problem.

There are concerns that lower entry standards and a shorter period of campus-based training will have a detrimental impact on standards, but in the case studies there was little reliable evidence to either support or refute this assertion. While there is as yet little objective evidence, the few examples where similar tests were used suggest that in practice there is little difference in performance. In-service teacher training may in some cases be a more effective method, as it is easier to link the training with the realities of the classroom. Where the in-service training is delivered by the same teacher-trainers as the pre-service training, there may even be beneficial effects for the trainers through increased contact with practitioners. However, there is still some risk of lower quality, and this may be especially true in the case of particular subjects, such as mathematics or international languages. Ensuring that in-service teacher training includes substantial blocks of residential time with access to expert tutors may be important in ensuring that there is no loss of quality in key subjects.

There may be a need for additional measures for teachers whose qualifications are too low to access in-service training courses. Despite the lower entry requirements for in-service courses, some countries had unqualified teachers whose qualifications were so low that they were ineligible for in-service training. In the absence of a strategy to either support or replace these teachers, they often remained in the system and continued to teach classes.

TEACHER UPGRADING PROGRAMS

Opportunities for teachers to upgrade their qualifications while participating in in-service programs were provided in most countries, and have potential benefits for teachers and for the system. Upgrading courses provide teachers with opportunities for career advancement and professional development, and offer a means to build the capacity of the teaching force. However, upgrading courses can also provide adverse incentives, encouraging teachers to neglect their duties to pursue their studies.

The implications of teacher upgrading need to be considered in planning for teacher supply and finance. Upgraded qualifications normally resulted in an automatic increase in salary and in some cases involved migration to a different type of school (from primary to secondary, for example). In Lesotho, the large-scale upgrading of teachers from certificate to diploma qualifications had significant fiscal implications, as the starting salary for a teacher with a diploma was 83 percent higher than that of a teacher with a certificate. In The Gambia, the expansion of the HTC, which allowed teachers to move from lower basic to upper basic schools, resulted in a loss of teachers from lower basic schools equivalent to 40 percent of the annual output of newly trained lower basic teachers.

Upgrading courses were not always under the control of the government. In Zambia, the private provision of upgrading courses for teachers on a large scale raised the possibility of large unanticipated increases in the teacher wage bill. Governments will need to monitor the provision of these courses to avoid teacher shortages or unexpected financial implications.

IN-SERVICE CONTINUING PROFESSIONAL DEVELOPMENT

Provision of ongoing professional development opportunities for teachers is likely to improve quality and motivation, but was poorly developed in the case-study countries. While most countries had some provision, it was often weak in terms of geographical coverage, consistency, and integration with accreditation systems. A great deal of the provision was by non-state providers, or linked with donor-financed projects of limited duration. Despite the international recognition of the importance of ongoing professional development opportunities (Villegas-Reimers 2003; Giordano 2008), most teachers, once qualified, had little access to further assistance with methodological or content difficulties.

The provision of continuing professional development opportunities can be divided into three main categories: (i) short training courses, (ii) support systems, and (iii) peer networks. The provision of short training courses was mainly through cascade training, with courses developed centrally and delivered locally through a network of trainers. The support services mainly consisted of individual support workers based at local centers and visiting schools to observe and support individual teachers and provide school-level training. Peer networks were in evidence in only a minority of cases, but provided opportunities for teachers to meet and determine their own training needs.

PART III

After They Are Qualified: Teachers As Professionals

CHAPTER 7

Supervision of Teachers

L ike any other professionals, teachers normally work within systems where they are supervised, monitored, and guided in their work. Well-functioning supervision and support systems play a pivotal role in improving the quality and efficiency of education systems. In most cases the supervision structures include a school head teacher or equivalent based at the school, some form of external inspection or monitoring of schools, and additional oversight from teachers unions and local communities.

This chapter examines the roles played by each of these in overseeing and guiding the work of teachers. Head teachers,[1] although well placed to have a strong influence on teachers, often did not give this role much priority, and often had limited management training. External inspection was in most cases too infrequent to influence behavior at the school level, and too poorly documented and analyzed to serve as an effective feedback mechanism for policy makers. Teachers unions, although associated mainly with their roles in collective bargaining, were in many cases also providing guidance and support services for teachers. Local communities were in many cases nominally involved in schools, but despite their obvious interest, there were only occasional indications of evidence of their impact on teachers. Taken together, the case studies suggest that in most countries the monitoring of teachers was not sufficiently robust to ensure quality of service delivery.

Nevertheless, there were some promising possibilities. Head teachers' contributions could be enhanced through in-service training, and management of their performance. External supervision was facilitated in a few countries, notably The Gambia, through provision of cluster monitors at a local level. Teachers unions, when engaged meaningfully in sector dialogue, seemed willing to play a constructive and supportive role in improving teacher performance. Local communities seemed to offer a strong source of both support for schools, and monitoring of performance of schools, although largely underused at present.

SCHOOL HEAD TEACHERS

As the most senior managers who are present in a school on a daily basis, head teachers play a vital role in the functioning of schools. Where they are effective, they can influence teacher attendance and performance, student behavior, and relationships with parents. A good head teacher can make a significant positive effect throughout the school. Given their importance, it is critical that effective systems for the selection, preparation, and supervision of head teachers be in place (Chapman 2005).

Too often, however, head teachers "look up rather than down." That is, they tend to focus their efforts on dealing with the district and central administration, rather than on managing the school for which they are responsible. These interactions with district and central administrations often involve absence from the school, sometimes for days at a time. In Uganda, provisional findings from a recent study on teacher absenteeism indicate that absence rates for head teachers are 50 percent higher than those of other teachers, and nearly half of the absences investigated were for officially sanctioned reasons (Habyarimana 2007).

Even when in the school, however, principals tend not to see pedagogical leadership as part of their role. In Lesotho, one secondary principal explained that managing the teachers was the responsibility of the deputy, although the deputy was expected to teach 20 periods a week (two-thirds of a normal workload). In Malawi, this withdrawal of head teachers from the daily management of teachers is more formal. Head teachers are expected to take responsibility for the overall management of the school, including communication with the community, ministry, and other stakeholders. Deputy heads are seen as curriculum managers, and are expected to take responsibility for managing the timetable and monitoring teacher attendance.

The tendency for head teachers to prioritize their work with district and central administrations over the work of managing their schools is encouraged by weak administrative systems. Head teachers often need to spend a great deal of time at administrative centers to arrange for routine transactions such as the transfer of new teachers or ensuring that existing teachers are on the payroll. Where transportation is difficult, as in rural Zambia, head teachers are often expected to travel to district offices to collect teachers' pay. Travel to district offices may also be more attractive than remaining in the school, offering head teachers in remote schools the opportunity to buy commodities, engage in other transactions, and maintain a visibility at the district office that may assist in the next promotion. Balanced against these enticements, there are few incentives to remain in the school and take care of daily management responsibilities.

The teaching load expected of a head teacher varies greatly (table 7.1). In Zambia, the post of head teacher is a nonteaching post in all but the smallest schools. In Lesotho, head teachers are usually expected to teach a class. In other cases, the teaching load is calibrated with the size of the school. In Eritrea, the

Table 7.1 Teaching Load of Head Teachers

Eritrea	In elementary schools, the director teaches reduced hours (15 periods) if the school has more than 15 sections (classes), and is excused from teaching if the school has more than 20 sections. In secondary schools, directors are not required to teach.
The Gambia	In the small schools (class A), head masters are expected to teach one class. In the class B schools, the head master is not required to teach, and in the largest schools (class C) both the head and deputy head are released from teaching.
Lesotho	In primary schools, head teachers teach one class. In secondary schools, heads of department are expected to work 25 periods, deputy principals 20, and principals 10 (normally secondary teachers are expected to teach 30 periods per week).
Malawi	In secondary schools, head teachers are expected to teach between three and six periods per week. Deputy heads are expected to teach nine periods per week, and heads of department teach full-time.
Zambia	In all but the smallest schools this is a nonteaching administrative and managerial role.
Zanzibar	Head teachers are expected to teach up to 12 periods per week.

director of an elementary school is expected to teach a reduced load (15 periods per week) if the school has more than 15 classes, and is excused from teaching completely if the school has more than 20 sections.

The positions of head teacher are sometimes advertised in open competition. In The Gambia, posts are advertised nationally, and the head teachers appointed can be posted to any school. In Lesotho, the post of head teacher is advertised by the school management body, for a specific school. In many other countries the posts are filled without open competition. In Eritrea, Zambia, and Liberia, school heads are appointed, largely at the discretion of local or regional education officials. These less-open procedures may provide opportunities for favoritism in selection, or even corrupt practices. Even if local officials choose well, the lack of transparency and competition may be demoralizing for teachers who are not selected. Some examples of the procedures for selecting head teachers in the case-study countries are provided in table 7.2.

TRAINING OF HEAD TEACHERS

Training of head teachers is not routine (see for example Bennell and Akyeampong 2007), and in the countries included in the study many head teachers (probably the majority) had not been trained for their role. Where training is provided, it most frequently takes one of two forms. Some training is provided in the form of short courses, typically of a few weeks' duration, for head teachers who are in-post. These are often financed through donor projects, and have often been provided for a limited period linked with external funding. In Lesotho and Malawi, head teachers

Table 7.2 Selection of Head Teachers, Some Examples

Eritrea	When a vacancy arises, a school director is selected by the zoba (district) management. Selection is, in theory, based on the performance of the teacher. Selection often occurs from within the school, but occasionally a director is transferred from within the zoba.
The Gambia	Where vacancies arise, they are advertised nationally, and eligible teachers can apply. To be eligible, teachers must have held a post for at least three years. Short-listing is based on qualifications, and the final selection on an interview. The selection process takes into consideration qualifications, length of service, posting (teachers in hardship posts are given preference in access to promotional posts), and performance. Letters of recommendation from their regional directors are expected, providing an opportunity for performance to be considered. Because vacancies are advertised nationally, newly appointed head teachers can be posted to any school.
Lesotho	Positions are advertised by the school management body, and selection is based on qualifications and an interview. The selection is reviewed by the senior education officer before the appointment is approved. If there is no qualified applicant, a teacher may be appointed acting head, and the post is re-advertised annually until filled. Primary head teachers are required to have a diploma-level qualification and five years of experience, while secondary head teachers are required to have a degree and 11 years of experience.
Liberia	School principals are selected at the county level, and selection is heavily influenced by the district and county education officers. Once a selection is made, the documents are sent to Monrovia, where the MoE decides the salary level at which the principal will be appointed.
Zambia	Heads are selected at the district level by district staff based on qualifications, ability, and experience. The usual route for promotion is via the positions of senior teacher and deputy head. Heads from smaller schools can be promoted to larger ones, where they receive a larger salary.

had been trained under a variety of different projects and training courses, although none of these remained in operation at the time of the study.

The second common approach was to provide management training through a university course, typically in the form of a one- or two-year diploma course in education management. These have limited capacity and typically reach only a minority of head teachers. Full-time courses of a year or more also result in the loss of head teachers from their posts for extended periods, and may in some cases be a pathway to further promotion into education management positions. Table 7.3 summarizes the practices for training head teachers employed in the case-study countries.

MONITORING OF HEAD TEACHERS

While the head teacher is recognized as a key influence on school quality and effectiveness, there is relatively little monitoring of their performance. Given the relatively low frequency of external supervision of schools, head teachers have relative autonomy. Even where there are monitoring systems, they frequently exclude school heads. In Zambia, there is an institutional monitoring form used by standards officers (inspectors) during school supervisions, but none of the

Table 7.3 Training of Head Teachers, Summary of Practices

Eritrea	A short training course is provided each year for newly appointed school directors, to give them basic skills in managing their schools. In addition, the Eritrea Institute of Technology (EIT) is providing a full-time two-year diploma in education management, which currently has 137 school directors enrolled.
The Gambia	A new one-year certificate course aimed at head teachers and focusing specifically on school management is hosted by the university. The head teachers are on study-leave for the year, paid by the Department of State for Education (DoSE), and bonded to work in a school for at least one year afterward. As part of the course, the participants spend two weeks working closely with an experienced head master. This course began in 2006–07, with 19 head masters or acting heads enrolled.
Lesotho	At present there is no training offered for school principals, although different courses have been offered in the past through various channels.
Liberia	There is no mandatory management training for principals.
Malawi	Provision of training is not routine, and not all newly appointed head teachers receive training. In the past, some training occurred, often as part of externally funded projects. For example, the Malawi School Systems Support Programme (MSSSP) provided training for three senior staff in primary school. Some secondary head teachers also undertook a three-week induction course, covering topics including finance, administration, HIV, and management of staff.
Uganda	Recently, short induction courses have been provided for head teachers.
Zambia	There is no mandatory training for heads. The national distance education college for teachers (NISTCOL) offers a two-year course by distance learning, but this currently has just 30 students. There are proposals in the teacher education directorate to expand the scope of training for head teachers.

headings refer to the head teacher and his/her effectiveness. In Lesotho, there is limited monitoring of school principals, and there are anecdotal reports of high absenteeism among principals. While no official records exist, one inspector estimated that about half of the school principals would be absent more than seven days a month. This encourages teacher absenteeism, which is likely to be higher on the days the principal is absent. In fact, the Teaching Service Department reported that in some cases, teachers who were faced with disciplinary charges responded with allegations of absenteeism by the principal.

Also in Lesotho, principals are nominally accountable to management boards, but in reality they frequently dominate these boards. Particularly in areas where the principal is the best-educated person in the community, management board members may have little confidence or ability to challenge a principal.

Recognizing the importance of quality school leadership, some of the countries studied had proposals to improve performance in that area. In Uganda the MoES was concerned that head teachers tended to remain in a single school for a long period, sometimes for their entire careers. In response, the government MoES began compulsory transfers of head teachers, to refresh the leadership in troubled schools and reduce the complacency of head teachers. Implementation of these transfers has been uneven, and there have been incidents of lobbying by head teachers and communities to reverse transfer decisions.

In Lesotho, the MoET had proposals to make principals more accountable through employing them on renewable contracts. This was intended to provide the MoET with the opportunity to remove a principal in the case of very poor performance. It was proposed that principals whose contracts were not renewed would revert to their positions as teachers. This relatively low-stakes penalty for nonrenewal was expected to make it more likely that principals who performed poorly would be removed.

SUPERVISION AND INSPECTION

Inspection of schools serves two main purposes. First, it is a supervision system, monitoring events in schools, identifying difficulties early, and ensuring quality. Second, it serves as a feedback mechanism, providing information to policy makers about the reality in schools. These two roles imply different coverage requirements. An effective supervision system should be able to supervise every school with a reasonable frequency. A feedback system may function effectively by examining a carefully chosen sample of schools, but must develop a synthesis of the findings of relevance for management and feed these to the appropriate points in the education management.

In most of the countries studied, the inspectorate was based either at a central location or decentralized to district level. In both cases the frequency of supervision visits was severely curtailed by the limited number of inspectors (table 7.4) and transportation and logistical difficulties, and most schools could expect an inspection visit less frequently than once per year. Where transportation is a major problem, the most isolated schools tend to be visited least frequently.

Liberia illustrates supervision difficulties common to many of the countries. Liberian county education officers are responsible for supervision of the schools in their counties, along with their managerial and administrative functions. The expectation is that each school will be visited once per semester, but the practice falls far short of that. One CEO interviewed reported that he had managed to visit

Table 7.4   Number of Teachers and Inspectors

	Teachers (primary and secondary)	Inspectors (primary and secondary)	Teachers per inspector
Eritrea	10,862	165	65
Gambia, The	7,707	54	142
Lesotho	13,741	44	312
Uganda	192,808	250	771
Zambia	59,076	326	181
Zanzibar	8,261	30	275

20 of the 189 schools in his county in the previous year. Another, who was fortunate to have a dedicated vehicle, had visited 65 of 110 schools in his county in one year. If these supervision frequencies continue, the average school may go between two and five years between supervision visits, and the most remote schools may have considerably longer supervision intervals.

PROMISING PRACTICES

A few countries have achieved more frequent supervision by having a highly decentralized inspection staff. In The Gambia a "cluster monitor" is allocated to every ten schools, and is expected to live at one of the schools and travel by motorbike to visit each school every two weeks. Both head teachers and teachers find the system helpful, noting the benefits of improved support for teachers and improved communication with district offices (VSO The Gambia 2007). There are indications that teacher absenteeism has been reduced following the introduction of these frequent external visits.

Eritrea reorganized its supervision system in 2005. Supervisors had been based at zoba (regional) offices, but there were acknowledged difficulties in supervision frequency, resulting mainly from transportation difficulties. In the reform in 2005, supervisors were deployed to clusters of schools (see box 7.1), each cluster comprising approximately 80 teachers, in between two and ten schools. These cluster supervisors were expected to live at one of the schools and travel on foot or by bicycle and visit each teacher three or four times per year. In reality, the frequency may be closer to twice per year. This reform has lowered costs by reducing the transportation requirement for supervision, and increased the frequency of visits. These cluster supervisors are supported and trained by a central quality assurance directorate, which visits a sample of about 100 schools each year.

BOX 7.1   ERITREA: THE TEACHER SUPERVISION SYSTEM

In Zoba Debub, Eritrea, there are 300 schools and 3,400 teachers. These are supported by 39 supervisors for basic education and three supervisors for secondary education, giving a ratio of one supervisor for every seven schools. Each secondary school is expected to receive two visits per semester, the first a short one-day visit, and the second lasting a week. In elementary education, supervisors are encouraged to concentrate on the weak schools, and schools with unqualified head teachers can be visited monthly, or in some cases multiple times in a month. Supervisors are not normally drawn into administrative work, and can devote 75 percent of their working time to supervision (including supervision of management). Supervisors live in their clusters, and generally get to schools using public transportation or walking.

Malawi had a decentralized supervision system similar to Eritrea and The Gambia, where 12–15 schools were grouped into zones, with a small teacher development center (TDC) and a primary education adviser (PEA). Each PEA was provided with a house, a motorbike, and a monthly fuel allowance (3,000 MWK). However, the frequency of visits was much lower, and many schools received only annual visits, despite expectations of visits three times a year. Two main factors appear to contribute to the disappointing supervision frequency reported in Malawi. First, PEAs are drawn into various other activities, many of which offer them opportunities to earn additional income. PEAs often organize courses at their centers, and can rent the center for other training activities and even community activities and weddings. The availability of a network of PEAs and centers is also attractive to other government agencies and NGOs, who frequently rent the facilities and involve the PEA in their activities. Second, PEAs frequently attributed the low frequency of school visits to a shortage of fuel for their motorbikes. In one case, a district education manager had decided to withhold fuel from PEAs who did not file reports on their school visits, resulting in an even lower frequency of visits.

Table 7.5 summarizes the current inspection systems and frequency of visits in the case-study countries, highlighting the countries that show promising practices.

Table 7.5   Inspection Systems and Frequency of Inspection Visits, Summary of Practices

	Deployment of inspectors	Frequency of school supervision
Lesotho	Central and district inspectors travel in official vehicles.	Frequency of less than once a year, some not visited for ten years.
Liberia	No separate inspection system. CEOs responsible for inspection of schools in their counties. Based in county offices.	Goal is to visit each school once each semester. In practice, most are not visited annually.
Uganda	Central, regional, and district inspectors. Average of 70 schools per inspector. Limited transportation.	Approximately one in 16 schools visited last year. Only four teachers observed in each visit.
Zambia	Standards officers at district, province, and central levels.	Approximately once a year (EMIS).
Zanzibar	Official complement of 30 inspectors, 15 on each island. One vehicle on each island.	The inspection service aims to visit each school every two years.
Countries with promising practices		
Eritrea	Cluster: one for every 80 teachers. Travel by bicycle or walking.	Visit each **teacher** twice a year.
Gambia, The	Cluster one for 10 schools. Travel by motorbike.	Expected once a week. In reality, maybe twice a month.
Malawi	PEAs, for every 12–15 schools. Travel by motorbike. 380 PEAs.	Expected three times a year. Many schools report only annual visits.

Table 7.6   Annual Report to Policy Makers, Summary of Practices

Eritrea	Supervisors report to the Zoba office twice a year, and this information is fed into the supervision workshops held twice a year for Zoba and central QA staff. The main problems reported by supervisors include (i) absence of lesson plans, (ii) insufficient assessment of student progress, (iii) use of a teacher-centered pedagogy, and (iv) some teacher absenteeism.
Gambia, The	The Standards and Quality Assurance Directorate is expected to compile a synthesis of the cluster monitors' reports and make this available to the senior management. At the time of the study, this had not been done.
Lesotho	Work is underway to compile the findings of inspection reports, but there is not yet a routine annual report summarizing the major inspection findings. Such a report is envisaged in the education bill currently before the government.
Liberia	Written reports are not routinely made of each inspection, and there is no compilation of the general trends observed in inspection.
Malawi	The EMAS is expected to produce an annual report to the principal secretary of the MoEVT, but the last report was in 2004.
Uganda	The standards agency produces reports on specific issues, but no overall report.
Zambia	Monitoring reports are gathered by officers at each district. Quarterly reports outlining achievements are produced at the district level with copies of completed monitoring forms attached. These reports are sent to the primary education officer (PEO), who then reports on behalf of the province to Lusaka. The standards directorate does not usually produce an annual report with an analysis of inspection findings.

FEEDBACK MECHANISMS

The mechanisms to provide feedback from school visits to policy makers were weak in many of the countries studied (table 7.6). No country had a routine summary of inspection findings provided to policy makers and teacher training institutions. Reports from inspection services were in some cases administrative reports, focused on the number of schools visited and reporting the work of the inspectors, rather than the findings from their work. There were some examples of successful feedback mechanisms. In Eritrea, workshops held twice a year provide a forum for cluster-based supervisors to feed back to zoba (regional) management and to staff from the quality assurance directorate. In Uganda, the education standards agency (ESA) has prepared reports on specific issues.

INSPECTION AND ITS IMPACT ON QUALITY

When inspectors visit schools, the extent to which they observe teachers varies. Some inspections concentrate on issues outside the classroom, such as student attendance, school finance, the condition of the buildings, and the presence of textbooks. The use of inspectors as the agents for data collection encourages them to focus on this nonpedagogical work. While these are important functions, they take away from the capacity of inspectors to monitor teaching and learning.

When inspectors do observe classroom teaching, there is little information on what they do, or what kind of feedback they provide. However, anecdotal reports suggest that many inspectors are poorly equipped to provide pedagogical support, and tend to focus on mechanical issues such as the use of textbooks instead of providing practical pedagogical advice. Malawi has prepared a classroom evaluation document for inspectors, to guide them to observe and examine pedagogy.

TEACHERS UNIONS

Teachers unions provide support to teachers through their ability to mobilize and represent teachers' interests nationally, as well as through their reach to teachers at the local level. All unions in this study had some role in advocacy for better pay and conditions for teachers—roles that have been criticized in the international literature as raising costs without improving the learning of students (Wößman 2003). However, unions also engaged teachers in other activities, including policy analysis, participation in the global campaigns for education, and advocacy for improvements in quality. At the local level, many provided services to their members, including continuing professional development, access to credit, and a recourse in the case of unfair treatment. In this way, teachers unions are evolving to function as both a support for teachers and an accountability check on the education system (Mundy et al. 2008).

In most countries, the majority of public teachers were represented by a union. Representation of private teachers was lower, and more varied. In most cases union membership was voluntary, although it was automatic in Eritrea and Liberia. Teachers unions were financed from member subscriptions of up to 2 percent of salary, mostly collected by the ministry through a payroll deduction and then passed on to the union. At least one union in most countries was also supported to some degree by "sister unions," predominantly from Norway, Sweden, Denmark, Ireland, and Canada. Support was often focused on capacity building of the union and training for teachers. The characteristics of the teachers unions in the eight countries of this study are summarized in table 7.7.

TEACHERS UNIONS AND ADVOCACY WORK

Advocacy work was an important part of several teachers unions' activities, although differing in form. In Zambia, the main teachers union had a full-time economist to monitor education spending and policy. In The Gambia, the teachers union had a desk officer for gender, with duties including encouraging girls to consider a career in teaching.

Teachers unions played prominent roles in the national campaigns for education in four of the eight countries. These campaigns were connected to the

Table 7.7 Characteristics of Teachers Unions in Eight Countries

Significant unions	Members	% of teachers (est.)
Eritrea: Teachers Association of Eritrea (TAE, est. 1958) Elementary, middle school, high-school, and teacher trainers	7,000	~64
Gambia, The: Gambia Teachers' Union (GTU, est. 1937) All levels (including non-teaching staff), both public and private. 80% of teachers	5,500	~71,
Malawi: Teachers' Union of Malawi (TUM) All levels—including primary, secondary and technical PSEUM—Private Schools Employees Union of Malawi	Over 40,000	~75
Uganda: Uganda National Teachers' Union (UNATU, est. 2003 Pre-primary to university teachers. Merger of two previous unions (private teachers now forming own union).	40–45,000	~20–23
Zanzibar: Zanzibar Teacher Union (ZATU, est. 2002) All levels: primary, secondary, teacher trainers, public, private, and unqualified teachers	4,000	~48
Lesotho: Association of Teachers (LAT, est. 1986) Primary and secondary	6,141	~45
Lesotho Teachers' Trade Union (LTTU, est. 1990) Primary and secondary Lesotho Preschool Teachers' Association Preschool only	2,000	~15
Liberia: National Teachers' Association of Liberia (NTAL, est. 1938) Mainly from public schools Monrovia Combined School System Teachers' Union	10,000	~76 (public)
Zambia: Zambia National Union of Teachers (ZNUT, est. 1953) All sectors (it was the only union until 1991, when liberalization of regulations allowed other unions).	39,000	~60
Basic Education Teachers' Union of Zambia (BETUZ, est. 2000) Open to all teachers in Gr. 1–9 who have primary teachers background	15,000	~28.6
Secondary School Teachers' Union of Zambia (SESTUZ, est. 1995) Secondary teachers Gr. 8–12	5,300	~27

Estimates based on teacher union reported membership.

Global Campaign for Education. Unions in Uganda and Liberia (NTAL) were the chairs of their national coalitions. Unions in Lesotho (LAT) and Malawi (TUM) were also active in their national coalitions, which undertook research and analysis on topics such as educational quality and monitoring government support to education.

TEACHERS UNIONS' TRAINING AND DEVELOPMENT WORK

At the local level, teachers unions provided grassroots services to their members. Training and continuing professional development was provided in most countries in a variety of areas, including content-based in-service courses in English, mathematics, and science; training for women; courses supporting improvement of teachers' formal educational qualifications; and training in professional ethics and school representation. Most unions had district or zonal branches, allowing for decentralized provision of training.

Credit services were offered through teachers unions in The Gambia, Lesotho, and Zambia. In The Gambia, the teachers credit union offered larger loans to teachers than they could get from banks, a lower interest rate (currently 1.5 percent per month), and repayment by salary deduction (which avoided penalty charges if salary payment was delayed). Zambia's basic education teachers unions was buying building materials in bulk and providing them to teachers, who repaid through salary deductions over a 36-month period. It also provided some grants to teachers to assist in paying fees for upgrading courses.

HIV/AIDS awareness training or research was also provided by several of the unions, including those in Eritrea, Lesotho, Liberia, Uganda, and Zambia. The Lesotho Association of Teachers had projects addressing awareness, prevention and voluntary testing, as well as gaining legal protection from victimization for its members. It published a book on life-skills education in partnership with the Ministry of Education and Training. Uganda's union has ongoing research looking at HIV, as well as developing a workplace HIV/AIDS policy for teachers. See table 7.8 for a summary of the grassroots activities of the teachers unions in the countries included in this study.

COMMUNITY INVOLVEMENT: PTAs AND SMCs

Local communities, and parents through parent teacher associations (PTAs) and school management committees (SMCs), have an important role to play in the quality, governance, and accountability of schools (Bray 2001). In contexts where external supervision of schools is limited, community bodies may be the only external agents with regular access to schools. However, despite its potential, some studies have found limited parental involvement in Africa, resulting from poor awareness and training, and existing school management practices (Pansiri 2008).

Most countries included in this study have some community involvement, either in the form of PTAs (Eritrea, Gambia, Liberia, Uganda, and Zambia), or SMCs (Lesotho, Malawi, and Zanzibar). Fund-raising emerged as the main activity undertaken by communities in the countries studied. Parents raise money for school materials,

Table 7.8   Grassroots Activities of Teachers Unions, Summary of Practices

Eritrea	• Seminars and workshops for teachers on professional ethics, HIV, and AIDS awareness; for school representatives of the association; and for female teachers. These workshops had all been supported financially by the sister associations.
	• Teachers' club in Asmara, as a venue for teachers to meet, with some recreational facilities (billiards, chess, etc.), a satellite TV, and a small library. The club was managed by an elected committee separate from the management of the association.
Gambia, The	• Extramural classes—formal intensive summer courses to improve teachers' educational qualifications.
	• Five-day training course for acting union representatives (teachers) in their schools, raising awareness of the teaching regulations and ability to act at the school level.
	• Training for women in leadership, promoting girls' education, making teachers aware of education policy, and liaising with other NGOs and education partners.
	• Development of training program for school head masters, to provide basic financial and management skills.
	• Providing credit services to teachers.
Lesotho	• In-service training to its members teaching English, mathematics, science, and art.
	• Centers for the training and support of teachers involved in further studies (e.g., teachers preparing for diploma course examinations).
	• Seminars for members on progress and achievements of the association and the education system.
	• Providing credit services to teachers.
	• HIV/AIDS awareness, legal protection from victimization, life-skills book.
Liberia	• HIV awareness training to teachers, with support from external donors, during 2008.
Malawi	• Hosts summer in-service courses for teachers with Junior Certificate to get a Malawi School Certificate Examination. Despite a fee of 3,000 MWK (approximately $20), the course was oversubscribed, and the numbers had to be restricted to 1,000 per year.
Uganda	• Hosts summer in-service teacher education (INSET) courses, on conflict resolution, classroom management, etc. The Canadian Teachers Federation provides support for these courses.
	• HIV/AIDS research, and developing workplace HIV/AIDS policy for teachers.
Zambia	• Courses on workers education and training, primarily helping teachers to understand their rights, and the structures of the education system and its management.
	• Provides credit services to teachers.
	• Training and mobilization of teachers for HIV/AIDS awareness and prevention.

operating costs (electricity and water), and school maintenance. These contributions serve an important function where there is very limited funding from non-pay-recurrent expenditures at the school level.

Some communities also contribute through paying or topping-up teachers' salaries. Parents in Malawi and Uganda use their contributions to employ additional teachers in public schools, both qualified and unqualified "volunteer teachers." Eritrean parents often top-up benefits to teachers in the form of accommodation, food, domestic help, and sometimes cash, although the scale of support varies widely. These extra contributions potentially result in distortions of the teacher labor market, as schools in more affluent areas (who can raise more funds through parent contributions) can attract and retain the better teachers, thus contributing to inequity in teacher distribution.

Although PTAs and SMCs have the potential to act as an extra accountability check on schools by discouraging teacher absenteeism and holding head teachers accountable, there was limited evidence of this occurring in practice. In Uganda, schools with strong parental involvement, as indicated by parental contributions and frequency of parent meetings, had lower teacher absence (Habyarimana 2007). In Malawi some school management committees are very active, in part because they have been trained by NGOs. As a result, misbehavior is reported, both to the school and the district education manager. As one official noted, "the office is under pressure from these people."

However, in many cases, parents play a very limited supervisory role. This may seem surprising, given their strong interest in the quality of education their children receive. It may be that poorly educated parents feel unable to challenge the relatively well-educated head teacher of a school. There were many examples in school visits of poorly educated groups of parents seemingly dominated by a better-educated and visibly more-affluent head teacher, reflecting experiences in West Africa (De Grauwe et al. 2005). It may also be that parents are unaware of their right to demand better performance. In Uganda, Eritrea, Lesotho, and Malawi, some training of school management committees was underway to prepare parents to know their responsibilities and rights.

While the community may sometimes help to make schools more accountable, there are other cases where parental involvement supports poor practices in schools. In Lesotho, community pressure may result in a school employing a local person in preference to a better-qualified outsider. In The Gambia and Uganda there were reports that head teachers might find it difficult to take disciplinary action against teachers living in the community. This is consistent with the statistics in Uganda which reveal that teachers working in their district of origin were more likely to be absent, by 3.5 percentage points (Habyarimana 2007).

DIRECTIONS FOR POLICY MAKERS

Head teachers have an enormous influence on the quality of schooling, and on teacher attitudes and performance. Yet systems for training, supporting, and supervising head teachers were relatively weak, and it seemed that many head teachers did little to actively supervise their teachers. It seems likely that the performance of head teachers could be enhanced by a formal orientation, making clear what is expected of them in terms of supervision of staff. As many head teachers remain untrained, provision of basic training providing practical managerial skills, and in particular the skills of managing people, would seem promising. In the context of limited training, provision of brief in-service training courses seems more appropriate than longer term training, which can reach only a minority of head teachers. Short in-service training for head teachers may also prove more flexible in addressing the different needs of head teachers (see DeJaeghere, Williams, and Kyeyune, in press), and may help to develop communities of head teachers, thus providing a support mechanism at the local level.

Once in position, there were few systems to either support or monitor head teachers. Given the relatively isolated role of head teachers, it seems likely that there would be benefits in providing head teachers with an opportunity to access some support, such as a peer-group of local head teachers. Increasing the accountability of head teachers also seems beneficial. The system proposed in Lesotho, where head teachers would be appointed on fixed-time contracts, after which they could either revert to their teaching positions or be awarded a new term as head teacher, seem to offer promising ways to enable removal of head teachers who are unable to effectively manage their schools.

While all of the countries had some supervision or inspection system, in reality the frequency of inspection was often so low as to be unlikely to deter malpractice. Reasonably frequent external supervision of schools was achieved only in cases where there were highly decentralized inspectors, such as the cluster monitors in The Gambia and Eritrea. In countries where transportation is difficult, this model of inspection decentralized to small clusters of schools offers the potential for regular monitoring of schools.

Teachers unions also provided support to teachers through a range of activities at the local and national level. While relationships with teachers unions have often been seen in terms of pay bargaining, those in the study were also involved in policy analysis, participation in the global campaigns for education, and providing professional development courses and HIV/AIDS and gender awareness training. This illustrates the changing role and/or perception of teachers unions from pure pay-bargaining organizations to professional organizations involved in both policy dialogue and service provision.

Parent teacher associations and school management committees played an important part in operating costs and school maintenance in many cases, but few had roles in accountability or monitoring tasks. Fund-raising for the school was one of their major activities, and in some cases parents also provided additional payment (in in-kind support) to government teachers or payment for extra non-government teachers. There were some, but few, reports of parents monitoring teacher attendance or taking action in cases where absenteeism was unacceptably high. In Uganda, one district officer reported pressure from parents to address teacher absence. In Malawi, some school management committees were very active, in part because of training through NGOs. This suggests that training of parent groups, combined with appropriate external supports, can enhance the ability of communities to monitor their schools.

NOTE

1. A note on terminology. The managers of schools are known by various titles including head teachers, principals, and directors. The term "head teacher" is used generally here, but other titles are used when referring to specific countries.

CHAPTER **8**

Teacher Absence,
Pay Distribution, and Discipline

I n any system it must be anticipated that some personnel will fail to live up to the professional standards expected of them. In low-income countries, one of the recurring concerns is the level of teacher absenteeism. High levels of absence undermine the quality of schooling, reduce parent confidence in the school, and tend to reduce student attendance. Failure to address teacher absenteeism further lowers teacher morale and sets low standards for other teachers. Yet some of the absence is caused by government systems, both through failure to deliver pay to teachers, and in withdrawal of teachers to participate in training. When teachers are absent without cause, the ability of disciplinary systems to respond in an appropriate and timely manner is key to reducing the negative impact. This chapter examines three aspects of the management of teachers: (i) teacher absenteeism and possible responses to it, (ii) systems for delivery of pay and their implications, and (iii) disciplinary systems.

TEACHER ABSENTEEISM

In every country included in this study, some degree of teacher absence was reported. Where teacher absenteeism is high, it undermines the quality of education, as pupils are left to study alone (figure 8.1). The impact on students' learning can be very significant; a study in Zambia showed that an increase of 5 percent in teacher absence reduced learning by 4–8 percent of average gains over the year (Das et al. 2005). Absenteeism also undermines confidence in public schooling, and is one of the drivers of the growth of low-cost private schools. Although private schools often have very poor facilities and badly qualified teachers, they attract parent resources because they are perceived to ensure more teacher contact time than public schools (box 8.1).

Figure 8.1   Uganda: Teacher Absenteeism

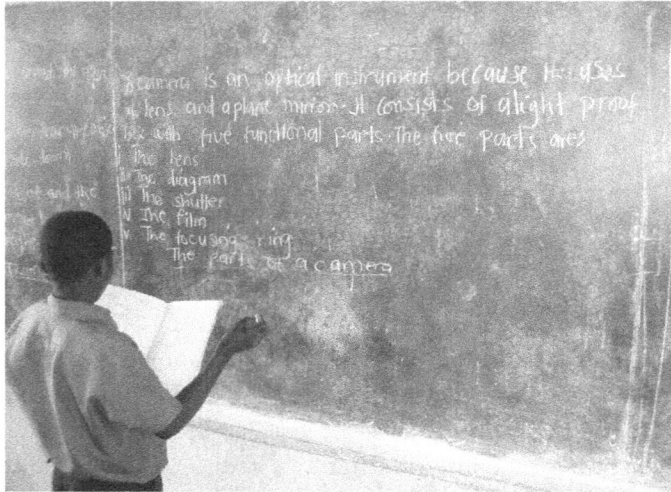

In Uganda, a student in primary 7 transcribes notes onto the board, as the teacher is absent

Despite the significance of the problem, it is difficult to get data about the extent of teacher absenteeism:

- None of the countries in this study had official teacher absenteeism statistics.
- None of the countries in this study included information on teacher absence in their annual education monitoring statistics.
- Teacher attendance was often recorded at the school level, but information was rarely analyzed or fed up to higher levels.

Nevertheless, some indication of the scale of teacher absenteeism can be found from attendance studies, usually based on unannounced visits by enumerators to a sample of schools.

BOX 8.1   WHY CHOOSE PRIVATE SCHOOLS?

Banda, a taxi driver in Lusaka, Zambia, has two sons aged seven and ten. Although not wealthy (he rents the 20-year old taxi on a daily basis), he pays 300,000 Zambian kwacha (ZMK) ($75) per term for each of his sons to attend a low-cost private school. When asked why, he explained that teachers in government schools are "too playful" and never in their classrooms.

Studies of absenteeism have found varied, but generally high, rates of teacher absence. A World Bank study of absence in six countries worldwide (Chaudhury et al. 2006) found an average of 19 percent of teachers absent when schools were visited. In Zambia a study conducted in 2005 as part of the public expenditure tracking study found that 18 percent of teachers were absent on the day of the visit (Das et al. 2005). A similar scale of absence was found in Uganda, where a 2006 study found that almost 20 percent of all teachers could not be found in the school at the time of enumerator visits. In addition, nearly *one-third* of teachers were at school, but outside of the classroom when the enumerators visited (box 8.2) (Habyarimana 2007). Combining the teachers who are absent with those who are "absent on the premises," it seems that less than half of the expected number of classes were actually delivered.

For the purposes of analysis, different types of teacher absence can be distinguished; nondiscretionary, employer-initiated, and discretionary. In the case of nondiscretionary absence, a teacher is unable to attend class as a consequence of factors outside of his or her control. Typical examples may include severe illness or injury, or failures of public transportation systems. In one school visited in Uganda, a seriously ill teacher had not attended the school for a number of months, but the school had not reported the absence to protect the income of their ill colleague. In Liberia and Northern Uganda, teacher attendance has been severely disrupted by civil strife; many teachers have left posts and as many as 20 percent of teachers in Liberia may have left the country.

Other teacher absence is employer-initiated. In this case the teacher is absent because of actions or opportunities of the employer, whether it be the school or the education administration. Examples include travel to collect pay, to attend courses, or to petition at education offices for a variety of benefits such as study leave, transfer, or payment of allowances. In Zambia and Liberia, some rural schools were closing for a number of days each month as teachers traveled to collect and spend their pay. In Malawi the overdeployment of teachers to urban schools left many schools with more teachers than classes, allowing each teacher to be absent a few days each week. In almost all countries, attendance at courses was a significant cause of teacher absence. In Zambia, the dates for the residential sessions of the distance training courses were not always synchronized with school holidays, causing significant absence during these periods.

Other absences are discretionary and teacher initiated. In these cases the teacher could attend the school, but chose not to. Examples include engaging in other income-generating activities, domestic activities such as caring for family members, community and cultural activities such as attendance at weddings and funerals, or simply absence because the teacher does not feel like working. A number of examples from Uganda highlight these occurrences: secondary teachers were often absent because of second jobs, often in private schools; teacher absence was reported to be

BOX 8.2 UGANDA: PATTERNS OF TEACHER ABSENTEEISM

A study in 2006, based on surveys of 160 schools in six districts from three regions in Uganda, found that:

- Nearly one-fifth of teachers were absent, and nearly one-third were present but not in their classroom at the time of enumerator visits.
- Schools with strong parental involvement, as indicated by parental contributions and frequency of parent meetings, had lower teacher absence.
- Schools with functioning teacher housing had lower teacher absence.
- Teachers living in the same parish as the school were absent less (by 9 percent).

Source: Habyarimana 2007.

higher at the start of term, when teachers with children were often absent to try to accumulate the funds to pay school fees; and finally, teacher absence was reported to be higher in harvest season and other peak periods in the agricultural calendar, when teachers may either work their own land, or work for pay on other farms.

RESPONSES TO ABSENTEEISM

POLICY RESPONSES

Nondiscretionary absences are less likely to be responsive to policy change, and addressing causes such as serious illness, war, and civil strife are far outside the scope of education policy. However, teacher absence resulting from travel difficulties may be reduced by provision of housing near to schools. A study in Uganda (see box 8.2, above) found lowered teacher absence associated with teacher housing and living in the same parish as the school. However, it is not clear that this is always a solution. In Lesotho, one rural school visited had empty teacher housing, as the teachers preferred to live in a nearby town and travel by public transportation each day.

Employer-initiated absence is highly amenable to change. The disruption resulting from salary collection can be reduced either by payment directly into teacher bank accounts or delivery of payment directly to schools (discussed later in this chapter). Ensuring that appointments, transfers, and promotions are implemented efficiently and without any need for petitioning in person at a district office could reduce the absence of teachers and head teachers. Absence to attend courses can be reduced by synchronizing training courses with school holidays and reducing the number of courses that can be provided within school time.

In The Gambia, head teachers are asked to use a quota system to reduce teacher absence. Head teachers are expected to monitor teacher absence and restrict the absence of each individual teacher to a maximum of two days per month. Any teacher who has been absent without permission is denied permission to attend training. This newly introduced policy seems likely to improve the distribution of training courses to teachers, and provide some incentive to improve attendance.

There are strong indications that discretionary teacher absenteeism can change significantly in response to changes in monitoring and the consequences of absence. Schools managed by nongovernment agencies often achieve lower teacher absence, even when teacher salaries remain similar or lower. Very low-cost private schools in Uganda and Zambia often have higher teacher attendance than government schools, as attendance is monitored actively by school managers whose income depends on public perception of their schools. In The Gambia, church-run schools are reported to have higher teacher attendance than government schools, although teachers have the same qualifications and earn the same salaries. These church schools may have more proactive managers driven by a sense of mission, and they also routinely withhold a portion of salary from teachers who are absent.

There are also examples of teacher absence responding to monitoring in government schools. In Uganda a 2004 study reported absence rates of 27 percent (Chaudhury et al. 2006). Following government efforts to improve monitoring, a study using a similar method in 2006 found absence rates of 19 percent (Habyarimana 2007). In The Gambia, teacher absenteeism fell following the introduction of the cluster monitors, who visited schools on a regular basis (typically twice a month) and monitored teacher attendance.

Figure 8.2   Zanzibar: Attendance poster

While these suggest that teacher attendance responds to monitoring, most of the countries in the study had weak mechanisms for monitoring and tracking teacher attendance. In most cases schools were expected to record teacher attendance, most frequently with a book in which teachers were expected to sign in daily (table 8.1). However, in most cases, there was no compilation, analysis, or reporting of this data, either in the school or at the central level. One exception was in Zanzibar, where schools were expected to compile records of attendance, and in some cases even displayed the teacher attendance data on public view (see figure 8.2). In The Gambia, regional offices have been developing a system to compile teacher attendance data from schools, but by 2008 this was still incomplete.

A poster in the head teacher's offices in a school in Zanzibar, showing average monthly attendance for students and teachers.

Table 8.1 Recording of Teacher Attendance

	Are all schools expected to record teacher attendance?	Is teacher attendance data tracked and analyzed centrally?
Eritrea	Yes	No
Gambia, The	Yes	No, but being developed.
Lesotho	Yes, but not all do.	No
Liberia	Yes	No
Malawi	Yes	No
Uganda	Yes	No
Zambia	Not always.	No
Zanzibar	Yes	No, but schools compile and some display average attendance.

External inspection visits did not always monitor teacher attendance data. In Zambia, standards officers are expected to complete an institutional monitoring form after each school visit, and a teacher monitoring form after each class supervised. Neither of these standard forms includes a place to comment on teacher attendance.

LEADERSHIP AND COMMUNITY RESPONSES

Head teachers are the most senior managers located at the school level, and should be expected to play a central role in monitoring teacher attendance and reminding teachers of their responsibilities. However, head teachers are absent from the school even more often than teachers, frequently for official business. For example, in Uganda, 27 percent of head teachers were absent, compared to 18 percent of regular teachers, with nearly half of the head teacher absences due to official duties (Habyarimana 2007). In Lesotho, one district inspector estimated that about half of the school head teachers were absent for more than seven days a month.

Even when head teachers are present, they are often reluctant to put pressure on teachers to attend their classes. Some head teachers do not see supervision of teachers as their role. Head teachers often live in close proximity to the other teachers, particularly in rural areas, and may find it difficult to take action against their colleagues. Akyeampong and Asante (2005) describe such a situation in Ghana, suggesting that head teachers may not have the necessary authority to enforce regulations due to the occupational culture of the schools.

The introduction of cluster monitors in The Gambia seems to have resulted in increased action by head teachers to enforce attendance rules. Since the cluster monitors began to visit schools, regional offices have reported an increase in cases of head teachers requesting salary stoppage or other actions in response to teacher absenteeism. It may be that head teachers felt an increased need to address teacher attendance in the context of greater external monitoring. It is also possible that the visible external monitoring made it easier for head teachers to address issues of absence with their colleagues.

Parents and the community should also be in a strong position to monitor teacher attendance. Parents generally have a strong commitment to education for their children, as demonstrated by the willingness of even relatively poor parents to pay for private schools. While parents are often not in a good position to judge the quality of education, they are normally aware of the frequency of teacher attendance, particularly in the smaller rural schools. Having the information and a system inviting feedback, as well as a strong personal interest in the outcome, should enable parents to monitor and encourage teacher attendance. There is some evidence that strong parent involvement is associated with higher teacher attendance. In Uganda, schools with strong parental involvement, as indicated by parental contributions and frequency of parent meetings, had lower teacher absence (Habyarimana 2007).

The impact of parent committees varies, however. In Malawi, it was reported that some committees were very active and kept teachers on their toes, but others did very little. It may be more difficult for parents in remote rural schools to monitor teachers because (i) they may be less educated than the teachers and so feel less able to intervene, and (ii) they may live in a small community and feel unable to cause tensions by addressing teacher absence.

In this context, official systems that collect information from parents, as well as training and support for parent groups, may help parents to play a role in addressing absenteeism. However, the case studies provided few examples of specific measures to encourage parents' participation, such as asking parent committees to endorse attendance records, or requiring inspectors to meet parents and specifically discuss attendance.

SANCTIONS AS A RESPONSE

Sanctions against teachers who are absent are possible through the mechanism of **formal disciplinary procedures,** but the long duration and unpredictable outcomes of these processes may be damaging to relationships and morale in a school and discourage their use. In Lesotho, most disciplinary cases are believed to go unreported, as principals are reluctant to get involved in a lengthy and complex process that ultimately may not result in any positive action. Disciplinary procedures are slow, and the majority of cases result in financial penalties or warnings. In some cases the regulations allow teachers to avoid disciplinary action using technicalities of terminology. For example, the regulations state that a teacher should not be "unreasonably absent." In one case, a teacher who was absent for a number of weeks while herding his cattle argued successfully that this was a "reasonable absence," as his family was dependent on the cattle.

In Uganda, disciplinary processes are also time-consuming, taking between six months and four years to reach a conclusion. Head teachers reported that taking disciplinary action could damage relationships in the school and cause conflicts with the staff or the community. Consequently, many head teachers avoid using disciplinary procedures, sometimes preferring to facilitate transfers for "difficult" teachers.

Two of the countries have **intermediate sanctions** that allow some action to be taken against an absent teacher without going through the formal disciplinary system. In Liberia, if a teacher is absent for more than three days in a month, the school issues a warning and the teacher's salary check is withheld until the teacher pays a fine of 150 LRD (Liberian dollars, U.S. $2.50) at the local revenue office. This relatively small amount is equivalent to about 4 percent of the monthly salary of a primary teacher, or less than one day's pay. Nevertheless, as all of the pay is withheld until the fine is paid, this penalty is a deterrent. One district education officer explained that this penalty is not always enforced, because the district management has some sympathy for the difficult conditions in which teachers work, but that nevertheless there is usually at least one fine charged each month.

In The Gambia, unqualified teachers and some qualified teachers are paid in cash at their school. Each teacher must be present in order to receive payment, as the recipient must sign for the pay, and head masters are not allowed to sign for absent teachers. This ensures that teachers must at least be present on payday in order to receive their pay. For other teachers, payment is automatic through electronic transfer. However, regional authorities have the power to request a salary deduction as a response to a period of unauthorized absence, or salary stoppage in cases where teachers have absconded. In region 2 there were approximately 2,400 teachers and 95 cases of either salary stoppage or deduction in 2006 (table 8.2). The largest category was stoppage of salary for those who failed to report to their posts at the start of the term. The regional office reported that teachers usually reappeared once the salary was stopped.

Table 8.2 The Gambia: Salary Deductions and Stoppages in Region 2, 2006

Salary sanctions	Number of incidents
Salary deduction (a response to a temporary absence)	20
Salary stoppage for existing teachers (teachers either left the school or had long-term absence without explanation)	34
Salary stoppage for failure to report (teachers who were transferred to a school failed to appear at the start of the term)	41

GHOST TEACHERS

Where teachers' management systems are weak, problems of ghost teachers can appear. Ghost teachers are those who appear on the payroll but in reality are not teaching. These may be deliberate fraud schemes, or result from teachers who died or left the school yet remain on the payroll. Ghost teachers draw resources from the system and result in local teacher shortages, where teacher allocation is based on the presumed existing number of teachers.

The scale of ghost teachers is difficult to determine, but the numbers can be quite substantial. In Uganda, ghost teachers were estimated to account for 20 percent of the payroll in 1993, but following a series of payroll cleaning exercises, this had fallen to an estimated 4 percent in 2006 (Winkler and Sondergaard 2007). In Liberia, there was a widespread problem of ghost teachers following the disruption of the war. Addressing this problem was made difficult by the poor records in the education sector and the weak linkage between the records in the Ministry of Finance (where payroll was managed) and the Ministry of Education. A payroll cleaning exercise conducted by the Ministry of Education in 2006 resulted in the recovery of 697 uncashed paychecks (from a teacher force of under 12,000) and the removal of a number of ghost teachers.

A number of countries have conducted activities to improve the accuracy of their teacher payrolls. In Zanzibar, the government arranged a one-day payroll cleaning, where all education personnel were expected to be at their posts on a specific date, to be checked by enumerators. This exercise was intended to remove both ghost teachers and teachers holding more than one post. In Liberia, payroll systems were restructured to improve accuracy (in addition to the 2006 payroll cleaning exercise). Each month a payroll list is sent to every principal, who certifies that it is accurate before payment is made. This monthly checking is intended to reduce the errors in payroll and provide a clear line of accountability in cases where fraud is detected.

DELIVERY OF PAY

The large number of teachers and their wide geographical distribution present logistical challenges in the delivery of payment. Payment systems differed both between countries and sometimes within countries. In some cases, different categories of teachers were paid in a different manner, and in some cases remote teachers were paid in a different manner. Payment systems differed in mode of payment, mode of delivery, and responsiveness to changes. Modes of payment included cash, check, and electronic transfer. Modes of delivery included direct bank transfer, delivery to school, and systems where teachers were expected to travel to collect their pay. As for responsiveness, in some cases payment could continue for months after the departure of a teacher, while other countries had mechanisms aimed at linking payment to teachers' presence. A summary of the methods of payment in the case-study countries is presented as table 8.3.

Payment delivery systems have significant implications for teacher performance. Late or unreliable delivery of pay results in hardship for teachers, lowers morale and loyalty, and encourages teachers to engage in secondary income-generating activities (Bennell and Akyeampong 2007). Systems where teachers must travel to collect their pay can increase absenteeism and reduce the real value of the payment, with disproportionately negative impacts in the most remote locations. The responsiveness of payment systems to changes, including the arrival and departure of teachers, has implications for teacher accountability.

BALANCING TRAVEL VERSUS LOCAL DELIVERY

Rural areas are more affected by the modes of payment and delivery than urban areas. In general, teachers in urban areas may receive pay in cash, check, or electronic transfer, because the travel costs remain at a minimum for all three. In contrast, requiring rural teachers to travel to collect their pay increased teacher absenteeism in many countries, with the most remote locations affected most negatively. This appeared to be the case regardless of whether payment was in cash, check, or electronic transfer. For example, in Zambia and Liberia, where teachers travel to district offices to collect their cash or checks, there were monthly closures of a few days or even a week in the most remote schools. In Lesotho and Uganda, where pay is by electronic transfer, teachers are required to travel to their banks to withdraw their pay.

Travel also often comes with additional costs in the most remote rural areas, further increasing the disincentives to accept a rural posting. In Liberia, some teachers report spending up to a quarter of their salary in travel costs to collect their pay. In other cases, teachers pay a percentage of their salaries to local intermediaries such as traders who cash checks or specialist intermediaries who take a number of checks and travel to the town to cash them.

Different strategies have been tried in several countries to mitigate the impact of travel. In Liberia some schools use a rota system, where one group of teachers goes to collect their check first, and the second group goes when they return, thereby allowing schools to remain operating during the pay period each month. Although a better alternative to closing the school, this still causes significant disruption to the schools. In Malawi and Zambia, some head teachers travel to collect the pay. This reduces teacher absenteeism, but can result in long absences from school for the head teacher. In Zambia, in one extreme case, a head teacher spends two weeks each month collecting the pay. This system also increases the risk of theft in transit, as the head teacher may end up traveling alone with the pay for the

Table 8.3 Payment Methods, Summary of Practices

Eritrea: Teachers are paid in cash. Each secondary school has a cashier, and teachers are paid on the premises. For middle and elementary schools, there is a cashier at the sub-zoba (a smaller unit of the zoba) level, and each teacher can go to the cashier and collect their salary. Because these cashiers are at the sub-zoba level, there is little disruption to the operation of the schools.

Gambia, The: Qualified teachers can be paid directly through bank transfer, and the majority choose this option. Even in the most remote region (region 6), there are banks in major towns that allow teachers to access their pay. Unqualified teachers are paid in cash at their schools. Each teacher must be present in order to receive payment, as the recipient must sign for the pay, and head masters are not allowed to sign for absent teachers.

The pay delivery system imposes a considerable burden on the regional offices. Each region sends a vehicle to Banjul to collect the paymaster, who travels to each school delivering the pay. In region 5, it is estimated that this process takes one full week each month. However, the direct payment system provides an immediate response to absent teachers, as each teacher must sign the salary receipt. For teachers paid through banks, it can take some months to stop payment if a teacher ceases to work.

Lesotho: Teachers are now paid through electronic transfer into bank accounts. In urban areas, this had reduced teacher absence to collect pay. In rural areas, there are often no banks available, thus forcing teachers to travel to withdraw their pay. In the most remote areas, this may take longer than a weekend and can result in some absenteeism.

Liberia: Teachers are paid by check. Normally there is one pay point in each county, and each teacher travels each month to collect his/her check. For the remote schools the loss of time for salary collection can be significant. In the extreme cases, it can take up to a week to travel to collect pay. Many rural schools close for two or three days for salary collection. There is a proposal to send checks directly to the schools. This would reduce the ability of teachers who are often absent from their school to collect pay, but might not reduce the disruption around pay collection time, as teachers might still need to travel considerable distances to cash the checks. A rota system was in place in some schools visited.

Malawi: Teachers can chose to be paid by check, in cash, or through electronic transfer, but more than 90 percent choose to be paid in cash. When teachers are paid in cash, the money is withdrawn from the bank by the district education manager (DEM), based on the verified list. Officially, the DEM should then distribute the cash to head teachers at a series of pay-points, usually the zonal TDCs. In practice, some DEMs require that all of the head teachers travel to the district office to collect the pay. Some districts have reported problems of either theft of the cash in transit or embezzlement by the head teachers.

Uganda: Teachers are mostly paid through electronic transfer. Since electronic transfer was introduced, pay usually arrives on time. Teachers are expected to travel to their bank to withdraw their pay, causing some absence in rural areas. Government policy is to encourage teachers to open an account in the nearest bank, but some teachers have accounts in banks in their home areas and tend to go home on a monthly basis to collect their pay.

The introduction of electronic transfer has reduced the immediate sanction of stoppage of pay for absent teachers. When teacher pay was distributed through schools, teachers who had not reported for duty could not receive their pay, and it was returned to the ministry. It is now reported to take some months to stop pay in the event of teachers failing to report for duty.

Zambia: Teacher payroll is managed at the district level. Each district office receives a block grant, and is responsible for the payment of salary and allowances to teachers. In urban areas, most teachers are paid through bank accounts. In rural areas, teachers are usually paid in cash, collected from the district office. Travel to collect pay causes some disruption. In the most remote schools, travel to the district office on foot can take a few days, and in one extreme case it was reported that it takes the head teacher six days to walk each way, resulting in absence from the school for two weeks each month. District offices have the ability to temporarily block the pay of teachers who have not been attending school, whether it was paid in cash or electronic transfer.

entire school. There is also the risk of embezzlement of the funds by the head teacher. In Uganda, the MoES is encouraging teachers to open bank accounts in the nearest bank, instead of traveling once a month to banks in their home areas. In Lesotho, the government is encouraging the expansion of banking services through the post office, to provide teachers with access to their electronic funds.

Local delivery of pay offers an alternative to requiring all teachers to travel. Delivery of pay to schools or to local pay-points (usually larger schools or teacher centers) is common in Eritrea, in rural Malawi, and for unqualified teachers in The Gambia. Delivery of pay to schools is a time-consuming and costly operation for the ministries (although it lowers costs for teachers). In some areas in rural Malawi, district education officers spend one week every month, with a vehicle and a police escort, delivering pay to schools. Inevitably, difficulties of weather, road conditions, vehicle maintenance, and fuel result in some disruptions of pay distribution. Despite the costs, this may be more efficient than the mass monthly absenteeism of individual teachers traveling to collect or cash their checks.

Delivery to local points may also provide an opportunity to verify teacher data and check on teacher attendance. In Malawi, for example, the district education managers are expected to verify payroll data while delivering pay. In The Gambia, unqualified teachers are paid in cash and must be present when the paymaster visits in order to collect their pay, thereby adding an extra accountability check.

ELECTRONIC TRANSFERS

Electronic transfer of funds to bank accounts is increasingly available in several countries, including The Gambia, Lesotho, Uganda, and Zambia. This allows efficient, simultaneous transfer of funds to teachers, while minimizing the risk of theft during delivery. Electronic transfer has also increased on-time payment in several countries. However, as mentioned above, electronic payment presents difficulties in rural areas where there is insufficient access to banks. As a result, in Malawi more than 90 percent of teachers choose to be paid in cash, although electronic payment is available.

Use of electronic payment systems before banking services are widely available may increase the difficulty of pay collection for teachers. In Lesotho, teachers in rural areas used to be able to cash checks in local shops. With the introduction of electronic payment they are forced to travel to the nearest town to withdraw cash, a journey that can take three days in the most remote schools.

Because of its highly centralized nature, electronic transfer may also reduce the responsiveness of the system to changes such as teacher absence. In The Gambia and Uganda, it can take months to stop the pay of an absent teacher paid through electronic transfer, but teachers paid in cash have to be physically present to collect their pay. Electronic payment can remove the ability of a head teacher to make immediate interventions to withhold pay. Thus, for example, a teacher who absconds or moves to another school without permission may continue to get paid. These difficulties highlight the need for efficient communications to ensure that the electronic payroll is responsive to school-level reality.

RESPONSIVENESS OF PAYMENT SYSTEMS

The responsiveness of payment systems to new teachers and teacher transfers, allowances, no-shows, and absences have implications on both teacher accountability and teacher morale. Although comparable research in Africa is unavailable, research from rural China indicates that consistent payment may be more important than salary amount (Sargent and Hannum 2005). Late or inconsistent pay continues to be an issue in several countries, regardless of whether teachers were paid at the school or at a central location.

There were serious delays in the payment of new teachers in some countries. Lesotho and Liberia both reported delays of up to six months in initial payments. These delays encourage, and in some cases force, teachers to take up other income-generating activities, possibly resulting in neglect of their duties. Once these practices are established, they are likely to continue even after salary payment commences.

Equally detrimental to teachers' morale and dedication are regular delays in additional allowances and mistakes in employment. At the time of the study, The Gambian hardship allowance had not been recently paid and the double-shift pay was delayed by a few months.

DISCIPLINARY SYSTEMS

Most countries have formal procedures for disciplining teachers. In most cases, these involve a series of warnings, followed by a formal process of review, after which disciplinary action can be brought. However, these disciplinary procedures are used in only a small minority of cases. It seems that school management is often reluctant to use the procedures for a number of reasons:

- The process takes a long time, and is burdensome for head teachers and district officials.
- During the process, the teacher may cause tension in the school. In most cases, the teacher may continue to work while the case proceeds. In Malawi the teacher is suspended either on half pay or no pay at all, but may remain in the same area, causing discontent. A suspended teacher may even work in a private school, and be as well off as they were before suspension.
- The outcome is uncertain, and in many cases disciplinary cases are rejected, returning the teacher to the school and potentially doing further damage to relationships in the school.

Table 8.4 Lesotho: Discipline Cases Brought to Adjudication, 2004 (TSC Data)

Reason	Number	%
Cases referred to adjudicator	33	
Cases returned for judgment	26	78.8
Not guilty	3	9.1
Fined	17	51.5
Dismissed	6	18.2

In Lesotho in 2004, only 18 percent of disciplinary cases resulted in dismissal of the teacher (table 8.4). Other cases resulted in the teacher being returned to the school.

In Malawi, the Teaching Service Commission (TSC) records over the previous three years show between 50 and 100 teacher dismissals each year (less than two per 1,000 teachers). The main reasons for dismissal were immorality (generally sexual relations with pupils) and absconding, accounting for 39 percent and 25 percent of all cases respectively. Given the widespread absenteeism and reports of sexual abuse of pupils, this seems to indicate that only a minority of cases of misbehavior actually reach the TSC.

Two examples of local and low-stakes interventions were reported—both dealing with absenteeism. In The Gambia, a head teacher can request temporary stoppage of salary of a teacher who has not reported for duty. Once the salary is stopped, many of the missing teachers return to their posts, and the salary is quickly reinstated. In Liberia, salary checks of absent teachers can be withheld at the local level, pending payment of a small fine. These simple interventions are more likely to be used, and to have immediate positive effects, than high-stakes and protracted disciplinary procedures.

DIRECTIONS FOR POLICY MAKERS

Some teacher absenteeism and misbehavior was reported in all countries, but monitoring and reporting of absenteeism or disciplinary occurrences were poor. Some promising practices for reducing absenteeism and misbehavior include:

- A requirement for schools to monitor, compile, and report teacher attendance. Monitoring teacher attendance may be one of the few low-cost, quick-win remedies available to education planners.
- Clear guidelines on absence. In The Gambia, head teachers are provided with guidelines that restrict the allowable number of absences for any reason each month. In effect, this means that teachers who are absent without cause lose opportunities to attend training or other potentially attractive events.
- External monitoring. In The Gambia, the introduction of cluster monitors who visit the schools regularly appeared to enable head teachers to be more diligent in both addressing absences and taking disciplinary actions, resulting in increased attendance.
- Development of "low-stakes" disciplinary interventions. Where teachers were absent without good cause, disciplinary systems were often seen as too slow,

cumbersome, and unpredictable to be of value. Given the understandable reluctance of head teachers to initiate disciplinary procedures that may lead to dismissal, the availability of more minor and immediate sanctions to deter misbehavior is more likely to be effective.

- Improved responsiveness of the pay system. It was frequently reported that teachers who had been absent reappeared when their pay was stopped. Systems that allow rapid pay stoppage in cases of continued absence seem likely to be highly effective in minimizing absence.

Surprisingly, parents were not often included in monitoring teacher attendance. Monitoring by parents, who are in situ and have a strong interest in the quality of the school, seems a promising backup to the formal systems. Another remedy involves ghost teachers: one simple action to address the question of ghost teachers might be to have each school display publicly the names of the teachers on the payroll. This public display of information would increase the number of people who would have to collude to maintain a ghost teacher.

At least a part of teacher absence was employer-initiated, either through failures in pay delivery systems or though provision of courses during school time. Both of these offer promising avenues to increase attendance. Access to courses in school time could be regulated, restricted to high-value courses, and rationed to ensure equitable access by teachers. Improvements in the delivery of pay to teachers, and the responsiveness of the pay system to absence or other changes, seem essential to improving attendance.

The need for more reliable pay distribution systems clearly goes beyond the issue of absenteeism. Unreliable pay causes morale problems and may force teachers to take up other income-generating activities, such as second jobs or informal fees. However, the best choice between electronic transfer, cash, or check, or between having teachers travel or having pay delivered locally, depends on local circumstances, including the availability of banking services. It is likely that the optimum pay system will call for different strategies in the most remote schools than those that are adequate in urban areas.

Pay systems also need to be responsive to changes, such as the arrival of new teachers, absences of teachers, and deaths or departures. Local control over pay creates more rapid response to these changes, but may allow some local collusion for improper practices. Electronic distribution of pay offers a reliable distribution, but few countries have developed corresponding processes that feed up information about local changes and ensure that the salary payment is adjusted rapidly in response to changed circumstances.

CHAPTER 9

The Teaching Career

For most professionals, opportunities for promotion or advancement provide an important motivation for performance and professional development; they also assist institutions in retaining skilled staff. Teaching is a profession that tends to have a relatively flat career structure, with comparatively few opportunities for promotion within the classroom. Internationally, many countries are struggling to develop career structures that will provide a flexible workforce, retain talent in the profession, and encourage teachers with a rewarding and attractive career path.

In the eight case-study countries, the dominant mode of employment for teachers was as public servants, with permanent, full-time employment on rigid salary scales. For teachers, this provided secure employment but little reward for improved professional performance. For the education systems, the promotion systems provided managers with little flexibility to retain talented teachers or address performance problems. The dominance of full-time permanent positions provided little flexibility to fill temporary vacancies (such as those that arise in the case of maternity leave or prolonged illness), provide for part-time staffing, or respond to a drop in overall teacher requirements. In the absence of flexible employment options, there was some use of unqualified teachers and retired teachers in temporary posts.

Promotional opportunities for teachers were relatively limited, and often involved leaving the classroom. In response to legitimate concerns about fairness and transparency, promotions were often based on qualifications and seniority. These provided an incentive for teachers to upgrade their qualifications. In some cases these opportunities risked encouraging teachers to neglect their duties in order to avail themselves of part-time study opportunities. Some countries provided generous opportunities for paid study leave, which provided opportunities for teachers to access further education. However, there were indications that these sometimes served to move some of the best educated teachers out of the profession.

Nevertheless, there were promising trends as well. Some of the countries were taking steps to revise career and promotion structures to enhance the linkage between performance and promotion. However, these countries were struggling with the challenge of linking career progression to performance while ensuring both fairness and transparency in the process.

THE DOMINANCE OF PERMANENT PUBLIC-SERVICE TEACHERS

In all cases, most public school teachers were employed as permanent public servants, with little or no provision for part-time or temporary employment (table 9.1). In contrast to the widespread use of contract teachers in Francophone Africa (see Fyfe 2007; Dembélé 2005; and Duthilleul 2005), there was no large-scale systematic use of contract teachers in public schools (i.e., qualified teachers employed by the government on temporary contracts). This gave teachers a measure of security in their positions, increasing the attractiveness of the profession. However, the full-time nature of the positions created some inflexibility in teacher provision. The inability to employ teachers on a part-time basis resulted in under-utilization in some cases, typically in small secondary schools, where there were optional subjects that required only a few classes per week.

In a few cases, teachers were employed through other employment arrangements, usually to address teacher shortages. In The Gambia and Malawi, retired teachers were allowed to remain employed on temporary contracts, as "month-to-month" employees, and received a fixed salary or gratuity payment along with their pensions. In a third case, Eritrea, there were large numbers of young people engaged in their period of compulsory national service.

UNQUALIFIED TEACHERS

In addition, in almost all cases there were significant numbers of unqualified teachers. The availability of unqualified teachers, usually employed on a temporary basis, provided some flexibility in the teaching labor force. Unqualified teachers were employed under a variety of tenure arrangements (table 9.2). In Eritrea, Liberia, Uganda, and Zanzibar, unqualified teachers were employed on a permanent basis

Table 9.1   Employment Status of Qualified Teachers in Public Schools

Country	Employment status of qualified teachers in public schools
Eritrea	Most were permanent civil servants
	Also large numbers doing a period of national service
Gambia, The	Permanent civil servants
	Some retired teachers return on temporary contracts
Lesotho	Permanent civil servants
Liberia	Permanent civil servants
Malawi	Permanent civil servants
	Some retired teachers return on temporary contracts
Uganda	Permanent civil servants
Zambia	Permanent civil servants
Zanzibar	Permanent civil servants

Table 9.2 Employment Status of Unqualified Primary Teachers*

Country	Unqualified teachers as a percentage of primary teachers	Unqualified teachers
Eritrea	15	Employed as permanent civil servants
Gambia, The	21	Employed on temporary contracts of 11 months. No pension rights, but can be re-employed each year.
Lesotho	39	Normally employed as temporary teachers. There is no limit to the duration of employment.
Liberia	56	Employed as permanent civil servants
Malawi	10	Unqualified teachers are no longer recruited. Existing unqualified teachers are permanent civil servants, but the government is trying to remove unqualified teachers from the system.
Uganda	32	Employed as civil servants, but on fixed pay scales (no annual increments)
Zambia	6.6	Information not available.
Zanzibar	13	Employed as civil servants

*Note that the percentage of unqualified teachers reported here, and the percentage of qualified teachers reported in chapter 1 do not always add to 100 percent, as some countries had other categories of teacher, including student teachers on placement, and teachers of unknown qualification status.

as civil service teachers. In The Gambia, unqualified teachers were usually employed on 11-month contracts, which carried no pension rights or terminal gratuity. In Lesotho, unqualified teachers were normally employed as temporary teachers. In both The Gambia and Lesotho, contracts for unqualified teachers could be renewed indefinitely.

The remuneration of unqualified teachers also varied widely, although it was usually substantially lower than the pay of their qualified colleagues (table 9.3). In The Gambia, unqualified teachers earned only 40 percent of the salary of a newly qualified teacher. Liberia appeared to be an exception, with qualified and unqualified teachers earning almost the same amount, but this was an unusual and temporary phenomenon, as all public servants were paid on compressed salary scales in an effort to address the financial crisis following the disruptive conflict.

Table 9.3 Comparison of Unqualified and Qualified Teacher Salaries

	Unqualified teacher salary (US$)	Qualified teacher starting salary (US$)	Unqualified teacher salary as a percentage of qualified teacher salary
The Gambia	284	707	40
Lesotho	1,796	2,366	76
Liberia	654	660	99
Uganda	857	1,412	61

TEACHER SALARY PROGRESSION

Public service teachers were normally employed on fixed salary scales, with salaries increasing in automatic annual steps until they reach a plateau (figure 9.1). The Gambia, Lesotho, Malawi, Uganda, Zambia, and Zanzibar used these incremental scales. In these scales, the salary typically rose by 11–23 percent over a period of seven to ten years (table 9.4). In The Gambia, there was an additional long service increment after 13 years, raising the pay to 36 percent above the starting salary. In Liberia and Eritrea, both in difficult budgetary conditions, there were compressed salary scales, with virtually no annual progression.

In the teacher salary scales, total growth for a teacher without a promotion was modest. Only two of the countries, Gambia and Lesotho, had total lifetime increases of over 15 percent. Research in the United States suggests that the relatively slow growth of teacher salaries makes teaching less attractive for mid-career teachers, and may encourage attrition of the most capable and most employable (Hoxby and Leigh 2004).

None of the countries offered performance-based incentive pay for teachers. There is some evidence from other regions that such additional bonuses can be used to encourage better performance among teachers (Vegas 2005; Lavy 2007). For example, research from Israel indicates that performance-based pay bonuses for teachers led to increases in student achievement, primarily through changes in teaching methods, additional after-school teaching, and increased responsiveness to students' needs (Lavy 2004).

Figure 9.1 Salary Progression of Qualified Primary Teacher (without Promotion), Expressed as a Percentage of the Starting Salary for a Qualified Primary Teacher

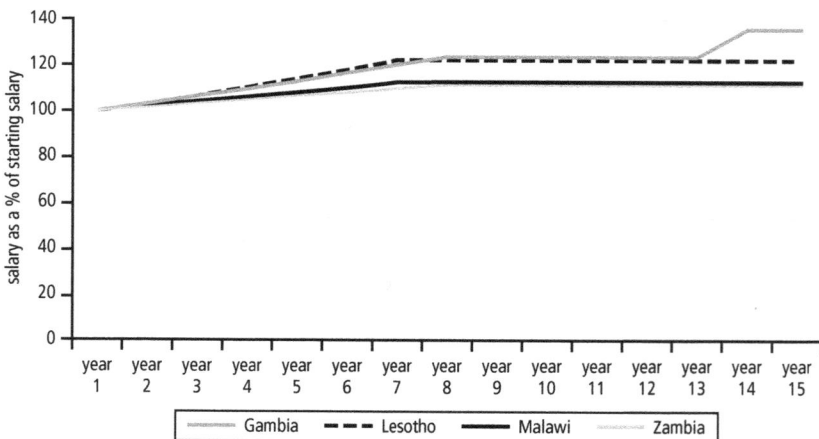

Table 9.4 Salary of a Qualified Primary Teacher as a Percentage of Starting Salary, Assuming Only Automatic Promotions

	Year 5	Year 10	Year 15
Gambia, The	113	123	136
Lesotho	114	122	122
Malawi	108	113	113
Zambia	106	111	111

However, it is acknowledged that teacher incentive systems tied to student performance require sophisticated mechanisms to avoid favoring privileged groups and further enhancing the incentives for teachers to locate in the schools in better areas. Research from Latin America shows that teachers respond to incentives, but not necessarily in predictable ways (Vegas 2005); while performance-based pay can improve teacher performance and morale, it can also lead to unintended and undesired consequences. A case in point is one school-based incentive program in Kenya that tied pay incentives to both teacher behavior and test scores (Glewwe, Ilias, and Kremer 2003). The result was a significant increase in student scores; but the gain was not attributed to improved teacher attendance, nor was there a change in homework assignments or pedagogy. Instead, there was evidence that teachers offered more test preparation sessions outside regular class hours, with no effect on dropout rates or long-term student results.

OPPORTUNITIES FOR PROMOTION

In the context of relatively limited and rigid salary progression, opportunities for promotion gain increasing importance in motivating and retaining staff. In all of the case-study countries, there were some opportunities for teachers to gain promotion to a higher salary scale. These opportunities for promotion may be classified into three types. First, in some cases there were opportunities for discretionary, merit-based promotions to posts such as senior teacher, which provided increased pay but retained the expertise in the classroom. Second, and more commonly, teachers had the opportunity for movement to different salary scales, based on improved academic qualifications. Finally, there were opportunities for promotion to nonteaching positions, usually in school management or inspection.

MERIT-BASED PROMOTION

Opportunities for merit-based promotion within the classroom are an important feature of teacher career structures. They can encourage teachers to strive for excellence and assist in retaining talented teachers. Where posts of senior teacher are

Table 9.5   Merit-based Promotions, Summary of Practices

Gambia, The	Positions were advertised nationally and teachers in any school could apply. Applicants were short-listed based on qualifications, and then selected for interviews. The selection process considered qualifications, length of service, posting (hardship posts given preference), and performance. This allowed teacher attendance and behavior to be taken into account. A performance appraisal system had been developed but not fully implemented, and was not currently in use.
Liberia	Teachers were selected for promotion at the discretion of the local district education officer and chief education officer. This process did not always allow for transparent decisions on promotions.
Malawi	The number of promotional posts available was determined annually, and selection was based on a written application and an interview. Interviews were conducted by a panel of three, including representatives of the Ministry of Education, the Teaching Service Commission, and an independent observer. Interviews used standard questions, covering areas of curriculum content, professional behavior, and record keeping. However, the panel did not have access to reports on behavior or performance from head teachers, primary education advisers, or inspectors.

linked with additional responsibilities, they can also provide a mechanism for in-school mentoring of less-experienced teachers. For promotional systems to have value in motivating teachers to improve their performance, the selection must be perceived to be genuinely based on merit. Systems that are perceived to be unfair may have a demotivating effect (VSO The Gambia 2007).

A few of the case-study countries had systems that allowed competitive promotion to positions of senior teacher. In Malawi and The Gambia, teachers were able to apply for promotional positions, with selection based at least partly on an interview (table 9.5). In Liberia there were positions of senior teacher, but these were filled at the local level and a competitive process was not always required.

Ensuring that career progression was perceived as fair was problematic. In Liberia, because promotions were at the discretion of the local district education officer and chief education officer, the basis for selection was not always transparent. This led to the perception that promotion did not fairly reflect classroom performance. In Malawi, although interviews were conducted by a diverse panel using standardized questions, the members of the interview panel did not have access to reports on behavior or performance from head teachers, primary education advisers, or inspectors when making their selections. This caused some concern that the interview system did not adequately recognize the best performers. As one Teaching Service Commission member noted, "A drunkard will get promoted if he talks well." In The Gambia, the formal selection criteria for promotion included qualifications, length of service, posting (hardship posts given preference) and performance. However, a study by VSO in The Gambia (2007) indicated that some teachers felt that promotions were conducted in an unfair manner.

In addition, there is a risk that access to promotion will be easier for teachers nearer to urban centers or regional administrative centers. Teachers in these areas may find it easier to get information about the availability of posts, and to make an application. They may also have more frequent contact with management and greater visibility. In The Gambia, despite the formal criteria, teachers reported fearing that they would be "forgotten or skipped over by the relevant authorities" while on rural postings (VSO The Gambia 2007).

SALARY DIFFERENTIATION BASED ON ACADEMIC QUALIFICATIONS

In most of the case-study countries, teacher salaries were linked to academic qualifications. Linking pay to qualifications may help to attract better-qualified candidates to teaching, and certainly provides an incentive for teachers to upgrade their qualifications. But the case studies suggest that overreliance on qualifications as a determinant of pay may have some negative effects, including encouraging teachers to prioritize upgrading their qualifications over attention to their duties. In addition, where teachers automatically receive large increases in pay with improved qualifications, it can be difficult for governments to manage and predict teacher payroll costs, particularly where private providers provide courses for large numbers of teachers.

In Lesotho, the starting salary for a teacher with a diploma qualification was 83 percent higher than the starting pay for a teacher with a certificate qualification (table 9.6). This created a strong incentive for teachers to participate in in-service upgrading courses. In the absence of effective measures to manage performance, this would appear to provide an incentive for teachers to neglect their teaching in order to pursue their studies.

Table 9.6   Lesotho: Primary Teacher Salary Scales, 2006

Annual salary in U.S. dollars	Min	Max
Teacher with certificate	2,120	3,774
Teacher with diploma	3,888	4,614

In Zambia, the automatic salary increase following improved qualifications had generated a market for in-service upgrading courses on a scale that had significant budgetary implications. Secondary teachers with a degree earned about 30 percent more than teachers with a diploma qualification (table 9.7). This difference in pay encouraged the growth of the Zambia Open University, offering an in-service upgrading course to teachers with a diploma qualification. This privately financed institution had plans to enroll as many as 6,000 students on its upgrading courses.

Table 9.7   Zambia: Secondary Teacher Salary Scales, 2007

Annual salary in U.S. dollars	Min	Max
Teacher with diploma	3,786	4,212
Teacher with degree	5,007	5,570

PROMOTION TO MANAGERIAL POSITIONS

Promotion to managerial positions, typically head teacher or deputy head, provides another major pathway for career advancement for teachers. Given the nature of education systems, the number of management positions in schools is relatively small. In The Gambia, for example, head teachers accounted for only 5 percent of teachers, while 83 percent of teachers are employed at the basic grade (table 9.8).

Table 9.8 The Gambia: Proportion of Lower Basic Teachers Who Are Promoted

Basic schools	Number of teachers	%
Qualified teachers	3,177	83.1
Senior masters	290	7.6
Deputy head masters	163	4.3
Head masters	191	5.0
Total	3,821	100

Source: The Gambia HR teacher database 2007.

The possibility of a promotion to head teacher should act as an incentive to encourage good performance among teachers. However, the selection systems used often limited this benefit, and in some cases provided adverse incentives. Where promotion to the post of head teacher was competitive, it was often linked to academic qualifications, rather than performance. In other cases, head teachers were selected by management without a competitive process. Such systems tend to favor those with high visibility to management, and create a perception that a remote location reduced the opportunities for promotion. Two of the countries provided enhanced promotional opportunities for teachers from remote schools. In The Gambia, preference was given to those who take hardship posts. In Zambia, head teachers were normally selected from within the school, providing greater opportunities for promotion in smaller schools.

PAID STUDY LEAVE

Most of the case-study countries provided opportunities for paid study leave for some teachers. The opportunity for study leave may help to build capacity in the system, and enhance the attractiveness of teaching as a career. For many young people without the financial means to pursue university courses, teaching may be an opportunity to finance a higher education degree (Hedges 2002; Towse et al. 2002; Akyeampong and Stephens 2002). However, in some of the cases the scale and terms of study leave made it a pathway to leave the profession, and increased attrition of some of the best-educated teachers.

In The Gambia, for example, a school leaver with three credits can enter The Gambia College and earn a certificate qualification. After two years of teaching, they can apply to return to the college and upgrade to a diploma. After a further few years of teaching, they can apply for further study leave, and upgrade to a degree. With a degree, the teacher has greatly enhanced opportunities for other employment. A bonding scheme is in place to require teachers to remain in service for the same number of years as they spent on study leave, but enforcement is weak.

Teachers in Uganda are entitled to apply for study leave if the ministry believes the system requires the skills taught in the course. In practice, it is reported that teachers in Uganda are able to get study leave for courses not directly related to their work. In Zambia, teachers who are confirmed in their posts are able to apply for paid study leave. Study leave is usually granted where the teacher has a confirmed offer of a place on a course, and the MoE believes that the system requires the skills taught in the course. This is widely used by teachers of basic education to do a diploma in secondary teaching, in order to migrate to secondary-level teaching. In Liberia, study leave is used to provide teachers with degree-level qualifications to fill the need in secondary schools, but despite a bonding scheme, few actually return to teach in government secondary schools.

The scale of study leave is quite significant. In Lesotho, more than 150 teachers per year are granted study leave, equivalent to approximately the entire output of new primary teachers from pre-service teacher training. In The Gambia, more than half of the students in the diploma course in 2007 were existing teachers using study leave to upgrade.

DIRECTIONS FOR POLICY MAKERS

The teacher career structure should provide opportunities for advancement in a manner that motivates teachers to work diligently and perform well throughout their careers, while building and retaining expertise within the teaching profession. This is a challenging task, as there are large numbers of teachers, working in a variety of contexts, and the system must balance the competing demands for flexibility and impartiality. Provision of incentives to influence teacher behavior is complex, and can create unintended consequences (Vegas 2005). Nevertheless, these cases suggest that in many countries the teacher career structure was not well designed to motivate performance or retain talent, and in some cases there were clear adverse incentives in the career structure. A series of promising areas for development of teacher career structures emerges from the cases.

SCOPE FOR MORE FLEXIBLE TEACHER CONTRACTS

Systems that allow for some employment of teachers on part-time contracts or on temporary contracts could be beneficial. The availability of part-time teachers could allow for more efficient teacher utilization, particularly in the context of optional subjects in small secondary schools. The ability to recruit temporary teachers could help to provide substitute teachers for cases of maternity leave or long-term illness.

A CAREER PATH FOR UNQUALIFIED TEACHERS

With the widespread use of unqualified teachers, and the reliance of many of the countries on them, there is a need to have a clear and planned route for unqualified teachers to become qualified. This is likely to be particularly important in rural areas, where recruitment of unqualified teachers may be one of the viable ways to find teachers for some schools. Developing a pathway to a qualification is likely to increase motivation and performance of unqualified teachers, but is likely to require careful design to ensure that opportunities to gain a qualification are available in all locations and that rigorous and appropriate standards are applied.

LINKING CAREER PROGRESSION WITH PERFORMANCE

In the context of the relatively compressed teacher pay scales, and the relatively limited promotional opportunities, opportunities for promotion are likely to be highly sought after. Stronger and more transparent mechanisms to take performance into consideration in promotion decisions offer an opportunity to encourage desired performance. Simple measures, such as tracking teacher attendance and using annual behavioral reports from head teachers, could be used to guide promotional decisions. The Gambia was clearly developing greater linkage between performance and career progression by ensuring that teacher performance was used as a criterion in making promotion decisions.

In other regions, particularly in Latin America, some countries have experimented with performance-based pay. Performance-based pay can offer some benefits, although it is clear that great care must be taken to avoid unintended undesirable consequences, such as exclusion of weaker students, overemphasis on teaching to the test, or providing an increased disincentive for teachers to take up posts in areas of educational disadvantage (Vegas 2005; Lavy 2007).

Mechanisms are needed to ensure the objectivity and transparency of performance monitoring systems. Promotions seen as unfair are likely to demotivate teachers. Where promotions are based on the judgment of district or regional officials, this may favor those with greater visibility at the district level. Promotions linked to head teacher reports may leave head teachers in a position to act as gatekeepers, making decisions based on personal relations, or even exacting a fee for a favorable report. Careful design of cross-checks and balances is needed to develop robust structures.

RISKS WITH QUALIFICATION-DRIVEN PROMOTION

Promotion systems based entirely on academic qualifications run the risk of creating adverse incentives. First, teachers may tend to neglect their duties in order to pursue study opportunities. Second, teachers in remote areas may have less access to opportunities to access upgrading courses, thus providing a further disincentive to accept a rural post. Third, qualification-based systems can create a demand for large-scale provision of upgrading courses, with consequences for the overall teacher wage bill. Unless carefully regulated, there is a risk that poor quality courses will be provided, resulting in increased recurrent pay costs but only marginal improvements in quality.

PART **IV**

Financing Teachers

CHAPTER 10

Teacher Finance

The policies related to teacher supply, deployment, training, and management are developed within the constraints of available resources. Teacher remuneration is the key cost driver in education, accounting for 94 percent of primary education expenditure in Eritrea and 99 percent in The Gambia (2006 data). Setting the appropriate level of teacher pay is particularly difficult, as policy makers need to balance the desire to provide attractive remuneration packages to recruit, retain, and motivate good teachers; the aim of universal access to education; and the constraints of public finances. This chapter examines the issues of teacher finance, in three main sections.

The first part considers teacher pay costs in the context of overall national finances and international benchmarks. Teacher finance is particularly challenging because of the very labor-intensive nature of teaching and the large numbers of teachers required. For example, in a country with 18 percent of the population in the primary school age range, and a pupil teacher ratio of 45:1, universal primary education requires four teachers for every thousand of population. The number of teachers required for universal basic education normally exceeds the number of workers required in any other public service, and in some countries teachers account for more than half of the entire public-sector workforce. As a result, teacher remuneration policy has a significant impact on overall public finances, and high teacher salaries can constrain the expansion of access to education.

The second part examines the remuneration of primary teachers. The case-study countries had already experienced the expansion to mass participation in primary education, and half had gross enrollment rates over 100 percent. The salaries paid to primary teachers varied a great deal, both in actual value and in relation to the GDP of the countries. These salaries are examined in comparison with salaries of other occupations, the poverty lines, and international norms.

The third part examines the question of the remuneration of secondary teachers. Most of the case-study countries had yet to provide secondary education for the majority, and had gross enrollment rates of under 40 percent. It is clear that the trend in the coming years will be the expansion of participation in secondary education, with consequent challenges for the financing of secondary teachers.

THE CHALLENGE OF EDUCATION FINANCE

Providing universal primary education tends to be more costly, relative to per capita GDP, in low-income counties than in high-income countries. Higher birth rates in low-income countries lead to a greater proportion of the population in the school-age range, and therefore a greater number of teachers. Teacher requirements are further increased by high repetition rates, combined with the enrollment of over-age pupils, often resulting in gross enrollment rates higher than 100 percent. In addition, the remuneration costs of teachers in low-income countries tend to be higher, relative to per capita GDP, than in high-income countries (box 10.1). Alongside this relatively higher cost, low-income countries frequently

BOX 10.1 TEACHER SALARIES RELATIVE TO GDP PER CAPITA

In general, "the average wage paid to teachers, as a multiple of country per capita income, tends to decline as countries develop economically. The average annual wage in the sample of very low income countries studied was in the range of 3 to 4 times per capita GDP (although with substantial variance, as we have noted). In middle-income countries in Latin America it is in the range of 2 to 2.5 times per capita GDP, and in the OECD it is currently about 1.8 times per capita GDP" (Bruns, Mingat, and Rakotomalala 2003, p. 69).

Two factors may contribute to this trend. First, with increasing development, the proportion of educated people in the country tends to increase, along with the proportion of jobs requiring levels of education comparable to teaching. Hence, while teacher pay continues to rise in real terms, it tends to fall relative to the national average. Second, as countries develop, there is an increasing requirement for universal primary education and reasonable class sizes. Teacher salaries that are high multiples of GDP tend to make universal education unaffordable and therefore tend to either reduce access to education or increase class sizes.

More recent data support this general trend. OECD data (OECD 2008, p. 444) indicate that in OECD countries, the salaries for teachers in primary and lower secondary education with 15 years of experience range from 0.82 times per capita GDP (in Hungary) to 0.88 times per capita GDP (in Sweden). Worldwide, average starting salaries for teachers are 1.42 times the per capita GDP (UIS 2007, p. 145). In the eight African countries in this study, the average starting salary for a primary teacher was 3.3 times GDP per capita.

Table 10.1   Model of Affordability of Universal Education, Simplified from EFA-FTI Indicative Framework

Number of teachers required		Finance available for teachers	
Proportion of the population in the primary school-age cohort	18%	Government spending as a % of GDP (i.e., amount of government revenue)	18%
Gross enrollment is 110% (including 10% repetition), but assuming 10% in private schools, enrollment in public schools is 100%	100	Allocation to education 20% of government spending, or 3.6% of GDP	20% (3.6% of GDP)
Pupil-teacher ratio	45:1	Allocation to primary education (assuming 6 years primary education)	58% (2.1% of GDP)
Number of teachers required per 1,000 of population 1,000 of population implies 180 school-age children, and at 45:1, 4 teachers	4 (0.4% of population)	Allocation to primary teachers remuneration of 67% of primary education budget	67% (1.4% of GDP)
		Affordable teacher salary if 0.4% of the population are teachers and 1.4% of GDP is available, average teacher salary can be 3.5 times GDP (1.4/0.4 = 3.5)	

raise a smaller proportion of the GDP in taxes, providing a smaller resource envelope from which to finance education.

The Education for All—Fast Track Initiative indicative framework (EFA-FTI 2004) provides a model of the resource allocations required to support the provision of universal primary education (table 10.1). This model suggests that a teacher salary of 3.5 times per capita GDP can be affordable if government revenues reach 18 percent of GDP, if 20 percent of revenue is allocated to education, and if a high priority is assigned to primary education.

This model is not intended to be normative, but to provide a series of comparisons against which the implications of resource allocation patterns can be clearly visible. Public expenditure on education in the eight case-study countries varied widely.

Three of the countries, Eritrea, Liberia, and The Gambia, devoted less than 10 percent of their budget to education, the first two because of their security situations, and The Gambia due to its recent economic crisis (figure 10.1). These low allocations to education suggest that in these three cases, it will be difficult to provide universal free primary education unless teacher salaries fall considerably below the level of 3.5 times per capita GDP. At the other end of the spectrum, public expenditure on education in Uganda and Lesotho was more than 30 percent of total government expenditure, leaving greater scope for increased teacher remuneration.

Figure 10.1 Percentage of Public Expenditure Allocated to Education Compared with FTI Benchmark

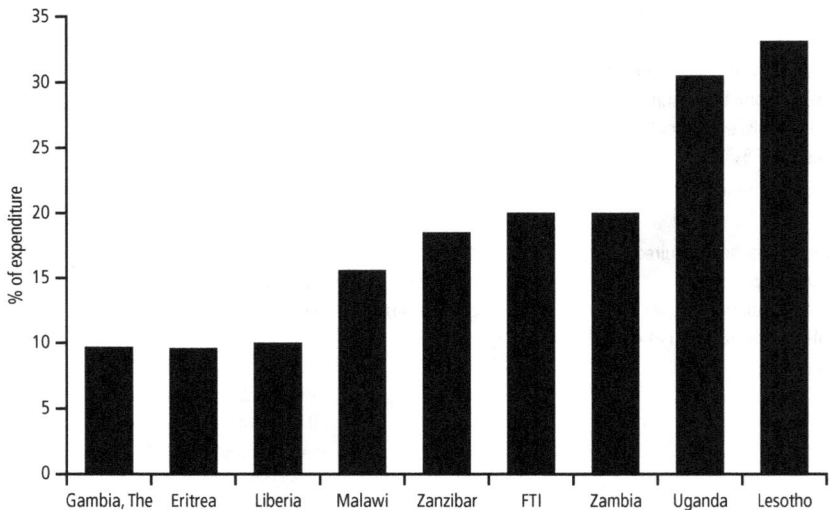

Table 10.2 Percentage of Education Expenditure Allocated to Basic Education

	Basic education as % of education expenditure	Years in basic education cycle	% allocated to primary education per year in cycle
FTI*	58.0%	7	Approximately 8%
Eritrea	19.7%	5	3.9%
Liberia	28.0%	6	4.7%
Lesotho	37.0%	7	5.3%
Uganda	66.3%	7	9.5%
Malawi	50.5%	8	6.3%
Gambia, The	70.9%	9	7.9%
Zambia	74.0%	9	8.2%

* FTI indicative figure is related to the length of the primary cycle: 42% if 5 years, 50% if 6 years, 58% if 7 years, and 64% if 8 years. Continuing this trend, 9 years would be just under 72%.

The share of the education budget devoted to basic education also varied widely across the countries, ranging from under 20 percent in Eritrea to more than 70 percent in The Gambia and Zambia (table 10.2). Comparisons are complicated by the variation in the duration of the primary education cycle, which ranged from five to nine years. Calculation of the proportion of education expenditure on a per-year basis reveals that only two of the countries, Uganda and Zambia, were allocating sufficient funds to primary education to match the FTI indicative model.

PRIMARY TEACHER REMUNERATION

The basic pay for a primary teacher in the eight case-study countries varied widely, both in absolute value and as a multiple of per capita GDP. For the purposes of comparison, the figures used are the starting salary for a qualified primary teacher with the most common qualification being provided at the time, which was in all cases either a certificate or diploma qualification.[1] In U.S. dollar terms, the annual salary ranged by a factor of six, from $490 in Zanzibar to $3,292 in Zambia (table 10.3).

When converted into purchasing power parity (PPP) dollars, an adjustment for the different costs in each country, the gap narrowed slightly, with salaries ranging from PPP$1,345 to PPP$6,082. The starting salary, expressed as a multiple of per capita GDP also varied, ranging from 1.5 times per capita GDP in Zanzibar to five times per capita GDP in Uganda (see table 10.4 and figure 10.2).

Two general trends might be expected in teacher pay. First, it might be expected that countries with higher GDP would pay higher teacher salaries (in dollar terms). This pattern was reflected to some extent. The teacher salaries were higher in the two countries with the highest GDP per capita (Zambia and Lesotho), but the pattern was not consistent. Uganda and The Gambia had very similar per capita GDP, but the teacher salary

Table 10.3 Starting Salary for a Qualified Primary Teacher (Excluding Allowances)

	Year	U.S. dollars	Dollars, purchasing power parity (PPP)
Eritrea	2005	728	2,330
Gambia, The	2007	707	2,672
Lesotho	2006	2,366	4,309
Liberia	2007/08	660	1,345
Malawi	2006	547	1,643
Uganda	2006/07	1,412	4,055
Zambia	2007	3,292	6,082
Zanzibar	2007	490	1,386

Table 10.4 Annual Starting Salaries for a Qualified Primary Teacher and Per Capita GDP

Country Ranked by per capita GDP	Year	Salary in local currency	U.S. dollar to local currency exchange rate	Salary in U.S. dollars	Per capita GDP in U.S. dollars	Salary as a multiple of per capita GDP
Liberia	2007	660	1	660	$160	4.1
Malawi	2006	76,548	140	547	$160	3.4
Eritrea	2005	10,920	15	728	$224	3.3
Uganda	2006	2,400,000	1,700	1,412	$280	5.0
Gambia, The	2007	19,080	27	707	$290	2.4
Zanzibar	2007	612,600	1,250	490	$330	1.5
Zambia	2007	13,167,780	4,000	3,292	$798	4.1
Lesotho	2006	16,536	6.98	2,366	$988	2.4

Figure 10.2   Starting Salary for a Qualified Primary Teacher and GDP Per Capita

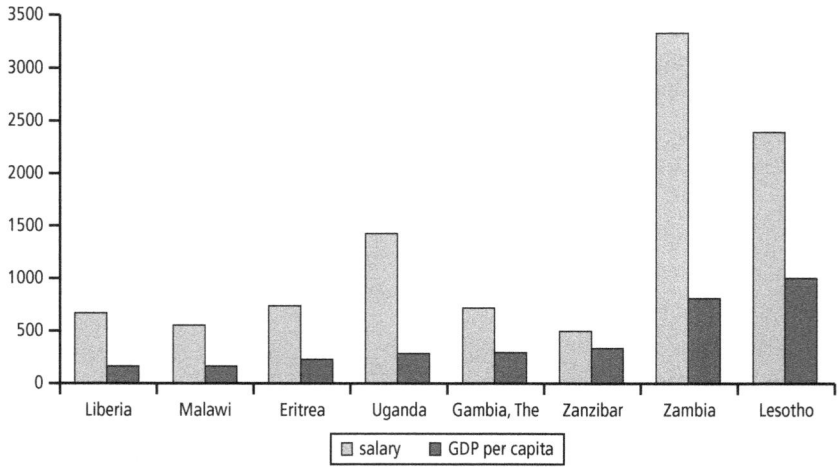

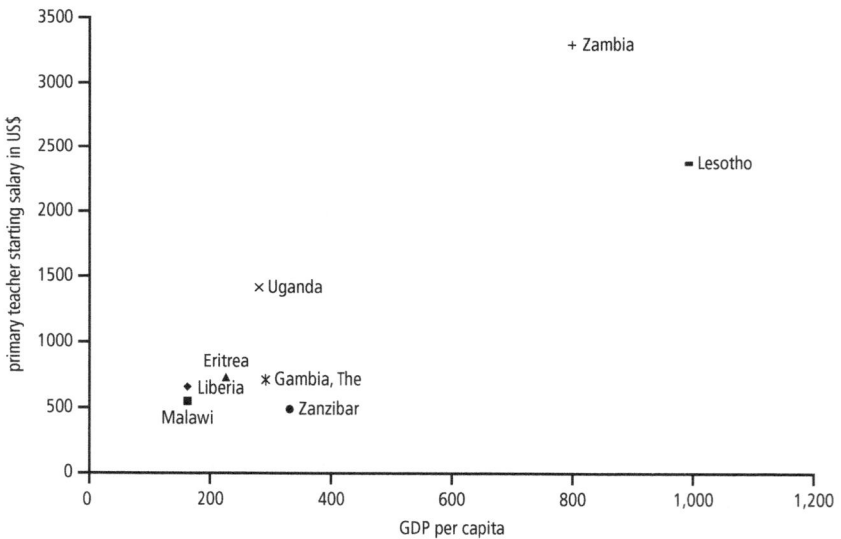

in Uganda was double that in The Gambia. Zanzibar had a per capita GDP double that of Liberia or Malawi, but paid lower teacher salaries.

Second, it might be expected that teacher salaries expressed as a multiple of per capita GDP would be lower in countries with a higher GPD per capita. This pattern was not evident at all: teacher salary as a multiple of GDP varied widely, and was not consistently lower in the higher income countries.

In addition to salary, most countries had a number of additional allowances paid to teachers. These including housing allowances, transportation allowances,

allowances for hardship locations, and double-shift allowances. These allowances can have a significant impact on total compensation. In The Gambia, additional allowances can add more than 50 percent to the basic salary (table 10.5). Two of the case-study countries, Uganda and Malawi, had simplified the salary scales by integrating housing allowances into the basic pay (table 10.6).

Table 10.5   The Gambia: The Impact of Allowances on Teacher Pay

Primary teacher, starting salary, U.S.$	Region 1	Region 6, hardship post
Basic pay	**59**	**59**
Regional allowance (0–17.5%)		10 (17.5%)
Hardship allowance (30–40%)		24 (40%)
Travel allowance	19	
Housing allowance		9
Total for a single-shift teacher	**77**	**102**
Double shift (50%)	29	29
Total for a double-shift teacher	**107**	**131**

Table 10.6   Summary of Allowances Paid to Teachers

Country	Additional allowances
Eritrea	Local communities often provide accommodation, food, domestic help, and, in some cases, cash
Gambia, The	Transport allowance 500 GMD ($18) per month (urban areas) Rent allowance 250 GMD ($9) per month (rural areas) Rural areas bonus between 7.5 percent and 17.5 percent of salary Hardship allowance between 30–40 percent of salary Double shift allowance, 50 percent of salary
Lesotho	Hardship location allowances of 275 LSL per month (about 31 percent of starting salary)
Liberia	Some housing provided by NGOs
Malawi	Housing allowance abolished in 2004 and incorporated into basic salary Housing is provided in a minority of schools The ministry operates a loan scheme that can provide loans at preferential rates to teachers. Commercial banks are reluctant to give loans to teachers, and teachers are required to seek approval from the Permanent Secretary of the MoEVT before entering into a commercial loan agreement.
Uganda	No housing allowance, as these were incorporated into basic pay in a salary reform Teacher housing is provided, but only in a minority of schools Hard-to-reach allowance of 15 percent of salary
Zambia	Subsistence allowance of 275–290,000 ZMK ($61–65) per month (approximately 22 percent of salary) depending on grade and marital status Double-shift allowance of 20 percent Responsibility allowance of 20 percent to certificate holders teaching upper basic classes or diploma holders teaching high school Recruitment and retention allowance of 20 percent of basic salary to degree holders
Zanzibar	Teaching allowance of 25 percent of salary Housing allowance of 6–10 percent of salary Transport allowance, either 5,000 TZS per month (about 5 percent of salary) or actual travel cost (whichever is greater)

In some countries there had been substantial increases in teacher remuneration in the preceding years, with teacher salaries outpacing inflation. In Malawi nominal teacher salaries tripled between 2000 and 2004, exceeding the rate of inflation and resulting in a real increase of 40 percent. In Uganda, in addition to the annual increase, primary teachers were awarded an exceptional increase of 33 percent of salary in 2006. In the period from 2000 to 2006, the Uganda consumer price index grew by 33 percent, while in the same period primary teacher salaries grew by 119 percent and secondary teachers' salaries grew 127 percent. In Zambia, salaries rose by 25 percent in 2004, followed by increases of 13 percent and 16 percent in the following years. In Liberia, the emergency basic salary for public servants was increased from about $20 per month in 2005–06 to approximately $30 per month in 2006–07, and to $55 for 2007–08.

Not all countries experienced an increase. In Lesotho, for example, analysis by Urwick, Mapuru, and Nkhoboti (2005) indicates that annual salary increases resulted in small increases in real income for the period 1990 to 1999, but lagged behind inflation a 1999, such that by 2005, the salary had approximately 95 percent of the value of the 1990 salary. In Eritrea salaries have also stagnated since 1997 and are believed to be falling in real terms.

HOW PRIMARY TEACHER SALARIES COMPARE

Teacher salaries relative to the poverty line: Teachers in the case-study countries were not highly paid, with starting salaries for a qualified teacher ranging from $41 to $274 per month. While in all cases the teacher salaries exceeded the absolute poverty line of one dollar in purchasing power parity per day (UNESCO-EFA 2008), a teacher trying to support a family on the starting salary could easily fall under $2 per day PPP. In Zanzibar and Liberia, the teacher salary was approximately $4 per day PPP, and a family with two teachers, both employed on government salaries, with two children, would find themselves living on $2 per person per day. A family with only one wage earner would be even worse off.

Even in the countries where salary appears relatively high, teachers reported considerable hardship. In Zambia, the starting salary was the equivalent of $17 per day PPP, but the teachers unions, using data from the central statistics office, showed that the starting salary of a primary teacher was roughly two-thirds of the cost of the basic needs basket for a family of six (table 10.7).

As well as causing hardship, low salaries provide strong pressures for teachers to seek other sources of income, whether through other income-generating activities or through imposing charges on their students. Conversely in Liberia, it was reported that recent increases in salary had been reflected in increased teacher attendance, and that private schools found it more difficult to attract teachers.

Primary teacher salaries relative to the private labor market: Comparisons with the salaries in the private sector are made difficult because of the limited size of the private sector, and the difficulty in obtaining reliable data. In Eritrea there were anecdotal reports that a shortage of manual labor has resulted in higher pay for casual laborers than for teachers. Some more objective data were available in Lesotho, where there are minimum wage levels for different grades of private sector workers (table 10.8). The salary of a qualified primary teacher was similar to the minimum wage for a construction machine operator, while the salary of an unqualified teacher was lower than the minimum wage for a trained security guard.

Table 10.7 Starting Salary for a Qualified Primary Teacher

	US$ per month	$PPP per month	$PPP per day
Eritrea	61	194	6
Gambia, The	59	223	7
Lesotho	197	359	12
Liberia	55	112	4
Malawi	46	137	5
Uganda	118	338	11
Zambia	274	507	17
Zanzibar	41	116	4

Table 10.8 Lesotho: National Minimum Wage, 2005, and Selected Teacher Salaries (in LSL)

	Monthly	Annual
Domestic worker	230	2,760
Textile general worker	643	7,716
General minimum wage	673	8,076
Trained security guard	934	11,208
Construction machine operator	1,400	16,800
Unqualified teacher with STD 7	880	10,560
Unqualified teacher with COSC	1,046	12,552
Qualified teacher with certificate	1,378	16,536

Primary teacher salaries relative to teachers in private schools: In most countries the better-resourced private schools were able to pay more than public service salaries, and to attract the best teachers and those in subjects where there is a shortage. Higher wages for private school were reported in Eritrea, The Gambia, and Malawi, although there were a limited number of opportunities available. Although pay in private schools is sometimes lower than in public schools in Liberia, the package of additional benefits (food allowance, travel allowance, and paid training) continues to make the private school remuneration more attractive. Attrition to NGOs was also an issue in Liberia, where it was reported that many of the graduates who qualify in education and the teachers who upgrade to degree qualifications have moved to the NGO sector.

Teacher remuneration relative to other public sector jobs: In both Malawi and Lesotho, the health service offered higher pay than the education sector, partly because of the need to retain expertise. As a result, students with science subjects at the National University of Lesotho were reported to prefer health courses to education courses. Urwick, Mapuru, and Nkhoboti (2005) argued that teacher remuneration was a less attractive package than those for other public servants with similar qualifications because they offered less access to loans, and because

Table 10.9   Lesotho: Comparison of Salaries in Health and Education (in LSL)

Health sector	Starting salary	Education sector	Starting salary
Nurse assistant	22,000	Certificate teacher	16,536
Staff nurse	34,000	Diploma primary teacher	30,324
Degree holders (public administrators, public accountants, etc.)	48,000	Graduate	53,364
Specialist (doctor)	137,256	School principal, high school	88,236

the initial pay is more often delayed because of the teachers' geographical locations (table 10.9).

In The Gambia, the Public Expenditure Review (PER) suggests that teachers' initial salaries may be comparable to (or exceed) those of other public service jobs, but may rise more slowly and attract fewer additional benefits:

> Whilst Graduate teachers are entitled to grade 8 in The Gambia Government pay scale, their counterparts with equivalent qualifications are appointed at grade 7 of the same pay scale i.e., economist. However where the cadet economist may be promoted smoothly to through the higher level of the administrative ladder i.e., to Senior and Principal or Director positions where they will enjoy in addition to their basic salaries other benefits i.e., car allowance, overseas training/trips (per diems), etc., the highest level the graduate teacher may reach is to be a principal and that even may take a much longer time before that really materializes. Graduate teachers may never enjoy travels and per diems that other professionals in other sectors may enjoy incrementally throughout their careers. (Emanic Consulting 2006.)

Labor market signals: Two general patterns emerged in a number of the case-study countries. First, teacher salaries seem insufficient to retain the most educated teachers, particularly those with qualifications in mathematics and science. In Liberia, most of the graduates from degree-level education courses do not return to public schools. In Malawi, Uganda, Zambia, and Lesotho there is reported to be higher attrition of the graduate teachers and those with mathematics and science. Second, teacher salaries seem sufficient to attract the less well educated, who typically have fewer alternative opportunities. In Lesotho, unqualified teachers work as volunteers (without pay) in government schools, sometimes for years, in the hope of getting a position as an unqualified teacher and later upgrading. In Malawi, when 2,900 positions in the teacher training colleges were advertised in 2005, there were 28,000 applicants. In Uganda, too, the positions in teacher colleges are oversubscribed.

Taken together, these suggest that the teaching profession is more attractive to those with lower academic qualifications, who may have fewer alternative opportunities. As a result, teaching tends to recruit those who did not get places in other courses. In Eritrea the entry qualification for primary teaching has been falling, as the best-qualified school leavers enter other professions. In The Gambia, the teacher training college has been unable to fill its courses in recent years because the best-qualified applicants chose places in other institutions. In Malawi, unemployment is high and the teaching courses are oversubscribed, but almost 15 percent of the students left the teacher training course in the first year, mainly to join the police and the Ministry of Agriculture.

FINANCING THE EXPANSION OF SECONDARY EDUCATION

For the case-study countries, the greatest fiscal challenges in education were likely to be at the secondary level. All of the case-study countries had made substantial progress in the expansion of primary education, and four had gross enrollment rates of more than 100 percent (table 10.10). Enrollment rates at the secondary level were much more modest, ranging from 32 percent to 58 percent for the lower secondary and as low as 6 percent in the upper secondary. The demand for access to secondary education is likely to rise, as the number of primary school leavers in Sub-Saharan Africa is set to double in the next ten years (Lewin 2008).

In some countries the cost of teacher provision at the secondary level was much higher than at the primary level, and seemed likely to constrain expansion (table 10.11). For the purposes of comparison, the cost of teacher provision was calculated per student, based on the average pupil-teacher ratio and the starting salary of a qualified teacher. In Malawi, for example, a primary teacher earning $547 per year and teaching a class of 76 pupils resulted in an average cost per student per year of $7 (table 10.12). At the upper secondary level in Malawi, a starting salary of $2,529 and an average class size of 21 resulted in a cost per student of $120.

Table 10.10 Gross Enrollment Rates in the Eight Countries Studied

	Year of data	Primary	Lower secondary/ middle school	Upper secondary
Eritrea	2004–05	72	48	24
Gambia, The	2005–06	85	59	35
Lesotho	2006	127	40[a]	—
Liberia	2006	87[b]	32[b]	11[b]
Malawi	2006	122	20[a]	—
Uganda	2006	112	22[a]	—
Zambia	2007	134	58	25
Zanzibar	2006	94	40	6

a. Secondary
b. Estimate

Table 10.11   Teacher Cost Per Student in Lower and Upper Secondary, Expressed as a Percentage of the Cost at Primary Level

CPS	Cost per student at the lower secondary as a % of cost per student at the primary level	Cost per student at the upper secondary as a % of cost per student at the primary level
Eritrea	111	169
Gambia, The	169	192
Lesotho	317	559
Liberia	432	480
Malawi	1,094	1,673
Uganda	417	536
Zambia	115	411
Zanzibar	250	260

Table 10.12   Teacher Cost Per Student (CPS) at Primary and Secondary Levels (in US$)

	Primary			Lower secondary			Upper secondary		
	Salary	PTR	CPS	Salary	PTR	CPS	Salary	PTR	CPS
Eritrea	728	53	14	960	63	15	1,160	50	23
Gambia, The	707	41	17	787	27	29	1,061	32	33
Lesotho	2,366	45	53	4,339	26	167	7,636	26	294
Liberia	660	32	21	677	8	89	693	7	99
Malawi	547	76	7	1,653	21	79	2,529	21	120
Uganda	1,412	48	29	2,328	19	123	2,997	19	158
Zambia	3,292	54	61	3,786	54	70	5,007	20	250
Zanzibar	989	35	14	1,017	29	35	1,054	29	36

Notes: Salary used is the starting salary for a teacher qualified to teach at each level. In Eritrea, middle school is used in place of lower secondary.

Not all countries had such extreme differentials between the primary and secondary levels. Table 10.11 shows the cost per student at the secondary levels as a percentage of the cost per student at the primary level. In Eritrea and The Gambia, the teacher cost per student at the upper secondary level was less than double that at the primary level. At the other extreme, in Uganda, Lesotho, and Malawi, the teacher cost per student at the upper secondary level was more than five times the cost at the primary level (figure 10.3).

The additional cost of teacher provision was driven by both higher salaries and lower utilization. The starting salary for qualified lower secondary teachers was on average 45 percent higher than the starting salary for primary teachers, and the starting salary for upper secondary teachers was on average more than double the salary for primary teachers. But an even greater additional cost resulted from the lower teacher utilization at the secondary level. Across the eight countries, the

Figure 10.3   Teacher Cost Per Student at Primary and Secondary Level

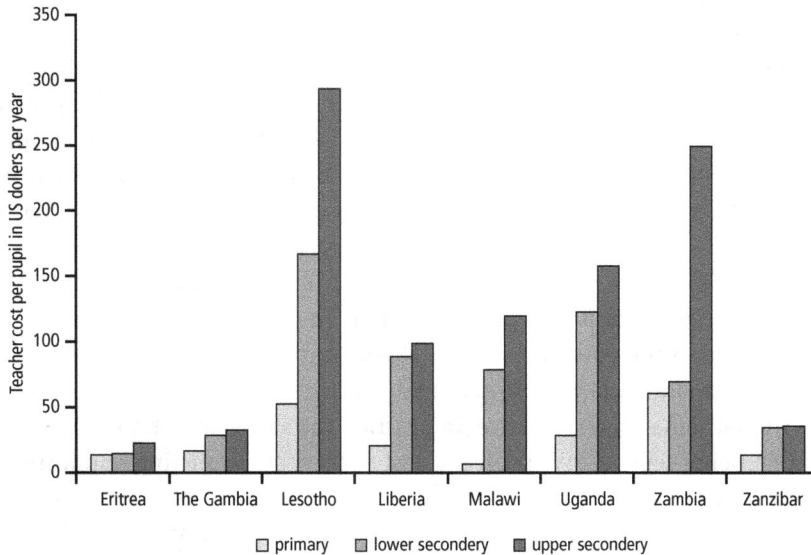

□ primary   ▨ lower secondery   ▪ upper secondery

average pupil-teacher ratio in primary schools was 48, while the average student-teacher ratio at the lower secondary level was 31, and 26 at the upper secondary.

These higher staffing levels in secondary schools result from three factors. First, secondary teachers normally teach for only a portion of the school day, resulting in a requirement for more than one teacher per class. In Lesotho, for example, secondary teachers are expected to teach 30 periods per week, while each class is taught at least 40 periods per week. Second, because teachers specialize in particular subjects, not all teachers are time-tabled for the full number of periods, particularly in subjects where there is an oversupply, or the less popular optional subjects. Third, high provision of optional subjects in secondary schools often results in small class sizes in some of the least popular options. These practices result in low student-teacher ratios, even when the class sizes are very high in the core subjects.

IMPLICATIONS FOR POLICY MAKERS

Most of these countries assign a high priority to education, and it accounts for a significant proportion of national expenditure. In all cases, teacher remuneration levels present difficult choices, and the need to balance the desire to increase teacher compensation with considerations of affordability and expansion of access. The case-study countries had starting salaries for primary teachers ranging from 1.5 times to five times per capita GDP. It seems that teacher salaries were largely determined politically. Teacher salary, as a multiple of per capita GDP, was not strongly related to either the proportion of national spending devoted to education or the per capita GDP.

Teachers were not well paid in absolute terms. Some teachers with a family earn salaries that put them not far above the poverty line. However, they are paid much more than average in their countries. Data from the Malawi Growth and Development Strategy (Government of Malawi 2006) suggest that even a primary teacher on the starting salary is in the top 5 percent of Malawians in terms of income.

These salaries were sufficient to attract teachers, and in many cases there were teachers in private schools and private teachers in government schools willing to work for less than the government pay. However, the salaries did not seem sufficient to attract and retain well-qualified teachers, in particular teachers with degrees in mathematics and science. In practice, the salary level had often resulted in teaching being seen as the "profession of last resort," attracting applicants who did not manage to get a place in their preferred course or career. This pattern has implications for policy makers, who must either mobilize more funds to raise teacher remuneration, or readjust their expectations to deal with attracting less-qualified teachers.

In parallel with the difficulty of providing sustainable and adequate finance for teachers, these countries all face the challenges of expected expansion at the secondary level. In each of these countries, enrollment was growing most rapidly in secondary education, in response to successful expansion in primary enrollment and increased primary completion. Current cost structures, both teacher salaries and utilization, make provision of teachers for the secondary level significantly more expensive than the provision of primary teachers. With these cost structures, reaching near-universal secondary education will require very substantial increases in finance for teachers, which is unlikely to be realistic. These suggest strongly that increases in teacher utilization will be required in order to attain mass secondary education.

NOTE

1. Note that starting salary is used here as the basis for comparison. The overall affordability of the teacher workforce is determined by the overall teacher wage bill, which will also be influenced by the rate of increase of salary and the proportion of teachers who are more experienced.

PART **V**

Conclusion

CHAPTER **11**

Challenges, Trends, and Promising Practices

Finding the right policies to address teacher issues is central to the challenges of both expansion and quality of education. The countries examined all faced challenges in providing a sufficient supply of teachers, in ensuring equitable deployment of those teachers, in developing sufficient quality in teachers, and in financing teachers. While it is tempting to view these dimensions of teacher policy in isolation, in reality they are interlinked, and developments in one dimension can have detrimental impact in another. Development of a balanced set of teacher policies requires a holistic view, balancing the desirable with the achievable in seeking to find the most appropriate solutions across the sector. This chapter begins with an overview of the primary challenges and trends in each of the main areas of teacher policy, and traces the interconnections between the competing priorities. Finally, it highlights some promising practices that may offer appropriate solutions for countries facing similar challenges.

SUPPLY

All of the case-study countries had a mismatch between the national requirement for new teachers and the current output of newly qualified teachers. In two of the countries, Lesotho and The Gambia, the annual output of primary teachers was less than the annual loss of primary teachers. In six of the eight cases, the annual output of trained primary teachers was less than 6 percent of the teacher workforce, which might be considered a normal attrition rate (table 11.1).

In most cases, the mismatch between supply and requirements had resulted in teacher shortages, but in three cases, Zanzibar, Uganda, and Zambia, there were excess primary teachers. Even in those three cases, there were shortages of qualified secondary teachers, and shortages in specific locations and specializations.

None of the countries had robust mechanisms to regulate teacher training to match requirements. Planning departments tended to project total teacher requirements, but rarely projected attrition of existing teachers and the required

Table 11.1 Output of Primary Teachers as a Percentage of the Primary Teacher Numbers

	Number of primary teachers	Newly trained teachers each year	Replacement rate: teacher output as a percentage of teaching force	Notes on teacher output data
Eritrea	7,154	644	9.0	2006–07
Gambia, The	4,477	256	5.7	2006
Lesotho	10,172	220	2.2	2006
Liberia	26,188	650	2.5	New course
Malawi	43,197	2,449	5.7	Intake 2006
Uganda	150,135	6,729	4.5	Intake 2006
Zambia	50,615	2,990	5.9	Output 2005
Zanzibar	5,781	1,907	33.0	Output 2007

supply of new teachers. In some cases, government ability to control teacher supply was being reduced, with increasing autonomy of the teacher training institutions. In Zanzibar, for example, the Nkrumah Teacher Training College had been transferred to the semi-autonomous State University of Zanzibar, resulting in a reduced output of primary mathematics teachers.

Adequate planning for teacher supply will require monitoring of teacher attrition. Primary teacher attrition rates varied widely, from 2 percent in Eritrea to 9 percent in Zambia. It seems reasonable to assume that, in a stable system, attrition rates of at least 6 percent are likely, as this assumes that the average teacher will teach for 16 years. The major cause of teacher attrition in most cases was voluntary resignation, presumably to take another job. As a result, attrition is likely to fluctuate with changes in labor market opportunities. Attrition was not even across all types of teacher. In all of the cases where data were available, the attrition rate of secondary teachers was higher than that of primary teachers. In Lesotho, for example, the attrition rate was 3 percent for primary teachers, and 10 percent for secondary teachers. In addition, there were reports that attrition was higher for better-educated teachers, and teachers of mathematics and science.

Also high levels of wastage (trained teachers not taking up teaching jobs) were reported in some cases, particularly for teachers with higher level qualifications, and those qualified in mathematics and science. In Zambia, for example, the number of teachers with degrees was approximately twice the annual output of graduates with degrees in education, suggesting that most of these graduates do not stay long in teaching if they started at all.

For all of these countries, secondary education enrollment was expanding more rapidly than primary enrollment. Planning for secondary teacher supply is more complex, as typically secondary teachers are specialized in two teaching subjects. While most countries expect a degree-level qualification at least for upper secondary teachers, few have an adequate supply of graduate teachers, and in practice most secondary teachers have diploma-level qualifications.

SHORTAGES

In most of the case-study countries, the inadequate supply of qualified teachers had resulted in large-scale use of unqualified primary teachers. In four of the cases, Liberia, Lesotho, The Gambia, and Uganda, more than one-third of primary teachers were unqualified. In six of the cases, less than half of the secondary teachers were qualified. Where the output of trained teachers is inadequate, there is no realistic alternative to widespread use of untrained teachers in the medium term. The level of education of unqualified teachers varied widely, but was in most cases lower than the level of education of the qualified teachers. The shortage of qualified secondary teachers was resulting in some upward migration of primary teachers to secondary schools, often replaced by unqualified teachers in the primary schools. In two cases, Eritrea and The Gambia, the domestic secondary teacher supply was so limited that the country was dependent on expatriate teachers for some subjects.

SECONDARY EDUCATION AS A CONSTRAINT

In some of the countries, the supply of new teachers was constrained by the limited number of school leavers with the required entry qualifications. In Lesotho and The Gambia, the teacher training colleges were unable to fill the available spaces due to a shortage of qualified applicants. In Eritrea, the entry requirements had been lowered to address the same problem. This arose because the total number of places in university courses and teacher training colleges was almost equal to the total number of school leavers with the required entry qualifications. Typically the best qualified went to the university courses, leaving a limited pool of potential entrants to teacher training.

MATHEMATICS AND SCIENCE

In almost all cases there was a more acute shortage of teachers of mathematics and the sciences. In Zanzibar, where primary teachers specialize, there was a shortage of primary mathematics teachers. In other countries, where primary teachers are not expected to specialize, there were reports of poor mathematical skills in primary teachers. In Lesotho, the inspectors were reporting cases of primary teachers skipping mathematics altogether, as they did not feel able to teach it. Unofficial teacher specialization was widely reported, particularly in the upper grades of primary school, and seemed to arise from concern that not all teachers were able to teach specific subjects. In The Gambia, Liberia, Lesotho, Malawi, and Uganda, schools frequently had informal arrangements to allow primary teachers to specialize.

The shortage of mathematics and science teachers was even more acute at the secondary level. Almost all countries reported shortages of teachers in these subjects, resulting in reliance on unqualified teachers and in a few cases expatriate teachers to teach these key subjects. In teacher training, the proportion of students being prepared for mathematics and science teaching was often inadequate. In Lesotho for example, only 8 percent of the student teachers in the Lesotho College of Education were studying mathematics as one of their two teaching subjects. In Zanzibar, Lesotho, The Gambia, Malawi, and Uganda, the colleges were unable to increase the number of student teachers in these subjects because of the limited number of applicants with the prerequisite mathematics and science qualifications.

This weakness in mathematics and science suggests a vicious cycle, where a shortage of school leavers with sufficient mathematics and science achievement results in a limited supply of teachers in these subjects, and thus results in poor teaching of these subjects in both primary and secondary schools.

DISTRIBUTION

Most countries had both teacher shortages in some schools and unemployed teachers seeking work in other areas. This coincidence of oversupply and shortage suggests that equitable teacher provision is unlikely to be achieved merely by continuation of current policies.

In almost all cases, there were very significant inequities in the pupil-teacher ratio, to the detriment of most remote rural areas. The intradistrict deployment inequities were often greater than interdistrict inequities, and often masked by the use of district averages in reported statistics. In one district in Zambia, the pupil-teacher ratio ranged from 22:1 to 210:1. These local differences in teacher distribution underline the importance of micro-geography in teacher deployment. Factors such as proximity to a road and availability of housing may make one school much more attractive than another.

Six additional general patterns emerged:

1. The best-qualified teachers were distributed more unequally than teachers in general. The remote areas had fewer qualified primary teachers and fewer graduate secondary teachers.
2. There was a gender dimension to the geographical distribution, with fewer female teachers in rural areas.
3. Those teachers in particularly short supply, such as teachers of mathematics and science, were underrepresented in remote rural areas.

4. Teachers with HIV were, in some cases, allowed to move to more urban areas, either formally or informally.
5. In centralized deployment systems, the mother tongue was rarely considered in the selection of teachers for particular areas. Consequently, teachers were posted to areas where they did not speak the local language.
6. Even in areas where the public authorities seemed unable to deploy teachers, there were people with some level of education willing to work as teachers, often as volunteers with low or minimal pay.

The deployment problem seems likely to become more acute as secondary education expands to more rural areas, as this will require the deployment of better-educated teachers, with greater employment options, to remote areas.

DEPLOYMENT SYSTEMS

Most of the countries used planned deployment systems, with deployment decisions made at the national or subnational level. In these systems a central agency is responsible for deployment of individual teachers to specific schools. In general, these systems are weakened by poor ability to enforce deployment, as teachers either fail to take up the unpopular posts or quickly arrange to leave these posts. The cumulative effect of these is a greater number of unfilled posts in remote areas, higher turnover, and less experienced staff.

Lesotho used a very different approach, with recruitment of teachers by school management committees. In this system, teaching posts are allocated to schools by the ministry, and the responsibility for selection of the teacher lies with the school. The effect of this local recruitment is that it creates a form of labor market for teachers. Teachers self-select the schools to which they will apply, and thus have some choice in location. Rural schools often recruit people already living in the area. This has resulted in a relatively even distribution of teachers and has avoided the high attrition often associated with remote schools; however, there remains an uneven distribution of the qualified teachers.

There is increasing use of more location-specific recruitment, in an attempt to address the deployment imbalance. In Zambia, teachers are given a choice of the district in which they will work. In Uganda, the government is piloting a system of advertising secondary teaching posts for specific schools. In some countries the practice of recruitment of unqualified teachers and subsequent provision of in-service training creates a form of local recruitment, and is an important mechanism for provision of teachers in the remote areas.

Most countries provided some financial incentives to encourage teachers to locate in remote areas, but these were often undermined by poor targeting. Despite these incentives, difficulty in attracting teachers to remote areas persisted.

The one exception to this pattern was in The Gambia, where a new incentive, of 30–40 percent of basic pay, seemed to be effective in attracting teachers to the most difficult schools. Within two years of the introduction of the incentive, 42 percent of the teachers in rural schools who were not receiving the incentive had requested a transfer to a hardship school. This suggests that financial incentives, if both substantial and well targeted, can attract at least some teachers.

There was some provision of teacher housing, but this covered only a minority of teachers, and the provision of housing was not always well targeted at the most difficult locations. While provision of housing may be particularly important in encouraging female teachers to accept a post at a school, housing alone may not be sufficient to overcome the disadvantages of a post in a remote location.

There were indications that there are some qualified teachers willing to work in rural areas. In Malawi, the NGO Development Aid from People to People (DAPP) operated a teacher training college specifically targeting young people willing to work in rural areas, which reported success in getting its graduates to return to rural schools. In part, this success depended on selection of interested candidates into the program.

For government teacher training colleges, selection was normally based on academic qualifications, rather than interest in teaching or willingness to teach in a specific location. This method of selection seems biased toward selection of students from areas where the level of education is already higher (such as urban areas), further exacerbating the distribution problem.

UTILIZATION

Teacher workloads varied widely. Primary teachers were expected (officially) to teach between 12.5 and 25 hours per week. In most countries, secondary teachers were expected to teach fewer hours per week than primary teachers. Official teaching hours were as low as 16 hours in lower secondary and 12 hours in upper secondary.

In most countries primary teachers were expected to teach all subjects to one class. In the one exception, Zanzibar, teachers were expected to specialize in one of three clusters of subjects: mathematics and the sciences, humanities, or Arabic and Islamic studies. In Zanzibar, the expected teaching hours were two-thirds of the school contact time, requiring three teachers for every two classes. In other countries, despite the policy of nonspecialist teachers, there was evidence of informal specialization in a number of countries, particularly in the older grades.

Multigrade teaching was widely used in most countries, particularly in rural areas. In some cases this was a result of a deliberate teacher deployment policy; in other cases it was a necessity resulting from failure to deploy teachers to remote schools. Despite the widespread use of multigrade teaching, initial teacher training did not always prepare teachers to teach in multigrade situations.

In practice, utilization was often lower than the official expectation. Utilization was reduced by oversupply of teachers in some schools through failures of the deployment system, and by other practices that reduced teachers' workloads (e.g., The Gambia's religious teachers). In secondary schools, utilization was further reduced as a consequence of the range of optional subjects, and teacher subject specialization. As a result, the teachers of the least popular subjects tended to have both a lighter workload and smaller classes.

TRAINING

Pre-service training of primary teachers ranged from 12 weeks to three years, normally following completion of upper secondary school (table 11.2). These courses varied in structure, with some including full years of work based in schools. For secondary teachers, most countries had dual systems, with diploma courses of two or three years, and degree courses of three or four years. There was a general trend toward inflation of the duration and certification of teacher training. In a few cases, the certificate courses had been replaced by diploma courses, and at the secondary level there were attempts to have all teachers trained to the degree level.

Table 11.2 Duration of Pre-service Teacher Training

Country	Primary teachers	Secondary teachers: diploma	Secondary teachers: degree
Eritrea	One-year certificate	Two-year diploma for middle school teachers	Four-year degree for secondary school teachers
Gambia, The	Three-year certificate, one in college, two in school	Higher Teachers Certificate (HTC), three-year diploma courses, of two years in college followed by one year of teaching in a school	Four-year degree course, normally an upgrade for an existing teacher, two years for an HTC holder, three years for a primary teacher
Lesotho	Three-year diploma, three years in college, since reorganized as a sandwich model (three years, but middle year in school)	Diploma in Education (secondary), a three-year diploma.	National university, four-year degree program
Liberia	12-week emergency course, but one-year certificate being introduced	Two-year certificate, no longer in operation	University, four-year degree courses
Malawi	Two-year certificate, one in college, one in school Formerly MIITEP (in-school)	Three-year diploma	Four-year degree
Uganda	Two-year certificate	Two-year diploma	Three-year degree
Zambia	Two-year certificate, one in college, one in school	Two-year diploma, increased to three years in 2005	Four-year degree
Zanzibar	Two-year certificate	Two-year diploma	Three-year degree

Entry to teacher training was normally based on academic performance. The academic performance required to enter teacher training was quite low, and in some cases declining. In Eritrea, for example, the entry requirements had fallen as expansion of alternative higher education opportunities reduced the availability of qualified school leavers.

In general, teacher training courses were seen as less desirable than other higher education options, and as a result, teacher training tended to absorb students who failed to get places in their first choice courses. In Eritrea, it was reported that the best students admitted to the Eritrea Institute of Technology tended not to select education courses, so the education courses tended to be filled with students with relatively low scores, for whom education was not their first preference. The education courses had particular difficulty in attracting sufficient students with qualifications in mathematics and science. The poor educational standard of entrants presented quality problems, reflected in high failure rates in some cases, and a more general concern about the level of education of students in others.

The teacher training curriculum was not always well aligned with the needs of the classroom. Three major observations emerge. First, training in pedagogical methods was often theoretical, making it less likely to have an impact on classroom practices. Second, the teaching of the content knowledge (that is, the subjects that a teacher would be expected to teach) was often not closely aligned to the school curriculum. Third, these difficulties were often compounded by students' poor proficiency in the language of instruction. Teacher trainers were not always well equipped to deliver training in a practical and relevant manner. Some, particularly in primary teacher training, had little experience teaching at the appropriate level.

In almost all cases, pre-service teacher training included a period of teaching practice. The duration of the period of practice teaching varied widely, from six weeks in Uganda to two years in The Gambia. At the secondary level, teaching practice was generally more limited, ranging up to a term in duration. In Malawi, Eritrea, and Uganda, there was no formal teaching placement for students in degree-level courses. The teaching practice was not always well integrated into the rest of the teacher preparation program, and student teachers frequently received limited pedagogical support while in school. Support systems in schools were relatively weak, and the training provided to those expected to mentor student teachers was very limited.

IN-SERVICE TRAINING

Most of the case-study countries had some system for providing emergency initial training and qualifications to unqualified teachers. These in-service training courses varied in duration and structure, but typically involved between two and four years of part-time study supported by some combination of residential training at a teacher training college, short courses provided at local centers, and printed self-study materials. The scale of the in-service teacher training courses makes it unlikely that all of the unqualified teachers can be trained quickly. In Lesotho, for example, each cohort of teachers taken into the in-service course was approximately 10 percent of the total of unqualified teachers.

The in-service teacher training courses usually, but not always, required lower entry qualifications than the campus-based courses. This made the in-service courses an attractive pathway into the teaching career for many who would not have reached the higher standards required in the pre-service course. Despite these lower entry requirements, there were some teachers who were unable to gain entry into the in-service courses because of their poor academic qualifications, and these mostly remained in service as unqualified teachers.

There is no clear evidence of relative quality of different programs, but generally anecdotal evidence suggested that the quality of the teachers with in-service and pre-service training was comparable, with some reports that the teachers from the in-service courses were more skilled in the classroom, and that those from the pre-service courses had better understanding of academic content, particularly of mathematics and English.

In addition to in-service training of unqualified teachers, there was in some cases significant in-service upgrading of qualified teachers encouraged by the substantial pay increases associated with improved qualifications. In a few cases, such as Zambia, large-scale teacher upgrading by distance education presented financial challenges for the government.

CONTINUING PROFESSIONAL DEVELOPMENT

Systems for continuing professional development of qualified teachers were relatively undeveloped. The most common modality was centrally planned delivery of short courses on specific topics, such as the introduction of a new curriculum. A few countries had developed alternative systems. In Zambia, for example, there were zonal resource centers, serving small numbers of schools and staffed by a teacher on a volunteer basis. Teachers within the zone were expected to identify their own training needs, usually drawing on locally available expertise.

MANAGEMENT

HEAD TEACHERS

The important roles of head teachers in managing schools, leading teachers, and establishing the culture of the school were all well recognized, but in practice, many head teachers devoted much of their time to relations with administrative authorities outside the school. Training for head teachers was sporadic and did not reach the majority of head teachers. In general, systems for managing head teachers were weak.

SUPERVISION AND INSPECTION

All countries had some kind of system of external supervision of schools, but in most cases the frequency of visits was too low to effectively monitor quality. In six of the eight countries, the average frequency of school visits was less than once per year, and the frequency of supervision of each teacher much lower. Two countries had achieved higher supervision frequencies. In The Gambia, schools were visited every week or two, and in Eritrea, each teacher was visited twice per year. Both had achieved this level of supervision through the use of decentralized inspection systems, with inspectors monitoring and living near a small number of schools. In The Gambia, cluster monitors were responsible for approximately ten schools each and traveled by motorbike. In Eritrea, cluster supervisors were responsible for 80 teachers each and traveled by bicycle or on foot.

Mechanisms to provide policy-relevant feedback from school supervision were also weak. None of the eight cases had a routine summary of inspection findings provided to policy makers. There were some good practices in Uganda, where the Education Standards Agency (ESA) had prepared reports on specific issues, and in Eritrea, where the cluster supervisors met twice a year to share findings and provide feedback to regional officials.

The extent to which inspectors and supervisors actually supervised and supported teaching varied. In some countries inspection visits concentrated on data collection and administrative issues. There was little evidence that inspectors and supervisors were adequately prepared to provide meaningful pedagogical support, and much of their feedback seemed to focus on more mechanical issues, such as lesson planning and the use of teaching materials.

TEACHER ABSENTEEISM

Some teacher absenteeism was reported in all countries, but in reality little was known about the extent and causes of absenteeism. In Uganda, where a study of absenteeism had been conducted, an average of 20 percent absence was recorded. In almost all cases, records of teacher attendance were kept at the school level, usually in the form of an attendance book that teachers signed on a daily basis. However, few of the countries had a system for compiling and analyzing this information. One of the exceptions was in Zanzibar, where some schools recorded monthly teacher attendance figures and displayed them in the head teacher's office. In The Gambia, a system for monitoring attendance was under development, with the aim of tracking teacher attendance at each school.

There was some indication that teacher absence was responsive to monitoring. In The Gambia, with the introduction of cluster monitors and regular external visits to schools, it was reported that teacher absence had fallen, and the incidence of head teachers requesting stoppage of pay for teachers who had absconded had increased.

Where teachers were absent without good cause, disciplinary systems were often seen as too slow, cumbersome, and unpredictable to be of value. In a few cases there were smaller, more immediate sanctions that could be used to deter casual absence. In Liberia, schools were able to withhold the salary of a teacher who had been absent until a small fine was paid at the local revenue office. In The Gambia, unqualified teachers were paid in cash, and head teachers had the discretion to withhold payment in cases of absence. Under a new system in The Gambia, no teacher was to be absent for more than two days per month for any reason, and an unauthorized absence might result in their inability to attend a training course.

Much of the teacher absence was attributable to employer behavior, most frequently salary collection, absence to address administrative issues, or absence to attend training. Improvements in administrative systems, and policies governing the amount of training that can be provided within school time, could significantly reduce teacher absence.

Delivery of pay was problematic in many countries, and had particularly adverse consequences for the most remote schools. In Liberia and Zambia, some remote schools routinely closed for up to a week each month as teachers traveled to collect their pay. Increasingly, countries (including The Gambia, Lesotho, Uganda, and Zambia) were migrating to the use of electronic transfer into teacher bank accounts. This improves the efficiency of delivery, but without adequate controls may reduce the responsiveness of the system to teacher absence or movement to other schools.

CIVIL SOCIETY

In most countries, there was some form of parent involvement in schools, either through parent teacher associations or school management committees. Where these were active, fund-raising for the school was one of their major activities, and played an important part in operating costs and school maintenance. In some cases parents also provided additional payment (in in-kind support) to government teachers or payment for extra nongovernment teachers. There were some, but few, reports of parents monitoring teacher attendance or taking action in cases where absenteeism was unacceptably high. In Uganda, one district officer reported pressure from parents to address teacher absence. In Malawi, some school management committees were very active, in part because of training through NGOs.

Teachers unions were also present in all countries, and in most cases the majority of public teachers were represented by a union. These teachers unions played a variety of roles. All had some role in advocacy for better pay and conditions for teachers, but many were also involved in professional development activities, providing training opportunities for teachers or helping to define codes of professional conduct.

THE TEACHER CAREER STRUCTURE

The dominance of civil-service career structures, characterized by permanent appointments, fixed pay progression, and promotion based heavily on academic qualifications provided little reward for excellence in the classroom. In all of the case-study countries, qualified teachers are employed as permanent civil servants. There was no significant use of contract teachers. Teachers were employed on short-term contracts only when unqualified, or in some cases where retired teachers were offered opportunities to work after retirement age.

There were large numbers of unqualified teachers, sometimes employed as permanent civil servants, and sometimes employed on temporary contracts. Most countries had some form of in-service upgrading course to allow unqualified teachers to become qualified. Entering as an unqualified teacher was a major pathway into the profession in most countries. In Lesotho, for example, the recruitment of unqualified teachers exceeded the recruitment of qualified teachers in some years.

For civil service teachers, pay was on rigid scales, with fixed annual increments and a plateau level after a number of years. A typical teacher could expect salary increments of 10–25 percent of starting salary over the first ten years of service. None of the countries had any system for performance-based increases.

There were limited opportunities for promotion within the classroom. Some countries had a grade of senior teacher, but few had robust merit-based systems for selection to these posts. In Malawi, performance reports from head teachers and inspectors were specifically excluded from the selection process. In Liberia and Eritrea, the selection was at the discretion of district officials and not transparent. In most cases, there were greater opportunities for additional pay through improved qualifications, which normally provided an automatic move to a higher pay scale. These automatic increases, when not balanced by other opportunities, provide an incentive to seek additional qualifications even if this involves neglect of duty.

The relatively easy entry to the teaching profession, and the opportunities for progression in academic qualifications, make teaching a route to other professions for some. Teaching is a profession that is open to many who, because of limited academic performance or financial means, cannot access other forms of postsecondary education. The increasing availability of upgrading courses to help teachers move from certificate to diploma qualifications, and to degree qualifications, makes teaching an attractive "stepping stone" to other professions. These options are particularly attractive in The Gambia, where large numbers of teachers avail themselves of full-time paid study leave after a few years of service. The impact of study leave is significant. In The Gambia in 2007, the number of teachers leaving to start full-time study leave was almost half of the number of newly qualified teachers recruited. In Uganda, study leave was the main reason for the departure of secondary teachers. In Lesotho, 150 teachers were granted study leave in 2005, more than half of the total number of new teachers trained.

TEACHER FINANCE

Teacher remuneration varied widely. Teachers were generally not well paid, yet were paid a multiple of per capita GDP, and much more than the average wage. Starting pay for a qualified primary teacher ranged from $490 per year in Zanzibar to $3,292 in Zambia. These are clearly not high salaries. In Zanzibar and Liberia, a teacher with one dependent would have a per-person income of less than $2 per day (purchasing power parity). Even in Zambia, the teachers unions, using data from the central statistics, showed that the starting salary of a primary teacher was only two-thirds of the cost of the basic basket of needs for a family of six. On the other hand, these salaries represented multiples of GDP per capita, ranging from 1.5 times in Zanzibar to five times in Uganda.

In general, when compared to other government jobs with the same entry qualifications, teaching was seen as having a slower pay progression, fewer opportunities for promotion, and sometimes fewer opportunities for additional benefits. Headquarters-based civil service jobs were generally perceived to offer easier working conditions and greater opportunities for promotion. Even jobs like the police force were seen as more attractive than teaching in some cases, partly because of the greater opportunities for earning additional income.

As a result, teaching tended to absorb those who attained the minimum qualifications but failed to get any of the jobs seen as more desirable. This pattern of recruiting contributed to the difficulty of attracting teachers for subjects where there was a labor market shortage, such as mathematics and science. Relatively low salary levels also appeared to contribute to attrition. In all cases where data were available, resignation was the primary cause of teacher attrition, most of which was presumably to move to alternative employment. There are some indications that teacher retention responds to salary movements. In Uganda, teacher attrition fell by 24 percent between 2005 and 2006, following a 33 percent pay increase.

In all eight cases, the expansion of lower secondary education was outpacing that of primary education, resulting in greater requirements for additional teachers at the secondary level. Current cost structures, driven by higher salaries and lower utilization, resulted in teacher costs that, on a per-student basis, were a multiple of the costs at the primary level. In Malawi, the cost of lower secondary teachers on a per-student basis was 11 times that of teachers at the primary level. In Liberia and Uganda, the cost at the secondary level was over four times the cost at the primary level. These high cost ratios are neither essential nor ubiquitous. In The Gambia, the cost at the lower secondary level was 1.7 times that at the primary level, while in Zanzibar the ratio was 1.25 times. For those countries with structures that result in high teacher costs at the secondary level, this is likely to prove a significant barrier to the expansion of secondary enrollment.

GENDER PERSPECTIVE

It is clearly desirable to have female teachers in schools, as they potentially increase the participation and retention of girls, both by making schools safer places for girls and by acting as role models of educated professional women. The proportion of female teachers varied, but was in all cases lower in secondary schools than in primary schools. However, there were strong geographical patterns in the presence of female teachers. There were more female teachers in urban areas, and a higher proportion of male teachers in the most remote areas. This was true even in Lesotho, where the majority of teachers were female.

Female teachers were reported to be less mobile than male teachers. In cultures where it is unusual for a man to move to follow his wife, married female teachers must either stay near their husbands or split up their families, with the consequent financial costs, risk of damage to their relationships, and possibly even increased risk of HIV infection. For unmarried teachers, there were reports of strong family and social pressure to avoid postings in remote areas, which were perceived as unsafe for single women.

The second pathway into teaching, through recruitment of unqualified teachers who later attain qualifications, may assist in recruiting more female teachers in the remote schools. As this mechanism normally recruits local teachers already resident in the area, it may be easier to recruit female teachers. In Lesotho for example, unqualified teachers in mountain areas are often women already living in the area.

HIV

HIV infection rates for teachers varied widely across the eight case-study countries, ranging from 1.2 percent to 27 percent (table 11.3). While this is primarily a human tragedy, it also had implications for the education system. The first and most obvious impact was the loss of teachers through illness and death. While specific causes of illness are not normally recorded, in the countries with high

Table 11.3   Summary of HIV Infection Rates and Teacher Attrition Rates

	Available data on HIV infection	Teacher attrition rate (all causes)
Eritrea	No data on HIV status of teachers	2%
	National infection rate estimated at 2–3%	
Gambia, The	No data on HIV status of teachers	3%
	National infection rate estimated at 1.2%	
Lesotho	Estimates of HIV prevalence among teachers range from 22% to 27%.	3% primary, up to 10% secondary
Liberia	HIV prevalence rate for the 15–49 age group was estimated at 2–5%	Estimated at 1.6%
Malawi	Infection rate among teachers is estimated at 15–25%	5% primary, 10% secondary
Uganda	Infection rate estimated at 6.4% in the general population	5% primary, 6% secondary
Zambia	Adult infection rate estimated at 16%	9%, though may be overestimated by interschool movement
	Voluntary testing of teachers in 2005–06, 18% of those who were tested were found to be HIV positive	
Zanzibar	No data on teacher infections rates	5% primary, 6–7% secondary

HIV infection rates, teacher death and illness accounted for attrition of between 0.66 percent and 3 percent of the teacher workforce annually.

In addition, HIV/AIDS was often a factor in teacher deployment, contributing to the inequity of deployment as more teachers were transferred to schools near medical facilities. For example, in Uganda teachers who are HIV positive are facilitated to either transfer to a location near medical facilities or to avoid redeployment in order to maintain linkage with their current medical providers. In Zambia, teachers who are ill are allowed to transfer to a school near a health clinic if there is not one near their post. Many of the sick teachers are referred to the University Teaching Hospital in Lusaka. In Malawi, the policy determines that a "reasonable accommodation" be made for staff with HIV. In practice, this means lighter duties and transfer to a location near a hospital. Teachers with HIV and AIDS are frequently transferred to urban schools to be nearer to medical facilities. As a result, the percentage of sick teachers in urban areas is higher, contributing to higher absenteeism in these areas.

The burden of the pandemic also fell on the education system in a variety of other ways (table 11.4). In Malawi, high attrition of district education officials was reported, reducing the management capacity in the system. Further, the deaths of teachers and their relatives cause significant disruption, as colleagues leave their posts to assist ill friends and attend funerals. In some cases there are other, less obvious impacts. In Malawi, when teachers die, the ministry pays for the purchase of the coffin and transportation of the body to the home area. When relatives living with a teacher die, the ministry also pays for the transportation costs. Given the

Table 11.4   The Contribution of Teachers' Death and Illness to Attrition

	Cause of attrition	Number	Total teachers	Percentage of teacher workforce	Death and illness as percentage of teacher workforce
Lesotho, primary and secondary, 2004	Died	131	13,500	0.97	
	Prolonged illness	4	13,500	0.03	1.00
Malawi, primary, 2006	Died	618	43,197	1.43	
	Prolonged illness	149	43,197	0.34	1.78
Malawi, secondary, 2006	Died	157	10,386	1.51	
	Prolonged illness	173	10,386	1.67	3.18
Uganda, primary, 2005	Died	721	144,832	0.50	
	Prolonged illness	443	144,832	0.31	0.80
Uganda, secondary, 2005	Died	191	42,673	0.45	
	Prolonged illness	91	42,673	0.21	0.66
Zambia, government schools, 2005	Died	607	48,125	1.26	
	Prolonged illness	121	48,125	0.25	1.51

large number of deaths, this imposes a considerable cost, absorbing much of the discretionary budget of some districts and reducing the availability of ministry vehicles for other purposes.

TEACHER ISSUES – AN INTERCONNECTED SYSTEM

Countries face a series of challenges in provision of teachers. First, there are challenges of teacher supply and ensuring an appropriate supply of teachers. Second, there are challenges of teacher distribution and getting teachers to the schools in the most disadvantaged remote communities. Third, there are challenges of teacher quality, including attracting suitably qualified people, providing the right training and support, and managing to ensure quality of service delivery. Finally, there are financial constraints, which present the challenges of supporting expansion of coverage and retention of teachers in the most efficient manner possible.

These four dimensions—supply, distribution, quality, and cost—are interrelated, and a balanced policy for teachers must consider its impact on each dimension (figure 1.1, on page 8). The obvious actions to address problems in one area often have negative impacts in other areas. The main policy options in each of these four areas, and their implications for other areas, are outlined below:

Figure 11.1   Teacher Policy: Four Interrelated Dimensions

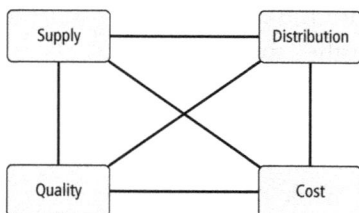

POLICY OPTIONS TO ADDRESS SUPPLY DIFFICULTIES

In order to increase the supply of qualified teachers, countries may seek to increase teacher remuneration or reduce entry requirements, with consequent implications for cost and quality. As much of attrition seems to result from movement to other jobs, increased salary is likely to assist in retaining teachers for longer in the profession. In addition, as the position of teacher tends to be perceived as less attractive than other public service jobs with similar entry qualifications, increased salary relative to other public servants is likely to attract a greater proportion of the available school leavers into teaching. However, this intervention will also increase the cost per teacher, with consequent risks to affordability.

In countries where the supply is constrained by the availability of suitable qualified applicants, the obvious reaction may be to reduce the entry standard. At the time of the case study visits, both Lesotho and The Gambia were experiencing shortages of qualified applicants to teacher-training courses. In both cases the entry requirements were subsequently lowered in pragmatic moves to recruit sufficient candidates. Of course, this has implications for the quality of teaching, and the duration and content of the training to be provided.

An even more difficult problem arises in the countries where there is a shortage of teachers of mathematics and the sciences. There are already lower entry requirements for students with these subjects in Zanzibar, Lesotho, and Uganda, yet a shortage remains. Further reductions in entry requirements may compromise quality of teaching. None of the countries were offering additional incentive payments to teachers of these subjects, but as these subjects are also in high demand in the labor market, an incentive payment would probably have to be quite substantial to be effective.

POLICY OPTIONS TO ADDRESS DEPLOYMENT

Hardship allowances (or other bonus payments) and the provision of housing may be considered in the attempt to increase equity of deployment, but both have cost implications. Additional payments and hardship allowances have not removed the inequity of deployment in most cases, but seem to have had a very positive impact in The Gambia, where the incentive is both strictly targeted and very substantial (30–40 percent of pay). Payments of this scale have obvious implications for teacher cost, and are likely to be realistic only where teacher salary is already low and a significant increase in average teacher cost could be considered.

Nonfinancial policies to address the deployment problem may have quality implications. In Zambia, teachers who have served for two years are allowed to apply for transfer, and the district offices are overwhelmed by requests for transfer from rural posts. This creates a cycle where young, inexperienced teachers work in the most isolated schools and then gradually transfer back to the more desired locations. In The Gambia, teachers working in hardship locations are given preference in competition for promotional posts. While this may provide an incentive to remain in a rural post, it reduces the ability to provide a merit-based promotion system. In Lesotho, schools recruit teachers directly, creating a labor market for teachers. While this results in reasonably even distribution of teachers, the best-qualified teachers are able to secure the jobs in the most desired locations.

Forced redistribution of teachers, which could ensure even deployment, is also likely to result in a great deal of loss of talent, and particularly female teachers, as those who are unwilling to move leave the profession to find alternative employment in the private sector or leave the workforce altogether.

POLICY OPTIONS TO IMPROVE QUALITY

Raising the level of academic qualifications to improve teacher quality has implications for cost, supply, and distribution of teachers. In many cases primary teacher qualifications are being upgraded from certificate level to diploma level. In Lesotho for example, the initial teacher qualification has been transformed from a certificate to a diploma program. This has resulted in a significant increase in teacher remuneration. The starting salary for a teacher with a diploma is 83 percent higher than that for a teacher with a certificate. It has also been accompanied by an increase in entry standards, resulting in restricted supply.

At the secondary level, the trend has been to increase the expected qualification from diploma to degree level. In Zambia for example, high school teachers are expected to have a degree, although in practice only 12 percent have one. The teachers with higher educational qualifications seem more reluctant to locate in rural areas, conscious of their status as graduates and the alternatives available in the labor market. Similarly, in Malawi it was reported that "graduates would not live in a mud house where they have to draw water from 2 kilometers away."

Quality may also be improved through better management, reducing absenteeism, and ensuring efficient operation of schools. But effective action to reduce absenteeism is also likely to be costly, and may reduce teacher supply. Effective measures to reduce absenteeism are likely to involve both greater monitoring within schools and greater external monitoring of schools, both of which carry costs.

MEASURES TO REDUCE COSTS OR IMPROVE EFFICIENCY

The key drivers of teacher costs are teacher remuneration and teacher utilization. Any reduction of teacher pay is likely to further reduce the attractiveness of teaching as a profession, thus reducing supply, increasing attrition, and reducing the quality of intake. Increases in teacher utilization may also reduce the opportunity for secondary earnings, thus providing a de facto fall in earnings for some teachers.

As illustrated by these examples, the highly interconnected nature of teacher policies means that any policy intervention may have negative implications for one of the other dimensions. This is not to suggest that none of these measures can be implemented—some are desirable and beneficial. However, no single policy intervention should be considered in isolation from the overall system. The development of appropriate teacher polices should involve a calculated series of trade-offs between these competing priorities. While it is clear that there is no single solution, some promising ideas and possibilities emerge, as described in the following paragraphs.

PROMISING PRACTICES

Planning for teacher supply: Most of the case-study countries did not have adequate systems for monitoring and regulating teacher supply. As a result, in almost all cases teacher supply was out of balance with requirements, either producing an inappropriate number of teachers or an inappropriate balance of subject specializations. Teacher requirements could easily be forecast, based on the projected requirements (already available in sector plans) and information on teacher attrition (which could be sourced through either human resource data or Education Management Information Systems (EMIS) surveys). An annual review of the supply balance for each level and subject specialization, and subsequent adjustment of the intake to teacher training could significantly improve teacher supply.

The second path into teaching: For many of the case-study countries, the current output of primary teachers is inadequate, so some recruitment of unqualified teachers is inevitable. The pattern of recruiting unqualified teachers locally and then providing opportunities to upgrade them to qualified status through in-service training has become a second path into the profession. If good-quality in-service training can be provided, this second path can help address the problem of teacher distribution by recruiting teachers already resident in the areas where there are teacher shortages. Building the capacity of people who are from the remote areas seems a better long-term solution than providing subsidies to encourage teachers from other areas to move to places they consider undesirable. This can contribute to addressing the teacher gender gap in rural areas, by providing access to teaching jobs for female teachers already living in the area, and thus avoiding the specific difficulties of deploying female teachers to remote areas.

Location-specific teacher recruitment: Central recruitment of teachers, followed by planned deployment, has consistently caused difficulties as teachers resist moving to the least desired locations. Some countries have moved to systems where jobs in specific locations are advertised and teachers self-select by choosing to apply for the jobs. In Uganda, since the completion of the case study, the government has begun to advertise posts in specific rural areas to address the uneven deployment of secondary teachers. These systems appear to assist in getting teachers into rural locations. In Zambia, the teachers who apply for jobs in a particular district are much more likely to take up the post than those who are transferred to a district they did not chose. It seems likely that this is effective because, even if teachers would prefer an urban post, they may feel much more comfortable moving to a rural area where they already have some relatives or friends. In The Gambia, student teachers rated a post near home or relatives as a much higher priority than a location in an urban center. Lesotho, where a system of recruiting teachers for specific locations has been in place for some time, has been very successful in achieving even distribution of primary teachers, although there remain problems in attracting mathematics and science teachers to rural secondary schools.

Specific interventions for mathematics and sciences: One of the most consistent patterns across these eight case studies was the shortage of teachers of mathematics and science. In general, there was a weakness in the mathematical skill of primary teachers, a shortage of teachers of mathematics at the secondary level, and a shortage of entrants to teacher training with expertise in mathematics and science. Breaking this vicious cycle is likely to require special measures. One option is the provision of booster courses in teacher colleges, to improve the mathematical and scientific understanding of student teachers. Such booster courses are planned in Lesotho and are being implemented in The Gambia.

Broader criteria for selection into teacher training: Selection into teacher training has traditionally been based mainly on academic performance. In some cases this biases the selection toward students from more urban and better-off backgrounds, who are more likely to have better academic results. These are less likely to see primary teaching as their long-term career goal, or to be willing to accept a post in a remote rural school. Yet the success of the teacher training college in Malawi operated by the NGO Development Aid from People to People (and similar colleges in Mozambique and Angola) in attracting students who want to work in rural areas demonstrates that there are people who both want to teach in rural schools and have the ability to succeed in pre-service teacher training. Broader selection criteria, including both academic performance and interview, offer an opportunity to draw into teaching more of those who want teaching as their career, more of those who are willing to work in rural areas, and more students from linguistic and ethnic minorities who are underrepresented in teaching.

Targeted incentives for teachers in remote areas: In the short term there is a need to attract more teachers to remote rural areas. The case of The Gambia illustrates that financial incentives, where considerable in scale and very carefully targeted, can significantly increase the willingness of teachers to work in difficult areas. In The Gambia, following the introduction of the incentives, experienced teachers were requesting transfers to hardship schools. In 2008, more than one-third of the teachers in regions 3, 4, and 5 who were not in hardship schools requested transfers to hardship posts.

Monitoring of teacher attendance: There were strong indications that teacher absenteeism could be reduced (though not eliminated) by monitoring. In Uganda, the absenteeism rate fell from 27 percent in 2004 to 19 percent in 2006, following increased measures to monitor attendance. In The Gambia, it was reported that church-run schools had higher teacher attendance than government schools because managers routinely monitored attendance and deducted pay from teachers who were absent without permission. Also in The Gambia, following the introduction of cluster monitors, who visited schools on a regular basis, it was reported that teacher absenteeism decreased and the number of cases of head teachers taking action to address absenteeism increased. Note that in both Uganda and The Gambia, no additional sanctions or penalties were introduced. The teacher absenteeism decreased simply in response to monitoring. In most of the case-study countries, teacher attendance was monitored at the school level through an attendance book. However, this data was rarely compiled or analyzed, either at the school or district level.

Decentralized monitoring: In most countries, schools were inspected by external officials less than once per year, and in some cases much less. In Lesotho, some schools had not been visited for ten years. This frequency of inspection is clearly insufficient to act as a quality assurance mechanism. Two countries had much more frequent external supervision of schools, and in both cases (The Gambia and Eritrea), this was achieved by having decentralized inspectors serving small clusters of schools, living in their cluster, and using low-cost transportation. In The Gambia, cluster monitors live at one of the ten schools in their cluster and are provided with a motorbike for transportation. In the context of the high cost of transportation and the shortage of vehicles, decentralization of supervision to the cluster level seems to be the most viable method to ensure reasonable supervision frequencies.

Practical training for head teachers: No matter how frequent the external supervision, the daily supervision of teachers falls to school management. Despite the acknowledged importance of school leaders, too often head teachers were ill-prepared for this role. Most countries had no automatic training for head teachers. Instead, short courses were provided, frequently with external funds, and small numbers were drawn into long-term university-based courses. Provision of routine, practical training to all head teachers at the time when they take up the posts seems a promising measure to improve the quality of management and supervision of schools.

References

Akyeampong, K., and K. Asante. 2005. *Teacher Motivation and Incentives: A Profile of Ghana.* Centre for International Education, University of Sussex.

Akyeampong, K., and D. Stephens. 2002. "Exploring the Backgrounds and Shaping of Beginning Student Teachers in Ghana: Toward Greater Contextualisation of Teacher Education." *International Journal of Educational Development* 22 (3/4): 262–74.

Andrabi, T., J. Das, and A. I. Khwaja. 2006. "A Dime a Day: The Possibilities and Limits of Private Schooling in Pakistan." Policy Research Working Paper 4066, World Bank, Washington, DC.

Appleton, S., A. Sives, and J. Morgan. 2006. "The Impact of International Teacher Migration on Schooling in Developing Countries—The Case of Southern Africa." *Globalisation, Societies and Education* 4 (1): 121–42.

Avalos, B. 2000. "Policies for Teacher Education in Developing Countries." *International Journal of Educational Research* 33: 457–74.

Bennell, P., and K. Akyeampong. 2007. Teacher Motivation in Sub-Saharan Africa and South Asia. DFID Educational Paper No. 71. Essex, United Kingdom.

Bray, Mark. 2001. "Community Partnerships in Education: Dimensions, Variations, and Implications." UNESCO, Paris.

_____. 2008. *Double-Shift Schooling: Design and Operation for School Effectiveness.* Fundamentals of Educational Planning 90, Paris: UNESCO International Institute for Educational Planning (IIEP).

Brock-Utne, B. 2007. "Language of Instruction and Student Performance: New Insights from Research in Tanzania and South Africa." *International Review of Education* 53: 509–30.

Bruns, B., A. Mingat, and R. Rakotomalala. 2003. "Achieving Universal Primary Education by 2015: A Chance for Every Child." World Bank, Washington, DC.

Caillods, F. 2001. "Financing Secondary Education in Selected Francophone Countries of Africa: Issues and Perspectives." In *Financing Secondary Education in Developing Countries: Strategies for Sustainable Growth,* eds. K. Lewin and F. Caillods. Paris: UNESCO, IIEP.

Chapman, D. 2005. *Recruitment, Retention and Development of School Principals.* Paris: UNESCO, IIEP/IEA.

Chaudhury, N., J. Hammer, M. Kremer, K. Muralidharan, and F. Halsey Rogers. 2006. "Missing in Action: Teacher and Health Worker Absence in Developing Countries." *Journal of Economic Perspectives* 20 (1): 91–116.

Das, Jishnu, Stefan Dercon, James Habyarimana, and Pramila Krishnan. 2005. "Teacher Shocks and Student Learning: Evidence from Zambia." Policy Research Working Paper, World Bank, Washington, DC.

De Grauwe, A., C. Lugaz, D. Baldé, C. Diakhaté, D. Dougnon, M. Moustapha, and D. Odushina. 2005. "Does Decentralization Lead to School Improvement? Findings and Lessons from Research in West-Africa." *Journal of Education for International Development* 1(1). http://www.equip123.net/JEID/articles/1/1–1.pdf.

DeJaeghere, J.G., R. Williams, and R. Kyeyune, R. In press. "Ugandan Secondary School Headteachers' Efficacy: What Kind of Training for Whom?" *International Journal of Educational Development* doi:10.1016/j.ijedudev.2008.03.001.

Dembélé, M. 2005. *A Study of Primary Teacher Education and Management in French Speaking West Africa: Comparative Synthesis Report.* Washington, DC: World Bank.

Dembélé , M., B.R. Miaro, II. 2003. "Pedagogical Renewal and Teacher Development in Sub-Saharan Africa: A Thematic Synthesis." Paper commissioned for 2003 ADEA Biennial Meeting. Paris: ADEA.

Duthilleul, Yael. 2005. "Lessons Learnt in the Use of 'Contract' Teachers." Synthesis Report. Paris: IIEP.

EFA-FTI (Education for All—Fast Track Initiative). 2004. "Education for All–Fast Track Initiative: Accelerating Progress towards Quality Universal Primary Education—Framework." FTI Secretariat, Washington, DC.

Emanic Consulting. 2006. Republic of The Gambia, Department of State for Education, Public Expenditure Review.

Fyfe, Alec. 2007. "The Use of Contract Teachers in Developing Countries: Trends and Impact." Working Paper 252, ILO, Geneva.

Giordano, E. 2008. *School Clusters and Teacher Resource Centres.* Fundamentals of Educational Planning 86, Paris: UNESCO International Institute for Educational Planning (IIEP).

Glewwe, P., N. Ilias, and M. Kremer, 2003. "Teacher Incentives." Working Papers: 9671, National Bureau of Economic Research, Cambridge, MA.

Government of Malawi. 2006. Malawi Growth and Development Strategy, For Poverty to Prosperity 2006–11.

Habyarimana, James. 2007. "Characterizing Teacher Absence in Uganda: Evidence from 2006 Unit Cost Study." Draft report.

Hedges, John. 2002. "The Importance of Posting and Interaction with the Education Bureaucracy in Becoming a Teacher in Ghana." *International Journal of Educational Development* 22: 353–66.

Hoxby, C., and A. Leigh. 2004. "Pulled Away or Pushed Out? Explaining the Decline of Teacher Aptitude in the United States." *The American Economic Review* 94 (2): 236–46.

Kadzamira, E. C. 2006. *Teacher Motivation and Incentives in Malawi,* Zomba: Centre for Education Research and Training, University of Malawi.

Lavy, V. 2004. "Paying for Performance and Teachers' Effort, Productivity, and Grading Ethics." Working Paper 10622, National Bureau of Economic Research, Cambridge, MA.

———. 2007. "Using Performance-Based Pay to Improve the Quality of Teachers." *The Future of Children* 17(1).

Lewin, K. 2008. "Strategies for Sustainable Financing of Secondary Education in Sub-Saharan Africa." Working Paper 136, World Bank, Washington, DC.

Lewin, Keith, and Janet Stuart. 2003. "Researching Teacher Education: New Perspectives on Practice, Performance and Policy." Multi-Site Teacher Education Research Project (MUSTER) Synthesis Report. DFID Educational Paper No. 49a. Essex, United Kingdom.

Liang, Xiaoyan. 2002. "Uganda Post-Primary Education Sector Report." Africa Region Human Development Working Paper Series, World Bank, Washington, DC.

Little, A.W., ed. 2006. *Education for All and Multigrade Teaching: Challenges and Opportunities.* Dordrecht, Netherlands: Springer.

McEwan, P., and L. Santibáñez. 2005. "Teacher and Principal Incentives in Mexico." In *Incentives to Improve Teaching: Lessons from Latin America*, ed. E. Vegas. Washington, DC: World Bank Press.

Michaelowa, K. 2001. "Primary Education Quality in Francophone Sub-Saharan Africa: Determinants of Learning Achievement and Efficiency Considerations." *World Development* 29 (10): 1699–716.

Mulkeen, Aidan, David W. Chapman, Joan G. DeJaeghere, and Elizabeth Leu. 2007. *Recruiting, Retaining, and Retraining Secondary School Teachers and Principals in Sub-Saharan Africa*. SEIA Thematic Study No. 4. Washington, DC: World Bank.

Mundy, K. Cherry, S. Haggerty, M. Maclure, R. and M. Sivasubramaniam. 2008. "Basic Education, Civil Society Participation and the New Aid Architecture: Lessons from Burkina Faso, Kenya, Mali and Tanzania." Canadian International Development Agency and the Ontario Institute for Studies in Education, University of Toronto, Canada.

OECD. 2005. *Teachers Matter: Attracting, Developing and Retaining Effective Teachers*. Paris: OECD.

———. 2008. *Education at a Glance*. Paris: OECD.

Pansiri, Nkobi. 2008. "Improving Commitment to Basic Education for the Minorities in Botswana: A Challenge for Policy and Practice." *International Journal of Educational Development* 28 (4): 446–59.

Ping-Man Wong, and Chi-Sum Wong. 2005. "Promotion Criteria and Satisfaction of School Teachers in Hong Kong." *Educational Management Administration Leadership* 33 (4): 423–47.

Sargent, Tanja, and Emily Hannum. 2005. "Keeping Teachers Happy: Job Satisfaction among Primary School Teachers in Rural Northwest China." *Comparative Education Review* 49 (2).

Schwille, J., M. Dembélé, and J. Schubert. 2007. *Global Perspectives on Teacher Learning: Improving Policy and Practice*. Fundamentals of Educational Planning, 84. Paris: UNESCO International Institute for Educational Planning (IIEP).

Shinyekwa, Isaac. 2006. *Report on Universal Post Primary Education and Training*. MoES, Uganda.

Towse, P., D. Kent, F. Osaki, and N. Kirua. 2002. "Non-graduate Teacher Recruitment and Retention: Some Factors Affecting Teacher Effectiveness in Tanzania." *Teaching and Teacher Education* 18: 637–652.

UIS (UNESCO Institute of Statistics). 2006. *Teachers and Educational Quality: Monitoring Global Needs for 2015*. New York: UNESCO Institute of Statistics.

———. 2007. *Education Counts: World Education Indicators 2007*. New York: UNESCO Institute of Statistics.

UNESCO–EFA (United Nations Educational, Scientific and Cultural Organization—EFA Global Monitoring Report Team). 2003. *Gender and Education for All, The Leap to Equality*. EFA Global Monitoring Report. Paris: UNESCO.

———. 2008. *Overcoming Inequality: Why Governance Matters*. Paris: UNESCO.

Urwick, James, Puleng Mapuru, and Michael Nkhoboti. 2005. "Teacher Motivation and Incentives In Lesotho." A research report prepared for the project Teacher Motivation and Incentives in Sub-Saharan Africa and South Asia. Lesotho College of Education, Maseru, Lesotho.

Vegas, E., ed. 2005. *Incentives to Improve Teaching: Lessons from Latin America*. Washington, DC: World Bank.

Verspoor, A. and SEIA team. 2008. *At the Crossroads: Choices for Secondary Education in Sub-Saharan Africa*. Washington, DC: World Bank.

Villegas-Reimers, E. 2003. *Teacher Professional Development: An International Review of the Literature.* Paris: UNESCO International Institute for Educational Planning (IIEP).

Voluntary Services Overseas (VSO). The Gambia. 2007. *Teachers Speak Out: A Policy Research Report on Teachers' Motivation and Perceptions of Their Profession in The Gambia.* VSO The Gambia, Banjul.

Winkler, Donald, and Lars Sondergaard. 2007. "The Efficiency of Public Education in Uganda." World Bank, Washington, DC.

World Bank. 2000. "Effective Schooling in Rural Africa, Report 3: Case Study Briefs on Rural Schooling." Working paper. http://go.worldbank.org/DLT1OA39W0.

_____. 2003. *World Development Report 2004: Making Services Work for Poor People.* New York: Oxford University Press.

Wößman, Ludger. 2003. "Schooling Resources, Educational Institutions and Student Performance: the International Evidence." *Oxford Bulletin of Economics and Statistics* 65 (2): 117–170.

Index

Note: *b* indicates boxes, *f* indicates figures, and *t* indicates tables

www.ingramcontent.com/pod-product-compliance
Lightning Source LLC
Chambersburg PA
CBHW080330270326
41927CB00014B/3153